CAN
WE STILL
BELIEVE
in
God?

CAN WE STILL BELIEVE *in* God?

ANSWERING TEN CONTEMPORARY CHALLENGES TO CHRISTIANITY

CRAIG L. BLOMBERG

BrazosPress

a division of Baker Publishing Group
Grand Rapids, Michigan

Published by Brazos Press
a division of Baker Publishing Group
PO Box 6287, Grand Rapids, MI 49516-6287
www.brazospress.com

Printed in the United States of America

Library of Congress Cataloging-in-Publication Data
Names: Blomberg, Craig L., 1955– author.
Title: Can we still believe in God? : answering ten contemporary challenges to Christianity / Craig L. Blomberg.
Description: Grand Rapids, Michigan : Brazos Press, a division of Baker Publishing Group, 2020. | Includes index.
Identifiers: LCCN 2019040459 | ISBN 9781587434044 (paperback)
Subjects: LCSH: Apologetics.
Classification: LCC BT1103 .B56 2020 | DDC 239—dc23
LC record available at https://lccn.loc.gov/2019040459

ISBN 978-1-58743-493-8 (casebound)

20   21   22   23   24   25   26   7   6   5   4   3   2   1

For Alicia Duprée
whose faithful loyalty to Jesus Christ despite many
personal challenges remains an inspiring model and whose
friendship remains a continual encouragement

CONTENTS

PREFACE

A significant part of growing up and maturing for many people involves discovering that what they assumed was normal about their childhood was just one of many different kinds of experiences they could have had. The same is true for Christian growth and maturity. I had a lot of wonderful education, discipling, and mentoring, both formally and informally, in my family, in my church, and through two amazing parachurch ministries in my high school and college. All my life I went to public schools, and my college, though private, was in the process of shedding much of its religious heritage when I attended it. I spent a year between college and graduate school teaching in a public high school. By the time I attended my first evangelical Christian institution, then, when I went to seminary, I was aware of all kinds of questions that my friends and acquaintances who did not share my Christian convictions asked. I knew the ways skeptics often countered Christian faith. I had devoured literature, tapes, and live teaching in numerous settings that in most instances gave me what seemed to be compelling answers.

My experience at seminary was therefore not like that of many of my peers. Oh, I learned an amazing amount, and, at times, I realized that what I had thought was "the" evangelical Christian viewpoint on an issue was just one of several. Nevertheless, unlike many who struggled to grasp the reasons we were required to study numerous topics in an academically rigorous fashion, I understood—based on my previous experiences inside and outside of the classroom trying to share my faith and make a credible case for following Jesus—why we needed to be studying all that we were. I had already been introduced to every issue, in one form or another, that I am addressing in this book. I had already discovered convincing answers to most of them, but

I realized I had much more to learn. It quickly surprised me, then, how many seminarians seemed uninterested in them and unprepared to address them.

After I moved on from seminary to doctoral study and completed my PhD in New Testament, my first teaching job was at a comparatively young undergraduate Christian liberal arts college where students majoring in religion were eager for all kinds of knowledge. What some of them lacked in sheer smarts they made up for with zeal. But it was not my lot to stay there for a long time; instead, I came to Denver Seminary, where I have now completed thirty-three years of teaching in a wonderfully congenial environment. Over the years, I have experienced some of the same disconnect I had as a seminary student. There is a "mercenary" attitude among more seminarians than college students that insists a topic be demonstrated to be relevant fairly immediately in their ministries, current or projected, or else we shouldn't foist it on them. Amazingly, even some of these top ten reasons for rejecting God are at times on their list of topics we shouldn't "bore" them with! If it won't preach on Sunday, titillate their youth group on Wednesday night, or help their clients in the counseling clinic, then they show little interest. Never mind that most of them will go on to have multiple, fairly distinct ministries throughout their careers, with responsibilities they never anticipated and, if they dare to talk about their faith with people who don't share it, they will run into these topics again and again. I therefore make no apologies, for example, for spending an entire chapter on the transmission and translation of the text of the New Testament. But I begin with a chapter that deals with the problem of suffering and evil, which I hope needs no justification for anyone.

Numerous people deserve my thanks and appreciation for their help in this project. Bryan Dyer and Jim Kinney from Baker Academic and Brazos Press have showed enthusiasm for the project from the first day I suggested it to them. James Korsmo and the team at Brazos Press shepherded the manuscript well. Denver Seminary has continued to afford wonderful facilities, library resources, and supportive conditions for my writing. My wife, Fran, who early in my career read and critiqued everything I wrote, was not able to keep up with all of it as our girls were growing up and then as she worked on the pastoral staff of two local churches we attended, in turn. Now that she is retired, she is reading my books again, and for that I am again grateful. Our two grown daughters put up with occasionally being "found out" to be related to me but more importantly give perceptive feedback whenever I bounce ideas and questions off them.

I continue to be grateful for the support of the administration and board of Denver Seminary and for their generous sabbatical policy, although this book was largely completed in between two sabbaticals that gave and are giving me the opportunity for researching and writing longer works. The distinguished professorship, which I have held since 2006, has provided an annual stipend for research assistants and assistance, without which I could not possibly have kept on publishing the quantity of scholarship that I have. The research assistant who has had the greatest amount of input in this volume is Alicia Duprée, who is now also my (adjunct) faculty colleague and a part-time PhD student in New Testament studies as well. I am profoundly grateful for her help in this project and wish to dedicate this volume to her.

INTRODUCTION

Blogs, tweets, podcasts, YouTube videos—these and other high-tech forms of communication allow people to express their commitments and convictions to a huge audience as quickly as ever in the history of the world. Because of self-publishing, books take a backseat in some people's minds to peer-reviewed articles, when it used to be the other way around. In any event, this means we must exercise even more critical care in separating fact from fiction, event from interpretation, and scholarship from rant. Nowhere is this discernment more crucial than in assessing the reasons why people choose not to believe in God.

In the middle of 2015, I scoured the internet for reasons people gave for being atheists. I tallied responses on websites that purported to give the primary reasons unbelievers in general rejected a God like that of Judaism, Christianity, and Islam, who is both transcendent and immanent, who discloses himself to human beings, and who longs for them to follow and pledge allegiance to him. I grouped a few of the reasons together when it seemed they were clearly related in some key respect. The table of contents of this book was the result, as it itemizes ten key questions (or clusters of two or three related questions) that appeared most commonly as reasons people gave for rejecting the God of the Bible.

Of course, trying to respond to skepticism at times resembles trying to nail Jell-O to the wall. It slips and slides all over the place. You answer one question, and immediately the conversation shifts to a related one, and then again and again. Or perhaps the better analogy is that of trying to keep the heads in a whack-a-mole game from constantly popping up. At some point in certain kinds of conversations, one realizes that one's conversation partners are not looking for answers to puzzling questions but simply seeing how many more puzzling questions they can pose each time they encounter an apparent answer to one of them. Thus not every topic that this book treats appears on every list I consulted in 2015, just as the top ten reasons for debunking God or Christianity today don't always match earlier lists. But the issues briefly addressed here are perennial questions that refuse to die and deserve thoughtful responses.

This book is hardly the first to undertake this kind of task. What makes it a bit distinctive is that it is written by someone whose academic training is primarily in New Testament studies. Most of the literature that addresses the kinds of questions tackled here is penned by theologians, philosophers, ethicists, and even Old Testament scholars. The New Testament, nevertheless, contains significant teaching on every topic considered herein, so that it is past time for a specialist in that discipline to author a comparatively short work like this one. Of course, the natural question quickly becomes, "If knowledge about the God whom I am commending comes first of all from the Bible, and especially the New Testament, then am I not arguing in a circle by using the New Testament, complete with all its worldviews and presuppositions, to explain the hardest features about the God disclosed therein?" I could be guilty of that if I were presupposing that whatever the New Testament said was inspired and therefore inerrant and authoritative. I personally believe that to be true but, for purposes of this exercise, I am bracketing those preunderstandings and suggesting we look at what the New Testament has to say about each of these topics whether or not we think it to be completely accurate or God-breathed. If, even when treated as a collection of books that narrate commonsense human wisdom only, the New Testament still proves to help us solve any or all of our problems, then how much more will it not function in that fashion if it is divinely given?

In 2014, the Brazos imprint of Baker Publishing Group published my book *Can We Still Believe the Bible? An Evangelical Engagement with Contemporary Questions*. There I chose six key topics that tended to be discussion stoppers rather than starters in various circles or, where discussions did begin and continue, often generated more heat than light. Brazos Press wanted a title for this work that would call to mind that earlier title—hence, *Can We Still Believe in God?* By definition we are speaking of the God of the Christian Scriptures, so that the title might have been *Can We Still Believe in the Christian God?*, but this too quickly excludes parallel questions in other theistic religions. The answers to our ten questions, then, are not comprehensive, nor are they intended to be. Only those portions of an answer that are clearly taught in the New Testament are offered for detailed scrutiny. But each of these questions finds enough New Testament responses, some of them not very well known, to make the endeavor worthwhile. I hope that readers will come to agree with this conviction too. I also hope that they will find those responses helpful in addressing the key issues.

ABBREVIATIONS

General and Bibliographic

AB	Anchor Bible
ASV	American Standard Version
b.	*Babylonian Talmud*
BECNT	Baker Exegetical Commentary on the New Testament
BNTC	Black's New Testament Commentaries
BST	The Bible Speaks Today
BTCP	Biblical Theology for Christian Proclamation
CEB	Common English Bible
CGTC	Cambridge Greek Testament Commentary
CJB	Complete Jewish Bible
CPNIVC	College Press NIV Commentary
CSB	Christian Standard Bible
EGGNT	Exegetical Guide to the Greek New Testament
ESV	English Standard Version
Gk.	Greek
HCSB	Holman Christian Standard Bible
ICC	International Critical Commentary
IVPNTC	IVP New Testament Commentary
KJV	King James Version
LEB	Lexham English Bible
NAB	New American Bible
NAC	New American Commentary
NACSBT	NAC Studies in Bible & Theology
NASB	New American Standard Bible
NCB	New Century Bible
NCBC	New Cambridge Bible Commentary
NCCS	New Covenant Commentary Series
NET	New English Translation
NICNT	New International Commentary on the New Testament
NIGTC	New International Greek Testament Commentary
NIV	New International Version
NIVAC	NIV Application Commentary
NJB	New Jerusalem Bible
NKJV	New King James Version
NLT	New Living Translation
NRSV	New Revised Standard Version
NTL	New Testament Library
par(s).	parallel(s)
PNTC	Pillar New Testament Commentary
REB	Revised English Bible
RSV	Revised Standard Version
SHBC	Smyth & Helwys Bible Commentary

SP	Sacra Pagina	TOTC	Tyndale Old Testament
THNTC	Two Horizons New Testament		Commentaries
	Commentary	UBS	United Bible Societies
TNIV	Today's New International	WBC	Word Biblical Commentary
	Version	ZECNT	Zondervan Exegetical
TNTC	Tyndale New Testament		Commentary on the New
	Commentaries		Testament

Old Testament

Gen.	Genesis	Eccles.	Ecclesiastes
Exod.	Exodus	Song	Song of Songs
Lev.	Leviticus	Isa.	Isaiah
Num.	Numbers	Jer.	Jeremiah
Deut.	Deuteronomy	Lam.	Lamentations
Josh.	Joshua	Ezek.	Ezekiel
Judg.	Judges	Dan.	Daniel
Ruth	Ruth	Hosea	Hosea
1 Sam.	1 Samuel	Joel	Joel
2 Sam.	2 Samuel	Amos	Amos
1 Kings	1 Kings	Obad.	Obadiah
2 Kings	2 Kings	Jon.	Jonah
1 Chron.	1 Chronicles	Mic.	Micah
2 Chron.	2 Chronicles	Nah.	Nahum
Ezra	Ezra	Hab.	Habakkuk
Neh.	Nehemiah	Zeph.	Zephaniah
Esther	Esther	Hag.	Haggai
Job	Job	Zech.	Zechariah
Ps(s).	Psalm(s)	Mal.	Malachi
Prov.	Proverbs		

New Testament

Matt.	Matthew	1 Tim.	1 Timothy
Mark	Mark	2 Tim.	2 Timothy
Luke	Luke	Titus	Titus
John	John	Philem.	Philemon
Acts	Acts	Heb.	Hebrews
Rom.	Romans	James	James
1 Cor.	1 Corinthians	1 Pet.	1 Peter
2 Cor.	2 Corinthians	2 Pet.	2 Peter
Gal.	Galatians	1 John	1 John
Eph.	Ephesians	2 John	2 John
Phil.	Philippians	3 John	3 John
Col.	Colossians	Jude	Jude
1 Thess.	1 Thessalonians	Rev.	Revelation
2 Thess.	2 Thessalonians		

If There Is a God, Why Does He Allow So Much Suffering and Evil?

As I begin to write this book in the summer of 2018, a seemingly endless civil war, exacerbated by the presence of foreign powers, continues to decimate Syria, with millions already killed or displaced, many of them outside of their homeland. In the United States, school and church shootings occur with record frequency, transforming what were once refuges of safety into danger zones. Cancer claims the lives of countless people annually, many of whom suffer horribly in their final days, weeks, and months. Volcanoes erupt and cover everything in their wake with lava, earthquakes swallow people and buildings whole, and forest fires ravage homes and property, while hurricanes and tornadoes kill and destroy even more. Corrupt governments and other authorities line their pockets with scarce resources while the poorest in our world die of disease and drought that could have been prevented or ameliorated. CEOs of multinational corporations become billionaires, while nearly 800 million of the world's inhabitants live in extreme poverty.[1] Somewhere around 133 million Americans alone have some kind of chronic illness or injury that causes varying degrees of suffering.[2]

The philosopher's age-old conundrum remains as acute as ever. If there is a God, it seems that he is either omnipotent but not omnibenevolent (all-powerful but not all-loving) or the reverse (all-caring but unable to prevent most of the world's evil). He apparently cannot be endowed both with complete power and with complete love; otherwise, he would do something, lots of things, to diminish the amount of suffering, even gratuitous suffering, that occurs in the universe. And all this canvasses solely the human realm. If we add in the suffering of animals and the rape of the environment, the amount of evil only grows exponentially. Little wonder that this is the biggest reason some people reject the idea of anything like the Judeo-Christian God.[3]

Most *philosophers* who defend the existence of God focus on the issue of human freedom. They argue that God so valued a freely offered love relationship with beings created in his image that he needed to allow them to have sufficient liberty to reject him as well as to accept him.[4] These philosophers then divide into those who believe in libertarian free will and those who opt for compatibilist free will. Libertarian freedom affirms that people have the ability to choose the contrary of what they most deeply desire, while compatibilist freedom insists that people necessarily have only the ability to choose what they do most deeply desire.[5] Either way, though, there must be the possibility for people to rebel against God, reject all of his loving overtures toward them, go their separate ways, and experience the consequences of their choices.

Ethicists rightly point out that if a person rejects the existence of an all-powerful, all-loving being, they still have no satisfactory explanation for evil in the universe. Of course, a Darwinian naturalism can postulate the survival of the fittest and acknowledge that the fittest often get that way by inflicting great harm on others. But where do the concept of evil and the idea that it is something to be alleviated come from in the first place? If neither revealed religion nor natural theology (ultimate truths that can be inferred from what exists) points to a transcendent God who concerns himself with the affairs of humanity, from where do the ideas of good and evil originate?[6] Put another way, if humanity is not qualitatively distinct from the rest of the animal kingdom, why has there never been a hint of evidence that suggests that other life forms reflect on the problem of evil? When a carnivore attacks another animal to kill it and eat its meat, it does so instinctively and not after pondering the morality of its attack. The very concepts of good and evil, of moral and immoral, require a source, which atheistic evolution does not provide.

Theologians often address our problem by focusing on the idea of sin and how it has shaped the human race. The amount of what people, theists and atheists alike, usually call evil that is produced by the callousness, selfishness, and cruelty of other human beings is staggering. Theologians may debate the extent to which God's image in humanity is marred by sin, the specifics of how sin originated and is transmitted throughout the whole human race, and the extent to which people (if at all) are *born* sinful.[7] But there is little debate that warfare, genocide, terrorism, rape, and violence of many other kinds are precipitated primarily by individuals and groups of people who defy the standards of decency taught in most world religions.

Old Testament scholars, finally, turn to the first three chapters of Genesis and observe how sinless humanity, given the power of choice, rebelled against the only prohibition God gave them in a world of seemingly endless delight, and the entire universe was affected in the process. The distinction between human evil and natural evil thus collapses; the former is seen as the ultimate cause of the latter. Human sin led to the ground being cursed as part of the man's punishment, making work that much harder for him. The woman experienced great anguish in childbirth, and the animal kingdom, through which Satan had seduced the first human couple, discovered that its existence became considerably more difficult as well (Gen. 3:14–19). And it is important to note that these are the abiding teachings of Genesis 1–3, no matter if one sees them as factual history, as archetypal myths, or as something in between those two literary forms.[8]

Yet none of these emphases captures the heart of *New Testament* teaching on our topic. To be sure, human freedom appears almost everywhere, but it is usually more presupposed than explicitly articulated. It is regularly balanced, moreover, with an emphasis on divine sovereignty.[9] This sovereignty can in turn be interpreted variously across a spectrum, from stressing God's acting on the basis of his knowing ahead of time everything that could or would happen, to an emphasis on God's own choices independent of anything about the nature or activity of humanity. In any event, God cannot be "let off the hook" for some responsibility in the matter of suffering and evil merely by emphasizing that he gave humans freedom to rebel against him, however important that is as a *partial* answer. Observing that atheism has no answer to evil should lead merely to agnosticism about embracing either theism or atheism, unless one can find more to say on the topic. Finally, as helpful as it is not to have to provide separate explanations for personal and natural evil, the sum total of the two remains astonishing and still requires an explanation.

What God Has Done, Is Doing, and Will Do

The New Testament's focus lies not nearly so much on the origins of evil and the suffering it produces as on what God is doing in the midst of these horrors. The distinctively Christian part of the Bible, in other words, often assumes that behind the question of why God allows suffering and evil is the follow-up add-on: "that is, without doing something about it." A simple but helpful way of categorizing much of the New Testament's teaching in reply to this complaint considers what it has to say about past, present, and future. Put another way, the New Testament insists that (a) God *has* done something about evil, decisively in the person and work of Jesus of Nazareth, (b) God *is* doing something about it in all kinds of ways in the present, and (c) God *will* provide its final eradication at some point in the future in conjunction with the return of Christ and the ushering in of judgment day.

Past Action

Christians often highlight the substitutionary theory of Christ's atonement in reflecting on what God did about evil in the crucifixion of Christ. They view Jesus's death as the necessary substitute for the punishment that sinful human beings should have experienced instead (e.g., Mark 10:45; Rom. 3:25). Central as this is to the Christian message, it is the so-called classic theory of the atonement that interests us here.[10] Jesus's death on the cross provided the decisive impetus for the conquest of Satan, suffering, and evil altogether (Heb. 2:14; 1 Pet. 3:22). Like the arrival of the kingdom of God, however, the demise of evil is "already but not yet." The decisive battle has been won, but there are major mopping-up operations still to undertake. It is intriguing but also very encouraging to see how consistently the New Testament refers to the fulfillment of Old Testament promises, even though some still await fulfillment at the end of history.[11] The biblical writers refer to the era from the ministry of Jesus onward as the "last day(s)" (2 Tim. 3:1; Heb. 1:2) precisely because everything has occurred that is necessary for God to usher in final judgment except for the final clusters of events inherently bound up with judgment day.

To the extent that the suffering and evil we long to have eradicated involve the persecution of believers, we should not be surprised that such persecution still exists. Jesus stresses in John 15:18–25 that the same hatred that he experienced in his day would be what his followers would have to endure. We are too intimately tied to our Lord to expect any less. Later Paul would state matter-of-factly that "everyone who wants to live a godly life in Christ Jesus will be persecuted" (2 Tim. 3:12). That persecution will vary in nature and in severity, but all who live a significant length of time will experience hostility for their faith sooner or later. But while faith in Jesus does not exempt us from suffering and could even lead to martyrdom, the book of Revelation repeatedly depicts believers as protected from *God's* wrath (e.g., Rev. 7:3; 9:4).[12] While those who spurn his grace can expect only judgment (Heb. 10:29–31), Jesus's followers need never experience eternal punishment nor fear physical death.

Christ's agony on the cross was acute enough in the physical realm. Descriptions of ancient Roman crucifixions make it clear that it was one of the cruelest forms of prolonged human torture ever invented.[13] In fact, the English word "excruciating" comes from the Latin *crux*, "cross." But the physical suffering undoubtedly paled in comparison to the spiritual agony of recognizing that the unbroken communion with his heavenly Father that he had experienced throughout his life was suddenly and completely ruptured while he hung from the cross. Thus he cried out, "My God, my God, why have you forsaken me?" (Mark 15:34 par.). Little wonder that in the garden of Gethsemane he prayed fervently that if there were any conceivable way in all creation that he would not have to suffer this kind of death, God would give him that alternative. Nevertheless, he committed to following God's will, even if that should turn out to be completely different from his desire to avoid the horrors of crucifixion (14:36).

Because Jesus was fully human, his sacrifice provided an adequate substitute for us in a way that the Jewish system of animal sacrifices could never accomplish (Heb. 10:4). Because he was fully God, his atonement could be infinite and therefore never needed to be repeated (cf. 9:12). That God would become human in order to provide all that was needed to reconcile people to himself (2 Cor. 5:19), if they would but commit their lives to him, demonstrates his amazing love and dramatically refutes the claim that he doesn't care or hasn't acted to initiate the process of doing away with all evil. But just as a snake with its head cut off continues to writhe uncontrollably for a surprising period of time before rigor mortis sets in, so too the devil is wreaking as much havoc in the world as he can in the short time he has left (cf. Rev. 12:12). Those who argue that two thousand years scarcely qualifies as a short time are almost always among those who also believe that *Homo sapiens* first roamed the earth as far back as one hundred thousand and even perhaps two hundred thousand years ago,[14] so in comparison two thousand *is* a short period. Moreover, Psalm 90:4, quoted in 2 Peter 3:8, reminds us that, as an infinite being, God calculates time differently than we do. From the vantage point of his infinitude, a thousand years are as a day, a mere drop in the bucket of eternity.[15]

Present Action

If Christ's death triggered the series of events that would begin to eradicate the world of evil, have things on earth improved? It is far too easy to bash Christianity for the blemishes that mar what is otherwise a remarkable record. It is astonishing to realize how much better Christians and their undertakings have made this world over the past twenty centuries and how it has been atheism that has spawned most of the massive and hugely cruel pogroms against entire people groups throughout recent history.[16] Events like the Crusades are the exception, not the rule, and, even then, are often misunderstood and misrepresented.[17] What is the norm is the amount of good that Christians have done, including laying the foundations for modern science, medicine, law, government, economics, education, relief work, humanitarian aid, and helping the poor and outcast in widely disproportionate amounts compared to other religions and worldviews.[18]

God continues to address evil in the present. For the most part, he does so through his people, who continue to gravitate toward the healing and caring professions in large numbers. On occasion, he intervenes more miraculously to cure someone of a physical malady or help them avoid imminent danger, displaying his glory thereby (cf. John 9:3; Acts 12:7).[19] Spiritual conversions lead to improved lives in numerous respects and to more productive individuals who become better citizens and incite less evil, though there always are unfortunate exceptions. But explicit New Testament teaching addresses how God works in believers' lives in the midst of pain and suffering far more often than it describes God as exempting them from evil circumstances (cf. 1 Cor. 10:13).

It is not just a random fact for a game of Bible trivia that Romans 5:3–5 juxtaposes Paul's first reference to suffering in this letter with his first reference to love. Here we read that "we also glory in our sufferings, because we know that suffering produces perseverance; perseverance, character; and character, hope. And hope does not put us to shame, because God's love has been poured out into our hearts through the Holy Spirit, who has been given to us." Precisely because he loves us, God allows his people to go through a certain amount of suffering because of the endurance and resilience, the maturity, and the hope for the future that it engenders when we respond rightly and draw closer to God rather than becoming embittered and running away from him.[20]

Several key New Testament texts repeat this concept. First Peter 1:6–7 reads, "In all this you greatly rejoice, though now for a little while you may have had to suffer grief in all kinds of trials. These have come so that the proven genuineness of your faith—of greater worth than gold, which perishes even though refined by fire—may result in praise, glory and honor when Jesus Christ is revealed." Without the crucible of suffering, a person's alleged faith may never be shown to be genuine or may never mature. It is probably not coincidental that the book of the New Testament that most warns against apostasy is Hebrews, most likely written at about the same time as 1 Peter, when believers in the first-century Roman Empire were experiencing greater and greater persecution. It was all still local and informal, but Nero's first state-sponsored pogrom against Christians was perhaps only a year or two away.[21]

James 1:2–3 presents one of the Bible's most challenging commands in this area: "Consider it pure joy, my brothers and sisters, whenever you face trials of many kinds, because you know that the testing of your faith produces perseverance." Lest we think this means we must put on a happy face, deny our true feelings, and disguise ourselves while we are in public, it is important to notice the two verbs of thinking. We are to *consider* or regard trials as joy-inducing, and we can do so because we *know* the maturity that we can obtain by responding rightly to them. Feelings cannot be commanded, as if one could shout at someone else loudly and long enough to "be happy" and it would work! But individuals can choose to change their attitudes or ways of thinking about difficult circumstances in their lives.[22]

In addition to growth in maturity, various other blessings come with suffering in a godly way. Second Corinthians is the New Testament book that is most punctuated by this theme. Right in his opening thanksgiving (2 Cor. 1:3–7), Paul explains that God comforts us in all our troubles and therefore gives us the ability to comfort others in similar situations. It is amazing, for example, when people who have contracted and survived a rare disease of some kind discover how many others suddenly come out of the woodwork who have something similar going on and can benefit from what those individuals have gained from the experience. Helping others also helps hurting people avoid focusing just on themselves. C. S. Lewis speaks of pain as God's megaphone to get people's attention that something is wrong that they need to address, and this can include spiritual as well as physical issues.[23] However, unless those who suffer can find some comfort and solace, their attention can just as easily be directed at something unhealthy or escapist.

In 2 Corinthians 4:7–9, Paul explains that "we have this treasure [i.e., the light of the knowledge of God's glory] in jars of clay [our fragile, decaying bodies] to show that this all-surpassing power is from God and not from us. We are hard pressed on every side, but not crushed; perplexed, but not in despair; persecuted, but not abandoned; struck down, but not destroyed." These important truths remind us that when God seems to dangle us over the edge of a cliff, so to speak, he will never let go. But why even dangle us? Paul continues: "We always carry around in our body the death of Jesus, so that the life of Jesus may also be revealed in our body. For we who are alive are always being given over to death for Jesus' sake, so that his life may also be revealed in our mortal body" (vv. 10–11).[24] No one pays much attention to people who maintain their faith during good times, but people are more likely to notice those who cling tenaciously to trust in Jesus even when their world is falling apart. I had a friend my mother's age, who has long since gone to be with the Lord, who was restricted for years to a wheelchair because of multiple sclerosis but was one of the most joyous people I knew. Hardly anyone who met her came away without asking why she could be so happy. Uniformly they would be told it was her Christian faith that made it possible. This may be exactly what Paul means in 2 Corinthians 12:8–9, where he declares that he rejoices in his weaknesses, for when he is weak (physically) then he is strong (spiritually), because Christ can use him more effectively.[25] Returning to 2 Corinthians 4, then, we see that Paul is able to conclude in verse 12 that even though "death is at work in us" (apostles), "life is at work in you" (Corinthian Christians). He has given all he has for the sake of others so that they might become believers and then grow in their faith.

Second Corinthians 6:4–10 contains another amazing catalogue of sufferings that Paul and his travel companions have had to endure. Some involve direct persecution for their faith, like beatings and imprisonments, but many reflect just the inevitable difficulties of itinerant ministry in the first-century Roman world—for example, sleepless nights and hunger. The same is true of another detailed catalogue in 11:23b–28. That list climaxes with Paul asserting, "Besides everything else, I face daily the pressure of my concern for all the churches" (v. 28). At first, that comment seems to pale in comparison to being flogged, pelted with stones, or exposed to death or to other items mentioned earlier in the passage. But concern for the churches is the one that never went away. A person could heal physically, but a caring pastor remains constantly concerned for his or her flock.[26]

The catalogue in 6:4–10 is preceded by Paul's insistence that he puts no unnecessary obstacle in the path of his audience, so that his ministry will not be discredited (v. 3). Instead, he submits to the list of hardships in a way that no one could ever legitimately claim that he was doing what he was doing for money, power, fame, or privilege. There may be no better personal disproof besides Jesus himself that the gospel is not about gaining health or wealth in this life. Indeed, when he was younger, Paul had a bright future as a Pharisaic leader, training to be a rabbi and "advancing in Judaism," as he puts it, "beyond many of [his] own age among [his] people" (Gal. 1:14). In Philippians 3:4–6 he expands on some of these credentials but then quickly stresses, "But whatever were gains to me I now consider loss for the sake of Christ. What is more, I consider everything a loss because of the surpassing worth of knowing Christ Jesus my Lord, for whose sake I have lost all things" (vv. 7–8a). Bible versions usually balk at translating the next clause too literally because of its crude language. What is it that Paul considers all his previous privilege to be? Options for the Greek word (*skybala*) that he uses include "garbage," "refuse," "filth," "dirt," and "rubbish." The King James Version perhaps came closest when it used "dung," though the word, while including human and animal excrement, was not limited to defecation. In today's vernacular, the Common English Bible maybe says it best with "sewer trash," but a four-letter word beginning with "sh" and ending in "t" may more closely approximate the vulgarity.[27] How ironic, then, when contemporary Christians think of the ministry or even faith itself as a means to prosperity.[28]

Still, Paul believes that the Spirit of Christ powerfully sustains him and even compels him to continue his new life as it has come to be characterized. He breaks from Jewish tradition and urges churches to pay those who spread the gospel full-time so that they can be completely devoted to that work (1 Cor. 9:1–14). Nevertheless, he refuses to be bound to anyone's purse strings himself, lest he feel limited in how he can preach and what he can say, and lest anyone suspect he is fulfilling his calling as a missionary for the wrong motives (vv. 15–18).[29] His reward is not material; he rejoices to see people come to share the faith that has transformed his own life and can renew theirs as well.

Indeed, in one of his most enigmatic passages, Paul declares that he is filling up what is lacking in Christ's sufferings (Col. 1:24). This has been taken as missional: Christ did not traverse nearly as much terrain as Paul would and so did not experience as widespread or extensive persecution. The verse has also been tied to the Jewish concept of messianic woes: a fixed amount of tribulation in the end times before the Messiah comes (now revised to apply to the time before the Messiah returns). Elements of both interpretations may well be present.[30] In both instances, Paul's union with Christ shines through clearly, just as elsewhere Paul generalizes to link our union with Christ to sharing in his sufferings (Rom. 8:17).[31]

The New Testament, then, sees God as having definitively overthrown the powers of evil in Christ's atoning death on the cross and working through his people throughout church history, despite enormous obstacles of many kinds, for the betterment of individuals and of society. Paul can even declare that "in all things God works for the good of those who love him, who have been called according to his purpose" (Rom. 8:28).[32] But if there were not a future hope as well—of a resurrected body and a re-created universe—Christians would be of all people most miserable (1 Cor. 15:19). That brings us to the third prong of the answer to what God is doing to minimize suffering and evil: he has promised one day to eradicate them altogether.

Future Action

One of the most remarkable statements in all of Scripture appears in Romans 8:18. Here Paul declares that "our present sufferings are not worth comparing with the glory that will be revealed in us." Is this the same person who penned the long lists of injuries, illnesses, and injustices that afflicted him, which we read in 2 Corinthians? It is indeed, and his encounter with the risen Lord on the Damascus road has left him confident of a glorious, eternal, embodied future life to come. In the same vein, 2 Corinthians 4:17 maintains that "our light and momentary troubles are achieving for us an eternal glory that far outweighs them all." It is amazing that Paul can think of his experiences in this life as "light and momentary troubles" from any vantage point. But when one considers the life span of any human with its finite amount of suffering, however severe, in the perspective of eternity, such evil approaches the vanishing point compared with the unending good and glory available to those who accept God's free gift of salvation in Christ, based on his atoning death on the cross and bodily resurrection from the grave.[33]

Revelation 21–22 depicts this eternal glory in more detail than any other part of the Bible. Appropriately, these are its last two chapters as well. Of course, Revelation is a book of prophetic visions—an apocalypse. Words prove entirely inadequate as John tries to describe what he has seen. Symbolism abounds, so that we are never quite sure which parts are intended to be literal, which parts metaphorical, and which parts both. But it is hard to miss the thrust of 21:3–4, where the seer rejoices because he has "heard a loud voice from the throne saying, 'Look! God's dwelling place is now among the people, and he will dwell with them. They will be his people, and God himself will be with them and be their God. "He will wipe every tear from their eyes. There will be no more death" or mourning or crying or pain, for the old order of things has passed away.'" Complete happiness, joy, and fulfillment will characterize believers' eternal experience, and they will understand what God's purposes were in all the enigmas of this life.[34]

What we have surveyed thus far confirms what other observers have noted as well. The New Testament, just like the Old Testament, does not attempt to explain God's purposes in permitting every evil act of human beings (or any other part of creation, for that matter). It insists that God has legitimate purposes, so that there is no reason to call any evil gratuitous.[35] As to the allegation that God isn't doing anything to ameliorate the problem, the New Testament affirms that he did the most important thing of all *in the past* through Christ's crucifixion, making it possible for believers in Christ *in the future* to live forever without any suffering or evil. But he will not force salvation on anyone who does not want it; humans are free to reject all of his loving provisions. Meanwhile, even now, *in the present*, he uses pain and suffering to help bring believers to maturity and to wake up the spiritually asleep so that they might turn to him. But again, these things happen only when people respond rightly to tough times; nothing requires them to move closer to God (cf. the two responses in John 1:9–13).

Additional Passages

A second collection of New Testament texts bears on our topic, even if not as directly. Some evil occurs because certain people seem to recoil and exhibit hostility when they encounter Christian claims, in ways that do not match their responses to any other religion, ideology, or worldview. Is this a back-handed compliment or tacit acknowledgment of the genuineness of the gospel that is not exhibited elsewhere in our world? When Jesus, for example, unrolls the Isaiah scroll in the synagogue in Nazareth and claims that the prophecy about the Servant of the Lord who will heal the sick, free the oppressed, and bring good news to the poor (Isa. 61:1) is being fulfilled in him, some are ready to throw him off a cliff and kill him (Luke 4:16–30). What makes otherwise ordinary people turn potentially murderous when an individual promises to do nothing but good? It is when they believe he has arrogated to himself exclusive claims and powers of divinity, which, if true, would require them to abandon their self-directed lives and surrender control to his leadership. Little wonder that the Beatitudes bless everything that is the opposite of what this world considers "macho" (Matt. 5:3–12 par.)![36]

When Jesus declares the paralyzed man's sins forgiven (Mark 2:5 pars.), one can easily imagine the man thinking, "That's not why my friends brought me here. I know how to have animal sacrifices offered in the temple precincts for the forgiveness of my sins. I came for physical healing!" Of course, Jesus gives him both, but in a way that makes it clear that forgiveness of sins is the more important of the two kinds of healing and that he has the authority to bestow it completely apart from the sacrificial system of the Jewish law.[37] Ironically, even while some of the onlookers praise God, a number of the religious authorities believe that Jesus is blaspheming by asserting God's unique prerogatives (vv. 6–12). It is remarkable even in today's world how much evil is caused by those who unjustifiably take out their anger against Christians (cf. Mark 8:34–36 pars.; 13:9–13 pars.), sometimes just for "showing them up" because they live better lives. Jesus's interchange with the authorities also implies what he will say more directly to his disciples when he sends them out to replicate his mission: "Do not be afraid of those who kill the body but cannot kill the soul. Rather, be afraid of the One who can destroy both soul and body in hell" (Matt. 10:28). In other words, there is an even more important question than, Why does God allow suffering and evil in this world? That question is, How can I be sure to avoid suffering and evil throughout eternity?[38]

The Bible never teaches, in so many words, that we will appreciate sinless perfection in eternity far more after having to endure a world filled with horrible evil, but theologians and philosophers have often speculated that this may well be true. Many people have had to work strenuously to overcome great obstacles in order to receive something they value highly, and few would deny that achieving the goal becomes far more precious after all the hard work they expended. Jesus seems to point in that direction with his metaphor about a woman in labor experiencing so much joy that she forgets all the anguish she previously had (John 16:21).[39] Would the disciples rejoice as greatly when Christ returns to usher in the eternal state if this life had not been filled with as much sorrow as it has? It seems unlikely.

The relationship between the evil that befalls an individual and one's personal sin is often misrepresented. The New Testament betrays no awareness of a direct tit-for-tat relationship between one's sinfulness and the amount of suffering one experiences. Most of the time the responsible answer to why God allowed a certain evil thing to happen is that we live in a deeply flawed and fallen world, and the vast majority of the time God does not overrule the natural laws of cause and effect. Yet, after healing the crippled man sitting by the pool of Bethesda, Jesus does say to him, "Stop sinning or something worse may happen to you" (John 5:14). The implication is that his malady has been due, at least in part, to his sin, and that such a punishment could recur.[40] But when people honestly examine their lives to see if there is serious, unconfessed sin and don't find any, they should not beat themselves up trying to figure out what *they* did wrong to cause something evil to come upon them. And others should refrain from making such a connection all the more, since they can't enter into the afflicted person's mind to know what they have or haven't thought or done.

A powerful example of this lesson appears in Luke 13:1–5. Jesus raises the issue of two recent disasters: Pilate calling for the execution of some worshipers in the temple precincts, and the collapse of a tower in Siloam that killed eighteen people. In each case, he asks if the people who died were worse sinners than those around them who were spared. In each case, he maintains they were not, but he does see each as an occasion for taking stock and repenting of whatever may be wrong in our lives.[41] For those who are not his followers, lack of repentance will lead to their perishing (vv. 3, 5). So often people ask, "Why do bad things happen to good people?" Strictly speaking, from a biblical perspective, there are no good people. At least from God's perspective, everyone falls so far short of his perfect, infinitely holy standard that the question we ought to be asking is, Why do good things ever happen to bad people—that is, to all of us? If the wages of sin is death (Rom. 6:23), and we are all sinners, then no one ever deserves that which is good. God's good gifts to human beings are always entirely by his grace or unmerited favor.[42]

A classic example of this appears in Acts 5:1–11, in which God strikes down Ananias and Sapphira for lying about the amount of money they gave to the apostles to help the poor in their midst. Not only does on-the-spot physical death seem like an amazingly harsh punishment, but also the crime seems comparatively trivial. There are numerous ways to partially offset these perceptions: the couple was free to give any or no percent of the proceeds of their sale; they were actually engaging in embezzlement; they lied not just to humans but to God; nothing suggests they lost their salvation; intermediate natural agency like a heart attack may have been involved; and the church was particularly fragile in this early period of its history and might have been seriously compromised by such duplicity. At the end of the day, however, the entire story seems anomalous precisely because God doesn't react like this in the vast majority of cases of grievous sins against him.[43] The same is true of the Corinthian Christians who had died because they had profaned the Lord's Supper (1 Cor. 11:30).[44] It is a tribute to God's overwhelming grace that these episodes seem so out of character for him; if we were honest, we would acknowledge that we deserved such judgment for every one of our sins.

Many other passages repeat the themes we have already uncovered. There may have been some tit-for-tat retribution in God's selection of Saul of Tarsus to suffer as much as he did for his ministry, because of all the persecution he had previously unleashed on believers (Acts 9:13–16). In light of all Christ has done for us, our priority must be to follow him no matter what the cost (Gal. 2:20; Phil. 1:21–25). He nevertheless always makes the endurance of hardship possible (Phil. 4:11–13). First Corinthians 10:13 has often been misinterpreted as if it taught, "God never gives you more than you can handle." What it actually says is that "no temptation has overtaken you except what is common to mankind. And God is faithful; he will not let you be tempted beyond what you can bear. But when you are tempted, he will also provide a way out so that you can endure it." In our fallen and finite humanity, there are many things that we can't handle, even if God gives them to us, but with his empowerment we can bear them. It is also easy to read "He will also provide a way out" without its sequel, "so that you can endure it." God does not promise to take away the suffering, but he does promise to help us cope in its midst.[45] Jesus can nevertheless relate to whatever we are going through because of what he experienced in his own life and death (Heb. 2:14–18; 4:15).[46] So we need to fear spiritual death far more than physical death or pain (Rev. 2:8–11).

More Opportunities for Repentance

There is one distinctive contribution of the New Testament that I have not yet addressed. In fact, it only rarely comes up in discussions about the problem of evil. It is the question of what it would take to do away with most or all of the causes of suffering and evil in our world. Precisely because humans themselves are the cause of so much of the problem, it would mean dramatically diminishing or doing away with the freedom we have to harm others or the rest of the universe. In short, it would mean bringing an end to this age of human history as we know it and proceeding directly to either the millennium, in which sin is drastically reduced, or the eternal state—the new heaven and new earth—in which it is altogether absent. It would mean the end of human opportunities to rebel against God and therefore the end of their opportunities to accept his gift of salvation.[47] Because freedom allows for both, a significant diminution in freedom of choice would affect both options. The objection that God surely could have created us all perfectly good and happy and yet without freedom to rebel claims to know what in fact we cannot. No human being has ever been in that situation, and not even Scripture describes beings of any kind who have ever been in that situation. It is true that God can establish the faithful angels in a happy, sinless state and promise to re-create believers in a happy state in which sin is no longer possible. Yet that by no means makes it self-evident that without the option to sin in the first place we would still have experienced the same kind of bliss or been able to have the same kind of freely chosen love relationship with God.[48] I may choose to board an airplane with the promise that I will not be able to choose to jump out of it as it is flying without my freedom being compromised, but if I am forced onto the plane in the first place, then that freedom most certainly has been overruled.

What does all this philosophizing have to do with the New Testament? It is precisely the logic that is implicit in 2 Peter 3. Not only is God not slow in bringing about the end of this age and the return of Christ, because a day with the Lord is like a thousand years and vice versa (v. 8 [recall the discussion above of God's past action]), but also "the Lord is not slow in keeping his promise, as some understand slowness. Instead he is patient with you, not wanting anyone to perish, but everyone to come to repentance" (v. 9). When the end comes, there will no longer be any chance for repentance, salvation, and becoming a follower of Jesus. There will be only judgment for those who have rejected him (vv. 10–12).[49] Hebrews 11:39–40 puts it more positively. None of the great people or heroes of pre-Christian times saw the fulfillment in their days of everything God had predicted. "These were all commended for their faith, yet none of them received what had been promised, since God had planned something better for us so that only together with us would they be made perfect." In other words, God cared enough about you and me that he allowed history to continue long enough so that we would be born and have the chance to be part of his eternal family![50]

Christians who reflect deeply on these claims should come to a number of conclusions. First, we should be very grateful simply to have been given both physical life and the opportunity for spiritual life. Second, God could have done away with suffering long ago, but then we never would have been born. Third, God could free us from all our suffering, but in doing so he would be excluding anyone else's chance to be saved. God did not end everything sooner but allowed us to be saved, so how could we possibly begrudge him allowing more time for others to come to him? Fourth, whatever else we do with our lives, we need to be actively a part of commending Christianity to others in the most winsome ways possible so that by as many means as possible the greatest number of people might come to salvation and the fewest scared off (cf. 1 Cor. 9:19–23). Fifth, and pursuing this last point further, we should take pains to avoid anything that would lead to our faith being legitimately criticized, mocked, and rejected—whether that be due to our tactlessness, our hypocrisy, or any other sin that brings God's people into disrepute.[51] Above all, we can be thankful for a God who can and does redeem even the worst of circumstances, and that our relationship with God can be profoundly deepened as we witness his provision in our times of need and his healing of our wounds.

All this, of course, presupposes that the New Testament is telling the truth when it repeatedly insists that not all people will be saved. In other words, some are lost for all eternity. That leads to the second common question we must address: What about all those people throughout history who never heard the gospel? Surely it is the height of injustice for God to damn all of them when they never had a chance. Indeed it is, and that is not the message of the New Testament! But the unpacking of that assertion must await the next chapter.

2

Must All the Unevangelized Go to Hell (and What Is Hell)?

I was speaking at an outreach event in the Round Church in Cambridge, England, in the fall of 2015. After my talk we had a time of questions and answers, and a venerable older gentleman with an impeccable English accent remarked thoughtfully and slowly that he just couldn't see how the Christian message could represent the only way to God, if there were a God, when countless people lived and died long before Jesus ever did and millions have not heard the gospel in the centuries since. Would a God, like the one Christians say they believe in, really send all those people to hell for not believing in someone they have never had a chance to hear about in the first place? I thanked him for his very perceptive question, but I replied that I did not believe that was the Christian message at all, even if some people have misrepresented it as though it were.

If one studies the history of Christian reflection on this topic, one discovers about a half dozen different main approaches.[1] A *restrictivist* approach argues that Jesus is God's only full and final provision for the sins of humanity.[2] However, I have never once met or even heard of a restrictivist who thinks that all of the ancient Israelites about whom the Old Testament writes in so much detail were lost. God had given them a system of offering animal sacrifices in the tabernacle and the temple as a temporary stopgap until the Messiah should come and provide perfect atonement. Nor are Israelites the only pre-Christian people who had the opportunity to become right with

God. The Old Testament is dotted with characters who were not Israelites but who came to know the God of Israel, including Melchizedek, the king and priest of Salem (before it became Jerusalem; Gen. 14:18–20); Rahab, the prostitute in Jericho who harbored the Israelite spies (Josh. 2:1–21); Ruth; Job; probably Bathsheba (assuming she was a Hittite; cf. 2 Sam. 11:3, which notes that she was married to one); and Naaman (2 Kings 5). Moreover, these individuals may just be a drop in the bucket of other unnamed and unsung Gentile worshipers of the God of Israel.[3] Moreover, almost all restrictivists with whom I have become familiar have believed that very young children not yet capable of believing in Jesus will be saved rather than lost if they die at an early age. Almost all have thought that people born with severe mental limitations, even if they live into adulthood, may fall into the same category. Therefore, the entire category of restrictivism needs more careful nuancing than it usually receives.

Many completely orthodox or evangelical Christians, however, have adopted other approaches altogether to the fate of the unevangelized. A *Calvinist* perspective argues that God has his elect or chosen people throughout time and throughout the world, and if human emissaries fail to reach them with the gospel, he can send word directly, especially through dreams and visions. On occasion, even an angel delivers the message. In recent decades, a significant percentage of all the Muslim converts to Christianity worldwide have had a dream, a vision, or an appearance of an angel or of Christ himself, which has led them to embrace Jesus as Lord and Savior.[4] One strongly Calvinist writer tries to preserve his understanding of God's sovereignty in election alongside God's compassion for children by affirming that all infants who die thereby demonstrate that they were among God's elect.[5]

A more *Wesleyan-Arminian* perspective appeals to God's foreknowledge and argues that God knows how every person who ever lived would have responded to the gospel had they heard it and treats each person based on that knowledge.[6] This guards against the charge that God's election is simply arbitrary, but it leaves itself open to the countercharge that human response trumps God's sovereignty. A mediating position between complete Calvinism and thoroughgoing Arminianism is *Molinism*, or middle knowledge. This is the view that God knows how every person who could possibly be created would respond under every possible circumstance. Of that infinite set of beings, he chooses actually to create a finite subset. This view preserves the Calvinist concern to prioritize God's sovereignty: he chooses which potential people to create and which not to. But it also preserves the Wesleyan-Arminian concern to avoid determinism: God does not create people to act a certain way but creates them after knowing how they would act in all possible situations of life.[7]

A few evangelical thinkers have argued for *postmortem evangelization.* This view affirms that God will give unbelievers an opportunity to receive the gospel in their postmortem state: those who did not hear the Christian message in this life will get to hear it in the next, and they will be judged based on their response to it at that time.[8] But for the most part this has been an option found among those who are heterodox in their views on various key Christian doctrines.[9] In addition, it seems to fly in the face of the key emphasis in Hebrews 9:27 that it is appointed for humans to die once and then comes judgment. In other words, there does not seem to be any place for some kind of "second chance" of salvation after death (on 1 Pet. 3:18–22, see "Postmortem Evangelization?" below).[10] Still others adopt *annihilationism,* the view that only believers live forever (or, in some versions, are re-created). Unbelievers die and simply cease conscious existence.[11] So if there appears to be some injustice in who gets to hear the gospel and who doesn't, the consequences aren't that bad for those who do not. Yet, if the glories of the new heaven and new earth even remotely approximate the depictions of Revelation 21–22, those who are simply annihilated are still losing out on an infinity of happiness.

An approach sometimes called *inclusivism* believes that general or natural revelation can disclose enough of the Christian message to people that they can make an informed response to it, even if they do not have access to the gospel message per se (special revelation).[12] Inclusivism should not be confused with *universalism*—the view that everyone will eventually be saved irrespective of what they have done or believed in this life.[13] Nor is it to be confused with *pluralism,* which maintains the perspective that people may come to God adequately through numerous world religions, even if every last person is not saved.[14] Rather, inclusivism suggests that the nature of the universe and of humanity may be sufficient in and of itself to convince people that God exists and that they could not possibly live up to his infinitely perfect and holy standards. If they then recognize that their only hope is to throw themselves on the mercy of that God, however they conceive of him, perhaps God will consider that adequate and save them by his grace, through the finished work of Christ on the cross.[15] Inclusivists, as a result, tend to believe not that anyone is saved by means of their non-Christian religion but that other religions can prepare the way *in some respects* for them to be open to God's general or natural revelation. This may in turn cause them to reject other elements of their religion in order to have a genuine faith in the living God, however partially they may know him. They also tend to stress that such possibilities for salvation are not nearly as good as if those people actually were to hear and believe the true gospel of Jesus Christ.[16]

All these perspectives are further intertwined with individuals' conceptions of "hell," the standard Christian term for the sphere of postmortem existence of those who never become believers. This classic Christian doctrine is another major stumbling block for many. Atheists and skeptics consistently note that they find the concept of a God who would torture anyone forever repulsive, so that they could not believe in that kind of God. The most important response whenever anyone says, "I could not believe in a God who . . . ," no matter how that sentence is finished, is to note that whether or not a person thinks they can believe in a certain kind of God has no logical relationship to whether or not that kind of God actually exists. I might decide that I could not believe that Lake Michigan could ever freeze solid enough for a person to walk across it from Illinois to Michigan. But whether I am able or willing to believe it is possible has no relationship to the truth of the matter. I might believe it even though it were impossible; I might not believe it even though it were possible.[17]

Fortunately, the Christian concept of hell does not require anyone to believe that God tortures people forever. That concept owes more to Dante's *Inferno* or Jonathan Edwards's "Sinners in the Hands of an Angry God" than to the Bible itself. Once again, there are several possibilities for hell that have been argued from Scripture by competent, godly exegetes. The pictures of outer darkness and fire, or of weeping and gnashing of teeth, may well be metaphorical and not refer to any kind of physical torture at all.[18] Some have argued that the words translated as "eternal" or "everlasting" are better rendered as "to the end of the age," while even "forever and ever" means "to the end of the ages of ages," so that hell has a finite and temporal boundary.[19] Others have envisioned an intermediate state of purgatory, which is also finite, with hell reserved only for the very most wicked.[20]

As with the problem of evil, certain key New Testament texts often get very little attention. *Philosophers* wrestle with the logic of whether infinite punishment is consistent with a finite amount of sin. *Ethicists* debate whether any of the viewpoints on hell can be said to be morally just. Certain kinds of *theologians* like to highlight that because we all deserve hell for our sins, it is an act of God's sheer grace and mercy that he brings the gospel to *anyone* so that some may escape it, even if it seems unjust that not all have had an equal opportunity to hear that good news. *Old Testament scholars* like to point out that *Sheol*, the Hebrew word for the place of the dead, can sometimes mean just "grave" and not necessarily refer to any kind of conscious existence after death. But for the Christian, who should factor in the New Testament as well, and pay attention in detail to what its most relevant texts actually say, is there any more than this to emphasize?

The Problem of the Unevangelized

We begin with the problem of the unevangelized. The single most important text in all the New Testament on the topic may be Romans 2:13–16. It merits citation in full.

> For it is not those who hear the law who are righteous in God's sight, but it is those who obey the law who will be declared righteous. (Indeed, when Gentiles, who do not have the law, do by nature things required by the law, they are a law for themselves, even though they do not have the law. They show that the requirements of the law are written on their hearts, their consciences also bearing witness, and their thoughts sometimes accusing them and at other times even defending them.) This will take place on the day when God judges people's secrets through Jesus Christ, as my gospel declares.

Needless to say, at first glance, this passage seems to fly in the face of the overall thrust of the theology of Romans, indeed of Paul more generally, and arguably of the entire New Testament, that salvation is entirely by grace through faith apart from the works of the torah (the Old Testament law). Some scholars in fact use this as one of several passages that suggest to them that Paul's view of the law is incoherent, or at least inconsistent at various points.[21]

Major Approaches to Romans 2:13–16

A substantial majority of scholars, who think Paul does have a coherent or consistent understanding of the role of grace and works in salvation, suggest one of three possible ways of articulating Paul's thinking on this topic. The first, the most common, and probably the best known is that Paul is speaking hypothetically, a view held by both Martin Luther and John Calvin.[22] Yes, if someone ever could keep the law perfectly, they would be saved by their works. But no one ever comes at all close to doing this, so judgment according to a person's works always leads to their damnation. Whether or not a person has heard the gospel of Jesus Christ, they should know both from the existence of the universe and from human morality that God exists. Romans 1:20 has already declared, "For since the creation of the world God's invisible qualities—his eternal power and divine nature—have been clearly seen, being understood from what has been made, so that people are without excuse." Intelligent design in the universe suggests an intelligence behind it. In fact, the very existence of anything rather than nothing cries out for an explanation of how it came into being.[23] Here are the seeds of what philosophers call the teleological and cosmological arguments for God's existence, respectively. Verse 32 then supplements these with the foundation of the moral argument: people "know God's righteous decree that those who do such things [the long list of sins in vv. 29–31] deserve death," yet "they not only continue to do these very things but also approve of those who practice them."[24] People throughout the world may not always agree on every detail of what is right and wrong, moral and immoral, but they have a striking amount of agreement. The very fact that morality exists, moreover, points to the existence of someone or something outside of humanity that established that morality. So God is justified in condemning everyone who does not live up to whatever moral standards their culture has established, and that indicts everyone.[25]

There are actually three passages in Romans 2, not just verses 13–16, that nevertheless all seem to cut against the grain of Paul's main point in 1:18–3:20 about the universal sinfulness of humanity that leads all to stand condemned before God apart from Christ. The first appears in 2:6–10 and the last in 2:25–29. Verses 6–10 form the passage that is most amenable to the hypothetical interpretation I have just outlined. In short, these verses teach that God will repay each person according to their works—eternal life to the one who has persisted in doing good but only wrath and anger for the self-seeking person who rejects the truth and persists in evil. It is not difficult to imagine Paul implying that "since no one falls into the first category, judgment by works leads only to damnation."[26]

At first blush, 2:13–16 could appear to be saying the same thing. Verses 11–12 form the hinge between the two sections, emphasizing that God does not show favoritism, so that both those who sin under the law and those who sin outside the law will perish. Nevertheless, verses 13–16 are making a different kind of contrast than verses 6–10. "When Gentiles, who do not have the law, do by nature things required by the law" (v. 14) sounds more real than hypothetical. The contrast in verse 13 is not between the one who does good and the one who does evil as in verses 6–10, but between the one who merely hears the law and the one who obeys it. This enables Paul to address the question about the salvation of the Gentiles: even though they have not heard the law, they might be obeying it anyway. If no one ever did obey it, then it is hard to see why Paul even introduces this second argument, since his point would have been made adequately in verses 6–10. In addition, he notes that the Gentiles' consciences also bear witness, alternately accusing and acquitting them. If Paul's point were merely that all Gentiles are lost because all are sinners and their consciences themselves testify to this reality, then he would be arguing at cross-purposes with himself to add that sometimes those very consciences do not condemn some Gentiles.[27]

When we turn to verses 25–29, it becomes virtually impossible to limit Paul to making a merely hypothetical argument. Now he is speaking straight-forwardly of certain uncircumcised people keeping the law's requirements sufficiently that they will condemn the lawbreakers within Judaism (v. 27). Verse 29 would appear to clinch matters: a person is a true Jew not through outward circumcision but through circumcision of the heart, by the Spirit. Here is language that echoes the prophecy of Jeremiah's new covenant in Jeremiah 31:31–34, which was very much a genuine experience, fulfilled in the coming of Jesus and the establishment of his church. Even Luther had to admit that at least verses 25–29 refer to real people who really lived—namely, new-covenant believers.[28]

That brings us to the second main interpretation of Romans 2:13–16. This view argues that Paul is not talking about Gentile unbelievers at all but about Gentile Christians. Both Karl Barth in the twentieth century and St. Augustine in the fifth century defended this approach.[29] This requires repunctuating the sentence, and since the oldest manuscripts lacked punctuation, we are free to do that if it makes better sense of the text. Instead of translating the Greek of verse 14 as "when Gentiles, who do not have the law, do by nature things required by the law," we would render it as "when Gentiles, who do not have the law by nature, do things required by the law." These Gentiles can then be understood to be believers who didn't originally have the law as Jews did, but now they do have the law because in Christ it has been written on their hearts. This could clearly fit verses 25–29 too. It would not be the most natural reading of verses 6–10, but once established in the later verses it could fit there.[30] The biggest problem with this perspective is that the whole thrust of 1:18–3:20 is precisely the pre-Christian state of humanity. Paul is building toward the huge transition between 3:20 and 3:21 that whereas no one is justified by works of the law, Christ has come to justify us apart from the law. It would be highly incongruous if he expected his readers to realize that he was jumping ahead to talk about believers after Christ's coming when everything else in 1:18–3:20 is about humanity's condition prior to that coming.[31]

Was anyone else, therefore, ever a Jew inwardly (Rom. 2:29) prior to the coming of Christ? Of course. Innumerable Israelites throughout Old Testa-ment history, though many more in some periods of time than in others, were faithful followers of Yahweh, recognizing that the law was given to live out one's salvation rather than to attain it. For them religion was not merely an artificial façade but very much an internal and internalized way of life. Romans 2:25–29 may certainly be applied to Christians after Jesus's life and death, but they are by no means the only people who were ever circumcised (purified and dedicated to their God) in their hearts.[32] The third approach, therefore, takes these various verses in Romans 2 to refer to pre-Christian Israelites (and others) who had a true relationship with God. Faithful Jews also fit nicely as a primary referent of those who are said to do good in verses 6–10. But the Gentiles who do the law by nature (reverting now to the standard translation of verse 14) cannot simultaneously be Jews. So Paul must envisage some Gentiles likewise recognizing the role of law to be a response to the spiritual rescue that God himself must effect. Paul may well have had God-fearers in mind—those Gentiles who had come to believe in Yahweh and in many instances attended synagogue services and kept large portions of the law but without getting circumcised or becoming full-fledged converts to Judaism. He may well have also had individuals like Job, Ruth, Melchizedek, Rahab, and Naaman in view. Indeed, he may well have envisioned still larger numbers of people who never had heard the gospel, recent as its arrival on the stage of world history was, falling into such a category. Christians down through the centuries holding this view have often spoken of these Gentiles as people who lived according to the light they had received even if they never received the full light of the gospel.[33] Sometimes that "light" came in spite of their religion, especially when people rejected certain parts of their belief systems that were inimical to God's truth.

Was Paul thinking exclusively of the epochs before the coming of Christ when he spoke of the Gentiles who did the law by nature? No doubt, he was thinking primarily of those eras, since they constituted the vast majority of history from his vantage point, as he wrote in what we call the late 50s of the first century. But it defies credibility to imagine him never giving any thought to the spiritual state of everyone alive in his day who might die before they heard the gospel. Indeed, he would have almost certainly known (or at least known of) people who died in the twenty-seven or so years since Jesus's death and resurrection in AD 30 without learning about Jesus. To put the question pointedly, we need to ask what he thought about the faithful Jews who were not trying to establish their own righteousness by the law (as in Rom. 10:3) but following it as the proper outgrowth of salvation and offering sacrifices for the forgiveness of sins when they failed. Were they right with God in the late 20s, but if they lived into the mid-30s and then died without hearing the gospel, were they then lost? Did their eternal destiny depend on the date of their death? The notion seems scarcely conceivable.[34]

Perhaps, then, spiritually speaking, we should think of the transition from BC to AD not as a fixed dividing point in world history but as the division in time before and after a group of people (or even a single individual) gains an understanding of the genuine gospel of Jesus Christ.[35] A friend of mine during my doctoral studies in the early 1980s was a fortysomething native of a rural village in West Africa. He could actually recall as a boy when missionaries first came to his village and there was a widespread outpouring of faith and many conversions. With others in his family, he put his trust in Jesus at that time also. But he had a nagging question he had to ask one of the missionaries. "My father," he told the man, "died last year. But he was just like the rest of us who are becoming Christians. I know that if he were still alive, he would be trusting in Jesus too. But he never had the chance. Where is my father now?" The missionary pointed him to Romans 2:13–16 and read the text to him. He went on gently to explain, "We can't be completely certain but it seems like there is a very good chance your father is with Jesus." The boy was very relieved and replied, "I am so glad you said that, because if you told me that he was in hell, then I could not become a Christian. I would have to go to be where my father is so I could be with him." Whatever theological immaturity the boy may have reflected in his comments, the missionary gave a very wise answer.[36]

Implications of This Third Approach

Above I spoke of an "understanding of the genuine gospel." I could have phrased it as a "credible presentation of the gospel." It is possible for someone to hear the name "Jesus" or the term "Christian" or even gain some knowledge of what some people claim is Christianity without understanding the genuine gospel. Perhaps this takes place because the message is so truncated or skewed an oversimplification of the true gospel that it really isn't the good news of the New Testament at all. Perhaps it is so contradicted by a person or group of people's actions (as with some supposedly "Christian" Nazis in twentieth-century Germany or some supposedly "Christian" Ku Klux Klan members even today in the United States) that the actual teaching of Jesus, even if quoted, cannot properly be heard. Perhaps even the terminology gets in the way, as in parts of the Muslim world today where a "Christian" is synonymous with a rich, decadent, sexually immoral Westerner! Better in such instances to discard the term altogether and use one that can be dissociated from the false stereotypes—for example, "follower of Jesus"—so that people can hear and respond to the genuine good news. Otherwise, even seemingly evangelized people may in fact be unevangelized![37]

At this juncture, thoughtful readers may be formulating a potential objection. If someone could be saved without ever hearing the gospel, might they not later hear the gospel, reject it, and become lost? If this is the case, isn't it better not to promulgate the Christian message at all? Whatever the first followers of Jesus may have thought about the Gentile world, they certainly agreed that there were some of their Jewish compatriots who were in right standing with God. Presumably, then, the only consistent answer to this question is that those who were right with God must have been among those who responded positively to the message about Jesus when they heard it. Furthermore, the urgency that all the apostles felt for getting the word out to the ends of the earth suggests that they did not think that huge numbers of people, Jew or Gentile, were already believers.[38] They may well have taken their cue from the temporary nature of the temple sacrifices to cleanse human consciences from sin, as the author to the Hebrews argues (Heb. 9:9). They most likely did not imagine that anyone had the assurance of salvation in the long term, since sacrifices had to be repeatedly offered throughout one's life (7:27). And they might not have been able to point to anyone—Jew or Gentile—who they could say with confidence was saved prior to hearing the gospel, as Paul discusses in Romans 10:14–17. Yet in the same breath Paul can argue that the gospel has gone out to the whole earth, presumably again thinking of general or natural revelation (v. 18, quoting Ps. 19:1–4, a classic passage on natural revelation; cf. Col. 1:23).[39]

Objections from the Right and the Left

Two specific New Testament verses that are probably the most commonly cited ones by restrictivists are John 14:6 and Acts 4:12. In John 14:6, Jesus declares, "I am the way and the truth and the life. No one comes to the Father except through me." Clearly, Jesus is denying that there are any other saviors or mediators between God and humanity besides himself (cf. 1 Tim. 2:5).[40] But that is not quite the same as claiming that people must have heard about him; otherwise, again, there would be no way that any faithful Israelite during the period of the Mosaic covenant could ever have been saved. Or to go back even further, if anyone was unequivocally stated to have been right with God in pre-Christian times it was Abraham, "who believed the LORD, and he credited it to him as righteousness" (Gen. 15:6). Abraham never had the story of Christ's life, death, and resurrection narrated to him nearly two thousand years beforehand; his faith was directed toward God, who had promised him land and legacy, including descendants who would form an elect nation culminating in a long-awaited Messiah (12:1–4).[41] The New Testament itself makes these verses foundational for its understanding of salvation (Rom. 4:3, 9, 22; Gal. 3:6–8; James 2:23). So everyone who is saved in every period of human history is ultimately saved because of Jesus's full and final atonement on the cross, but that is different from saying everyone has to have heard the name "Jesus."[42]

Ah, but what about Acts 4:12? Doesn't Peter here explicitly declare, "Salvation is found in no one else, for there is no other name under heaven given to mankind by which we must be saved"? Of course, but one's "name" in biblical times often stood for a person's power, authority, or identity.[43] Even if "name" additionally preserves some sense of the literal appellation by which Jesus was called, Peter still stops just short of saying everyone has to have heard the name.[44] It is simply that God in Christ brooks no rival. If a person trusts in God to deal with them according to his mercy or grace and not according to the person's own merit, and if it turns out to be the case that God does indeed save such a person even if they haven't had a chance to hear the gospel or the name "Jesus," it will still be solely by the death and resurrection of Jesus Christ that the person is saved.[45]

This kind of inclusivism must be clearly differentiated from universalism, the belief that sooner or later, in this life or in the next, all people will be saved. Various texts are sometimes marshaled in support of universalism, perhaps none more often than Romans 5:18 and 1 Corinthians 15:22. The first of these two passages reads, "Consequently, just as one trespass resulted in condemnation for all people, so also one righteous act resulted in justification and life for all people." Out of context, especially since Adam's sin did lead to universal sin and condemnation, it is easy to assume that Paul is teaching universal forgiveness and salvation. But a glance at just the two verses immediately before and immediately after Romans 5:18 refutes this assumption. Verse 17 reads, "For if, by the trespass of the one man, death reigned through that one man, how much more will those who receive God's abundant provision of grace and of the gift of righteousness reign in life through the one man, Jesus Christ." Here it is clear that those who reign in life are those who *receive* God's gift of salvation. And in verse 19, Paul shifts from talking about justification for all to "many" being made righteous. The "justification and life for all people" about which verse 18 speaks, therefore, must be the *opportunity* for everyone to be saved. Still, it is not forced on those who are unwilling to receive it.[46] First Corinthians 15:22 reads, "For as in Adam all die, so in Christ all will be made alive." Again, it is easy to understand those who reason that since everyone without exception died in Adam, everyone without exception will be made alive in Christ. But again, the immediate context should disabuse us of this notion. Verse 23 adds, "But each in turn: Christ, the firstfruits; then, when he comes, those who belong to him." The "all" who will be made alive are clearly all those who belong to him.[47]

Two other passages frequently cited in support of universalism are Philippians 2:10–11 and Colossians 1:20. The so-called Philippian hymn contains the promise that sometime after Jesus has been reexalted to the Father's right hand, every knee in the universe will bow to him and every tongue acknowledge that he is Lord. The so-called Colossian hymn speaks of Christ reconciling all things in the universe to himself. But the verses in Philippians allude to Isaiah 45:23b–24, which declares, "Before me every knee will bow; by me every tongue will swear. They will say of me, 'In the LORD alone are deliverance and strength.'" These gestures of subservience, moreover, are not salvific ones, because Isaiah immediately adds, "All who have raged against him will come to him and be put to shame."[48] Given the overall similarities between the Philippian and Colossian hymns, it is likely that Colossians 1:20 should be understood similarly. Here "reconciliation," then, most likely refers to a person putting someone or something else back into its appointed place in the universe. The possibility of being made right with God in redemption is available to all, but not its actuality.[49] No one will be forced into being saved against their will.

While we cannot, therefore, say simply that everyone who has never heard the gospel is lost for all eternity, we see that at least some are. To claim otherwise would be to fly in the face of Paul's (indeed, the whole New Testament's) repeated emphasis on salvation by grace through faith rather than the works of the law (or any law). Put differently, hell will be populated by more than just the devil and his minions. There will be human beings there as well. But there may not be as many as some restrictivists think, and we certainly do not have to try to defend the claim that everyone who has never heard the gospel is automatically damned for all eternity.

The Problems of Hell

The moment we raise the topic of hell, however, we have to answer the question of what kind of hell we are talking about. The "outer darkness" (Matt. 8:12; 22:13; 25:30 NRSV) and "lake of fire" (Rev. 20:14–15) cancel each other out if either is absolutized.[50] So what is the literal reality behind these awful metaphors? Second Thessalonians 1:9 gives one probable answer: "They will be punished with everlasting destruction and shut out from the presence of the Lord and from the glory of his might." Exclusion from God *and all things good* is a key nonmetaphorical summary of the nature of hell.[51] This is agonizing enough. "Weeping and gnashing of teeth" (e.g., Matt. 8:12; 13:42, 50) suggests anguish and even anger, but not necessarily physical torture.[52] The key Greek verb for "torture" or "torment" in the New Testament, *basanizō*, is used for eternal suffering only once, and then only of the fate of the unholy "trinity" of the devil, the beast, and the false prophet (Rev. 20:10). Matthew 18:34 does use the cognate noun, *basanistēs*, for "torturer," but this may have just become a synonym for "jailer," and it comes in the context of a parable, the details of which should not all be allegorized.[53]

What, Then, Is Hell Like?

In fact, the most common description in the New Testament of the fate of the wicked or unbelieving is some form of destruction or ruin, as in 2 Thessalonians 1:9. (Consider, for further examples, Matt. 7:13; Luke 6:49; John 17:12; Rom. 9:22; Gal. 6:8; Phil. 3:19; 2 Thess. 2:3; 2 Pet. 2:1, 3; 3:7, 12, 16.) One can understand where annihilationism finds its support. But something can be ruined and yet still live, and the key terms in the Greek can be taken both for cessation of existence and for destruction of a current form of existence to be replaced by an undesirable one.[54] More significant are the places where Jesus stresses that it would be better for the wicked not to have been born than to have committed various sins and gone to hell. Matthew 5:29–30 twice says, for example, that it would be better to lose a sinning body part than to be thrown whole into hell. But if hell is just lack of conscious existence, there would be a lot of situations in which people would find that to be more desirable than suffering as a maimed person in this life (see also Matt. 18:6, 8–9). In Mark 14:21 and parallels, Jesus proclaims that it would be better for the one who was going to betray him never to have been born. Yet again, if before his birth, Judas had no conscious awareness of anything, and after death that was his state once more, neither condition seems any better or worse than the other.[55]

As for the idea that hell is finite in duration, we need to turn to those passages where the language of eternity is used for life after death in a positive sense and see how it is paralleled with life after death in a negative sense, without any contextual indicators that the two are to be taken differently. The classic example is in the so-called parable of the sheep and the goats (Matt. 25:31–46), where one group of people goes away to eternal punishment and the other to eternal life (v. 46). If eternal life is a conscious existence that continues forever, presumably eternal punishment is also (cf. Dan. 12:2 for similar language and probable background).[56] John 5:29 offers a very similar picture of the resurrection of all people, in which "those who have done what is good will rise to live, and those who have done what is evil will rise to be condemned."[57]

Can This Be Fair?

But how is infinite punishment congruent with a finite amount of sin over a finite life? And surely once those who have rebelled against God and rejected

Jesus see what separation from him and all things good is actually like, they would have a change of heart and want to repent. How can God be just if he refuses to forgive them in such a situation? The problem may lie in the assumptions behind the question. Maybe no one ever will want to leave hell for heaven. One of the most remarkable passages in Scripture that is almost never commented on in the context of discussions about heaven and hell is Revelation 20:8. On any view of the millennium, Revelation 20 portrays Jesus reigning over earth more beneficently than any monarch or politician in human history, as Satan is kept locked in the Abyss (v. 3) so that he cannot wreak the havoc on earth he was used to doing. Yet the moment he is let loose for one last fling (v. 7), innumerable people from every corner of the earth assemble under his leadership to fight against God and his people one last time (v. 8).[58] It seems that there are many people who simply will not release control of their lives to a supremely good Being, even though they will readily give in to seduction by diabolical powers. As C. S. Lewis has phrased it so memorably, if the "doors of hell" are locked, they are "locked on the inside."[59] Or as he puts it in another place, "There are only two kinds of people in the end: those who say to God, 'Thy will be done,' and those to whom God says, . . . 'Thy will be done.'"[60] In any event, there is no example anywhere in the Bible of God refusing someone who sincerely repents and wants to turn to him.

Another little-used text is Luke 12:47–48. Here Jesus announces that "the servant who knows the master's will and does not get ready or does not do what the master wants will be beaten with many blows. But the one who does not know and does things deserving punishment will be beaten with few blows. From everyone who has been given much, much will be demanded; and from the one who has been entrusted with much, much more will be asked." Over the centuries, Christians have debated whether there are eternal rewards in heaven. With Luther, and against Calvin, it is at least arguable that salvation by grace precludes the kinds of rewards that would lead to eternal differentiation of status of believers, even though everyone will have a very unique experience of judgment day with the kind and amount of praise and censure they receive.[61] But it should be much easier to agree that since judgment is according to works, those who are lost should indeed have gradations of punishment, which is exactly what these verses assert.[62]

What, then, of the charge that it seems entirely unfair to envision the proverbial "little old lady down the street" who never hurt anyone (but still as an atheist thumbed her nose at Jesus) having the same experience in the life to come as the mass murderers and brutal dictators of world history? The proper reply should be that she will *not* have the same experience! She will still not be in heaven, but compared to the Hitlers and Idi Amins of world history, her punishment will be comparatively light. Metaphorically put, she will be beaten with few blows. This clearly biblical teaching should address at least some of our need for justice in ways that annihilationism, certain very generous forms of inclusivism, and universalism cannot. To the skeptics who lampoon the notions of heaven and hell by saying that if the worst of the televangelists are in heaven, they wouldn't want to be there with them and would prefer to be with their buddies in hell,[63] at least three responses prove crucial. First, they drastically underestimate the harshness of life apart from all the moderating influences Christians have had on society. Second, they ignore the Christian doctrine of glorification, which says that the truly repentant person will be transformed into a perfect, sinless individual, so that even the most annoying features about some genuine Christians will disappear. Finally, if, as seems likely, in at least a few cases the most egregious and distasteful of those who peddle religion in public are not true believers at all, then those same skeptics may find that they haven't avoided the people they most dislike but are stuck with them forever!

Postmortem Evangelization?

The two passages in the New Testament that have most commended the idea of a second chance to repent after death appear in 1 Peter 3:18–22 and 4:6. Space prohibits us from going into detail on all the different approaches that interpreters have taken with these texts over the centuries. Suffice it to say that there is a fair consensus among scholars today that 3:18–22 refers to Christ proclaiming his victory to the demonic realm by virtue of his death and resurrection, rather than offering the gospel to those who didn't accept it in this life.[64] First Peter 4:6 seems most likely best taken, with the NIV, as referring to the gospel having been proclaimed at the time that those who are now dead were still alive, in order that they might experience spiritual life after death.[65]

One final observation, however, should ameliorate some of the concern that leads to theories of postmortem evangelization. Only recently, thanks to advances in medicine, have we been able with any frequency to bring people back to life, often on the operating table, who have actually lost all vital signs and even been pronounced dead. In many such "near-death experiences," as they have come to be called, individuals have described some kind of out-of-the-body experience of an existence they understand to be heaven (and in rarer cases, hell), or at least they encounter an angelic figure or even Jesus himself. In some of these experiences, they are able to report accurately on what was happening and even spoken in the operating room, other places in the hospital, and even other places outside of the hospital while they were flatlined. In many instances, those who were not believers became Christians, while nominal believers became much more committed Christians.[66] Yet the vast majority of everyone in the world who dies is never brought back to life, so for all we know, God could be revealing himself to many, many more just before they pass away. But we will never know this until eternity, because they don't come back from death to tell us. "Deathbed conversions" may actually be far more common than we might ever guess![67]

Conclusion

Be that as it may, at the end of the day we should be able to turn Abraham's rhetorical question in Genesis 18:25 ("Will not the Judge of all the earth do right?") into a resounding affirmation that God will indeed do right by every person who has ever lived. What is much more amazing and significant, though, is how often his mercy will triumph over his judgment (James 2:13).[68] We don't want God merely to be fair; we want him to be very gracious! He will have solved the problem of the unevangelized graciously and fairly, and there will be no one in hell who would prefer to repent and turn over control of their lives to God. To paraphrase the eighteenth-century ex–slave trader and author of the words to the hymn "Amazing Grace," John Newton, there will be three surprises in heaven—who's there, who's not there, and that I'm there![69]

3

Slavery, Gender Roles, and Same-Sex Sexual Relations

O ur next topic combines three issues that are closely related in many people's minds. For modern Bible readers, God appears to discriminate against slaves, women, and lesbian/gay/bisexual/transgender/queer (LGBTQ+) individuals. In a highly egalitarian age, at least in the Western world, this is almost the unforgivable sin. In cultures in which tolerance is the highest virtue, the only thing that cannot be tolerated is the appearance of intolerance.[1] The Christian church has at times condoned slavery. Far more often than not, it has limited women's roles in the church and home. In addition, its attitudes and actions toward the LGBTQ+ community have at times proved downright hateful. If these behaviors faithfully represent the Christian God's perspectives, then such a God cannot be believed in or trusted. In fact, he must not exist at all. Or so the argument goes. Once again, we frequently hear the refrain, "I cannot believe in a God who . . . ." In this case, the sentence is completed with something like "would discriminate in this fashion against people who are already oppressed." Of all the issues raised in this book, this may well be the most sensitive at this point in history.

As we noted in the last chapter, whether certain people can bring themselves to believe in a certain kind of God has no logical relationship with whether such a God exists. It is the age-old distinction between ontology (the study of what exists) and epistemology (the study of what I can know exists). Whether I believe a mammal exists that lays eggs, has a bill like a duck, a tail like a beaver,

33

and feet like an otter has no bearing on whether a platypus actually exists. If in fact God does exist, a person's disbelief does not disprove his existence; it only shows that that person is alienated from him. But as it turns out, the oppressive kind of God whom many disbelieve is not the God who appears in the New Testament. *Philosophers* may debate whether the concept of ontological equality (equality at the very essence or core of all human beings) can be preserved alongside functional subordination (one category of people consistently submitting to another voluntarily).[2] *Ethicists* may debate the best ways to oppose slavery.[3] *Theologians* may speak of redemptive trajectories and see patterns of growing openness to certain freedoms as one proceeds through the Scriptures chronologically.[4] *Old Testament scholars* have the difficult task of trying to explain some of the harsher laws and practices on these topics · and then wrestling with how they apply, if at all, in today's world.[5] But what should *New Testament scholars* stress? Do they have anything distinctive to contribute to each of these three topics? We will consider them one at a time.

Slavery

Skeptics often turn to the Old Testament passages that legislate the treatment of slaves without ever calling for their emancipation and throw them in Christians' faces, accusing the biblical God of being immoral.[6] They seldom note that, compared with the practices of the other ancient Near Eastern cultures surrounding Israel, the Hebrew Scriptures moderate and tone down the approaches of their world.[7] Skeptics typically say nothing about the laws to set slaves free in sabbatical years (Exod. 21:2–11). Even more importantly, they usually don't observe that Christian believers should never implement any Old Testament teaching without understanding if and how the New Testament modifies it.[8] Those same critics, of course, can turn to individual New Testament passages, most notably Paul's "household codes" (Eph. 5:21–6:9; Col. 3:18–4:1; see also 1 Pet. 2:13–3:7), and make similar accusations.

Several general points should be made in response. Slavery in the ancient Roman world was a much more diverse phenomenon than, say, slavery in antebellum America or human trafficking today.[9] Slaves in prosperous households or with kind masters more resembled indentured servants. Some rose in society to become reasonably well off. Slavery was based not on one's race or the color of one's skin but on other factors, such as whether one belonged to a subjugated nation that Rome had conquered. Many slaves had the opportunity to be manumitted (or manumit themselves) by about age thirty, after the peak of their working years. On the other hand, plenty still led miserable lives, whether in the underground mines or rowing the famous triremes for long hours day after day. Slaves were at the mercy of their masters as well for any heterosexual or homosexual "favors" that their masters might demand. Moreover, those masters could give other harsh orders and expect them to be followed unquestioningly.

Not surprisingly, then, slave revolts occurred in ancient Rome. But they were all squelched with horrible massacres of the rebels. Why might New Testament authors not have more directly opposed slavery? It is quite possible that they could scarcely have conceived of creating an entire empire without slaves, especially when Christians wielded no social or political power in that empire at all. A key point to make about the epistles' commands to slaves to obey and submit to their masters is that this was a commonplace ethic in the ancient world; few would have even batted an eye at it. The gospel, furthermore, was first and foremost about spiritual rather than political liberation, and the apostles no doubt wanted to keep first things first.[10] If a person is liberated from physical slavery but still has no spiritual hope for life beyond this one, they are actually worse off than the person who remains a slave but has a vibrant hope for spending a glorious eternity with God and all of his people, redeemed and perfected.

On the other hand, a fair amount of shock would have ensued when people heard Paul's commands to the Christian masters in Ephesus and Colossae not to threaten their slaves (Eph. 6:9) and to provide them with what is fair (Col. 4:1).[11] The male head of a household in the ancient Mediterranean world under Rome was the *paterfamilias*—the father of the family. Slaves were included in this definition of the family, and fathers had the right to punish wives, children, and slaves in any way they wished, including in extreme instances with death. Threats and injustice would have been routine, but Paul would have none of these. What is more, he would have well understood that the Hebrew Scriptures supported disobeying authorities whenever their demands violated God's will. He would have known about the midwives' refusal to obey Pharaoh and kill the baby boys in Moses's day (Exod. 1:15–21), as well as Daniel's refusal to eat the king's food in Babylon (Dan. 1:8–21) or bow down to Nebuchadnezzar's giant idol there (Dan. 3). He would have also likely known about the apostles' refusal to obey the Sanhedrin when they were commanded not to teach about Jesus anymore (Acts 4:19–20; 5:29). So his commands to slaves to obey their masters could not have been unconditional but rather were a generalization that admitted of numerous exceptions. It may be that the comparative clause in Colossians 3:23 is pointing precisely to this state of affairs when it calls on slaves to serve wholeheartedly "as working for the Lord." In other words, it may not mean that they should serve earthly masters *to the same extent* as they serve God; that would fly in the face of God being all Christians' highest priority (recall Luke 14:26 par.). Rather, it may mean that they should serve earthly masters *in the way* that they serve God, doing only that which is moral and consistent with worshiping and paying homage to Jesus.[12]

Galatians 3:28 is also a key verse for understanding Paul's views on slavery (along with gender roles and ethnic divisions) among God's people. He writes, "There is neither Jew nor Gentile, neither slave nor free, nor is there male and female, for you are all one in Christ Jesus." The concept that Christians are all "one" (rather than, say, "equal" or "the same") suggests that the theme of this verse is unity rather than absolute equality in all respects.[13] At the same time, a common Jewish prayer among the rabbis thanked God that he had made them male, Jewish, and free.[14] So it seems that Paul is deliberately countering this gratefulness for privileges with an affirmation that significantly levels any distinctions among the various categories of individuals mentioned. And it would certainly be more difficult to have any true spiritual unity across a sharp divide between slaves and free persons if Christians themselves continued to be slave owners.

If the New Testament passages surveyed thus far do not prove entirely conclusive, one verse and one entire book nevertheless strongly support the emancipation of slaves and foreshadow the abolition of slavery. In 1 Corinthians 7, Paul is stressing that just because one becomes a Christ follower does not mean they must immediately seek to change their social or physical status in this world. He illustrates by explaining, "Was a man already circumcised when he was called? He should not become uncircumcised. Was a man uncircumcised when he was called? He should not be circumcised. Circumcision is nothing and uncircumcision is nothing. Keeping God's commands is what counts. Each person should remain in the situation they were in when God called them. Were you a slave when you were called? Don't let it trouble you" (1 Cor. 7:18–21a). At first it seems that Paul is going to treat slavery the same way he treats circumcision, as a matter of theological indifference. But in the second half of verse 21 he quickly takes a different tack: "although if you can gain your freedom, do so." Verse 22 returns to the theme of spiritual status trumping social status, but then verse 23 reverses matters again: "You were bought at a price; do not become slaves of human beings." The language of "bought at a price" uses the very imagery of purchasing slaves to speak of spiritual redemption, so it is as if Paul were saying that the one who has been spiritually freed should not become physically enslaved.[15]

For many centuries, Christians debated the exact meaning of 1 Corinthians 7:21b because of its elliptical nature. If one were to translate one word at a time in this short half verse, the result might be: "but if indeed you can become free, more use!" More use? Use what? Use what more? Proponents of slavery once argued that Paul was saying, "Even if you can become free, stay a slave and use your position within your household that much more to model Christian behavior and witness to your faith."[16] But this requires the cryptic clause to go back to the first part of verse 21 rather than its nearest antecedent—the clause "but if indeed you can become free." Much more likely is the interpretation that Paul is telling slaves to use the opportunity all the more to become free. A detailed study a generation ago of these two words ("more use") in combination (Gk. *mallon chrēsai*) made this second option all but certain. The grammar throughout this half verse—the strong adversative "but" (*alla*), the "if indeed" (*ei kai*) that is not normally a concessive ("even if"), the normal meaning of "make use of" as "take [positive] advantage of," and the intensifying force of "rather" (*mallon*) as "all the more"—all points in that direction. Plus there is no evidence that slaves were ever allowed to refuse manumission.[17]

Even more decisive is the little letter to Philemon. Here Paul is advising his close friend how to treat his runaway slave Onesimus, who met up with Paul (probably when he was in house arrest in Rome) and became a Christian.[18] In his letter, Paul shows himself to be the master of tact and persuasion by ancient Mediterranean standards to try to convince Philemon to welcome Onesimus back and not punish him.[19] Paul praises Philemon's partnership with him in the faith (v. 6) and how he is known for having "refreshed the hearts of the Lord's people" (v. 7). He makes a play on words, since the name Onesimus means "useful," and he stresses how much more useful Onesimus now is as a believer (v. 11). Paul is sending Onesimus back to Philemon's household, which is also the site of a house church (vv. 1–2), presumably in Colossae. But as soon as Paul announces this, he adds that he would have preferred to keep Onesimus with him as one of his helpers (v. 13). Legally, this could take place only if Onesimus were granted his freedom.[20]

Paul all but requests Onesimus's manumission in verse 16 when he speaks of him returning "no longer as a slave, but better than a slave, as a dear [Christian] brother." Yet some have argued that the second phrase, "better than a slave," suggests that he could have still been a slave even while not treated like one.[21] If verse 16 doesn't quite clinch the argument, verse 21 should. Here Paul sums up, "Confident of your obedience, I write to you, knowing that you will do even more than I ask." If Paul hasn't explicitly requested Onesimus's freedom up to this point, he has certainly asked that he not be treated as a slave. What else is left but to manumit him if Paul expects Philemon to do *more* than he has asked for in so many words?[22]

The differences between the Old and New Testaments remind us that we must always read these two parts of the Christian Bible in terms of progressive revelation. One cannot simply quote individual Old Testament passages in isolation and reject Christianity on the grounds that those texts are objectionable. One has to take New Testament teaching into account as well. Especially when one sees movement in a given direction throughout the Old Testament and then sees that trajectory moving even further in the New, one has to judge the Christian faith based on where the Bible ends up, when the writings are complete at the end of the first century.[23] To the retort that this means that God changes, the appropriate answer is no, *he* doesn't. But the way his revelation expresses his will for humanity does progress, as human beings and societies develop. What might not have been realistically possible in the first century—the abolition of all slavery—certainly is today. Where it still exists, especially, for example, in human trafficking, Christians should be more committed than anyone to help abolish it. They have certainly been at the forefront of abolition movements in other centuries.[24] Those who actually support slavery simply disclose a sinful attitude (cf. Rev. 18:13) that does not reflect God's will. So it does not logically follow that a person should blame God and therefore reject him because of the misbehavior of a few believers.

Gender Roles

Possibly no topic in New Testament studies has elicited more scholarship in the past half century than gender roles in the church and the home. Is the husband an authority over his wife? Are certain positions in the church reserved for men? Understandably, much of this flurry of study was spawned by the secular women's liberation movement in the 1960s and 1970s. But many people don't realize the number of leadership roles gifted women have had in the church over the centuries. The more independent, charismatic, or revivalist the Christian movement or the less institutionalized or ossified the church structures, the more likely at least a few women held leadership roles every bit as significant as those held by the men who were their peers.[25] A hundred years ago the fundamentalist-modernist controversy led some thoroughly evangelical institutions and churches to pull back from ordaining women, and today one might never guess at their earlier views.[26] As recently as twenty years ago, vigorous debate still engulfed the evangelical world at both scholarly and lay levels.[27] Today, unfortunately, the sides have tended to harden, decide the matter is settled (despite the lack of a consensus), form their own tribes of like-minded Christians, and engage very little in serious give-and-take with the other side. This often leaves Christian women in the lurch wondering where they belong or fit into God's plans.

It is impossible in one-third of one chapter in a short book to survey all the wide-ranging debates on gender roles. After extensive study, I am convinced that there are really only two viable positions: one complementarian (not all roles are equally appropriate for both men and women) and one egalitarian (all roles are equally open for appropriately gifted men and women). I have sketched the one viable complementarian position elsewhere,[28] so I will only summarize it briefly here, referring to the most significant biblical texts. While some of the issues resemble those that emerged in the debate over slavery, the situations are not entirely parallel. Slaves are not a genetic category of human beings. Even when certain cultures have enslaved entire races, emancipation has always been a possibility, even if only theoretically. Until the recent surgeries that have made possible what is sometimes called gender reassignment, men and women had no way to be emancipated from their gender. Moreover, the debates about gender roles are not about being freed from a condition in which one was born but about having equal access to leadership roles while remaining within a given gender.

In the Old Testament, even if some examples only rarely occur, women do hold every leadership role or office in ancient Israel except the priesthood. In the New Testament, Jesus affirms and encourages women in countercultural ways in numerous contexts, even though he never selects one to be among his twelve closest followers—the apostles. Paul and the other letter writers positively portray women in every ecclesiastical context except that of elder or overseer. Biblically speaking, if one decides on a complementarian perspective, therefore, one should not restrict women in church leadership from anything other than the highest office in a given congregation or denomination. One should also observe that the New Testament concept of elder involves men who both teach and exercise authority over a Christian congregation. Many people today who get called elders are not actually the authoritative teachers of their churches because they rarely if ever teach publicly. In other words, they are not elders as the Bible defines and describes them at all. In a multiple-staff church, often the only person in a position fully equivalent to that of a New Testament elder is the senior pastor, because everyone else looks to that person as the sole, fully authoritative teacher in the congregation.[29] Everyone else holds a subordinate or derived authority.

Even in this complementarian context, therefore, women should be allowed to lead and teach under the authority of the senior pastor, including preaching. Spirit-filled preaching is one form of the exercise of the spiritual gift of prophecy,[30] which Paul permits men and women alike to exercise so long as they have the culturally appropriate clothing and/or hairstyles that do not suggest they are sexually unfaithful to their spouses, if married, or religiously unfaithful to God (1 Cor. 11:2–16).[31] Women should participate with the entire congregation in evaluating the ministries of others who exercise gifts of teaching and leadership in their midst, but the final say still has to reside with someone. If Paul is assuming that these would be the elders, and that elders were all men (as arguably with 1 Tim. 2:12 below), then 1 Corinthians 14:35–36 could be referring merely to the women staying silent as the elders determined which prophecies to accept, rather than refraining from speaking in all ecclesiastical contexts.[32] When Paul writes that he does not permit a woman to teach or assume authority over a man, he is speaking not of two separate activities, teaching and exercising authority, but of two aspects of one related activity—authoritative teaching—made possible by virtue of that person occupying the office of elder, that is, senior pastor (1 Tim. 2:11–15, esp. v. 12).[33] Paul then supports this restriction by appealing to the sequence of the creation of the man and woman and of the sin of woman and man in Genesis 2–3 (1 Tim. 2:13–14), suggesting that he sees his commands as timeless, not bound by the specific contexts of his letters.

In the home, complementarians insist that wives should submit to their husbands (Eph. 5:22–24). Husbands meanwhile must love their wives sacrificially, as Christ loved the church (vv. 25–33). Paul designates the husband as "head" of his wife. In context, however, this suggests no unique privilege but rather a unique responsibility, since husbands must sacrifice themselves for their wives as Christ did for the church (v. 25).[34] In 1 Peter 3, Christian wives are to submit to unbelieving husbands to maximize the likelihood of their becoming Christians (vv. 1–6). However, Christian husbands must treat their wives with great respect as joint heirs of salvation lest God choose simply not to answer their prayers (v. 7)! Already in the preceding passage on slaves and masters (2:18–25), we read that Christ suffered for us, leaving us an example, so that we might follow in his steps (v. 21). We cannot imitate Jesus's atonement, since his death was a once-for-all provision for sin (Heb. 9:26). On the other hand, prior to the time for his death that God had shown him, Jesus's only reaction to hostility was to run away from it, when it came on him for any more than a brief period of time (e.g., Matt. 4:12; 12:15; 14:13). Therefore, Peter's commands for wives to submit not only do not allow spousal abuse but actually imply similar withdrawal from harm's way.[35]

In Ephesians 5, Paul's injunction to wives to submit to their husbands (v. 22) follows immediately after his call for mutual submission (v. 21). While it is true that all Christians cannot submit to all other Christians in the same way at the same time, this does not mean that verse 21 refers merely to the submission of the subordinate person to the authority figure in each of the three pairs of relationships addressed in 5:22–6:9 (wives-husbands, children-parents, slaves-masters). All believers may find occasions when it is important for them to submit to numerous other believers, even if the relationships of submission and authority are reversed in other contexts.

Over the years, I have worn numerous hats, so to speak, at the seminary where I teach. We used to rotate the responsibility of chairing a department among the tenured members of each department. Not long after I received tenure, therefore, I had certain kinds of "authority" over my colleagues in New Testament studies, which they had previously exercised over me, and would again when I rotated out of the chair. Among Christians of good will who are eager to defer to others as we did, this never created any kind of problem. The same model of deference can and should work in a Christian family as well.[36]

A second way of understanding this same set of texts leads to egalitarian conclusions. I have already referred to the unity and derivative equality implied by Galatians 3:28, which includes men and women just as it mentions slave and free. Jesus's not choosing a female apostle may have been just an accommodation to his day and age. It was scandalous enough that a larger group of supporters, including women, sometimes traveled on the road with him (Luke 8:1–3). Allowing them to share his most intimate moments, as the Twelve did, could have pushed the cultural envelope too far and simply proved counterproductive to his overall agenda. Paul may never unambiguously refer to a woman elder, but he knows of a female deacon (Rom. 16:1)[37] and a female apostle (v. 7).[38] He has numerous female "co-workers," a term that suggests some level of parity with Paul (e.g., Rom. 16:3; Phil. 4:3). Priscilla possibly took the lead, over her husband, Aquila, in teaching Apollos Christian truth (Acts 18:2–3), since Luke mentions her first.[39] Even most complementarians agree that 1 Corinthians 11:5–6, in which women are allowed to speak and instruct Christian congregations through prophecy and tongues, must qualify the apparent injunctions in 14:34–35 to absolute silence in the church.[40]

That leaves only 1 Timothy 2:11–15 to stand in the way of Paul countenancing a fully egalitarian position, at least with respect to gender roles in Christian circles. These verses thus require more study. The recent publication of a mid-first-century novel, *Ephesiaca*, by Xenophon of Ephesus (also known by the names of its two main characters as *Anthia and Habrocomes*), in a standard, scholarly series of ancient Greco-Roman classics, gives us greater insight into the religious milieu of the city in which Timothy was ministering when Paul wrote him.[41] Artemis, the patron goddess of Asia Minor, whose enormous temple pierced the city's skyline, had a profound impact on society in Ephesus. She was the goddess of the hunt but also of fertility; her large statue in the temple depicted her with a myriad of breasts. In some of her mythology, she herself was portrayed as the creator of all things. In other lore, it was said that woman was created before man. First Timothy 2:13–14 could be countering these claims rather than supplying timeless "creation ordinances." As for verse 12, it is clear to all scholars (and most ordinary readers!) that Paul is having to combat false teaching in Ephesus (1:3; 4:1–3; 6:20–21). It is a short step, then, to assume that too many women were caught up in this false teaching, probably about Artemis, so that Paul bans women teaching in the Ephesian church at this time but would not necessarily do so in other times when the context was quite different.[42]

As for relationships in marriages, it is telling that no biblical author ever commands a wife to "obey" her husband, despite that language being used in countless wedding ceremonies over the centuries. Instead, she should "respect" him (Eph. 5:33).[43] Children must obey their parents (6:1), and slaves their masters (v. 5), but this language is not repeated with respect to wives and husbands. Paul does want all three categories of individuals to submit to their heads, but when husbands, fathers, and masters put first the best interests of those for whom they are responsible, even submission is transformed. The result is that each person puts the other's interest above their own (cf. Phil. 2:4). Mutuality, rather than hierarchy, then prevails.[44]

This is not the context for further discussion about these two main options with respect to gender roles in Scripture. The point here is simply that no one should reject Christianity or its understanding of God on account of the Bible's teaching on gender roles (or anyone's misrepresentation of that teaching). For those who, for whatever reason, cannot envisage religious life without full equality between the sexes, there is a very viable form of egalitarian Christianity in which they can participate. For those who, for whatever reason, cannot envisage religious life without at least a modicum of male hierarchy, there is a very viable form of complementarian Christianity in which they can participate. What must be avoided are the extremes—those views that focus either on putting women "in their place" or on anger and aggression in the campaign for women's rights. A combative spirit is precluded by the very nature of the gospel. Believers must regularly affirm their views with humility and admit that they could be wrong.

Same-Sex Sexual Relations

One might have expected this chapter to be entitled with parallel nouns for the three historically oppressed categories of people we are considering: slaves, women, and homosexuals.[45] Such a title, however, would obscure the differences among the three topics. In the first, the classic debates have surrounded the institution and the question of whether slavery should be abolished. In the second, however, few have ever lobbied for the abolition of gender. The issue is what is perceived to be discrimination on the basis of gender. Put another way, egalitarians long for a world in which men and women have equal opportunities to serve in the ways God has gifted them. But abolitionists do not look just for slaves and free persons to have equal opportunities to serve; they look for the eradication of the institution of slavery altogether.

Distinctions attach themselves to the topic of sexual orientation as well. Of course, there are similarities in terms of discrimination and even oppression, which are obvious, but the differences are not nearly so widely noted. It is also true that there are people who wish that homosexuality would go away altogether, but that is the *opposite* of what the LGBTQ+ community is advocating, as they seek gay pride. So it is not the abolition of an institution that people can be put in or taken out of (like slavery) that is the issue here any more than it is for gender roles. There are further parallels with the gender-roles debate in that the issue is often access to church leadership or equal opportunities for and in marriage. But there are important differences as well. Most Bible scholars recognize that Scripture says nothing about homosexual or heterosexual *orientation*; the issue is rather the role and purpose of sexual relations.[46] So whatever combination of factors of nature and nurture ultimately explains sexual orientation, the issue is whether all consenting adults should have the moral right to engage in sexual relations with all other consenting adults irrespective of their gender or identification. From a biblical perspective, this is an issue of freely chosen behavior that can also be voluntarily limited, which has no analogy in the debates about slavery or gender roles. Readers who did not live through the social sea changes of the 1960s and 1970s may not be aware of the billions of dollars spent to "reeducate" Americans, especially through the public school systems, so that they would think of sexual orientation as something parallel to race or gender in ways that previous generations could never have imagined.[47]

There are also differences in the ways Scripture addresses sexual relations from the ways it addresses slavery and gender roles. On the issue of slavery, there are no passages in either Testament that ever command it. Some legislation assumes the continuance of the institution at least for a time, but overall the trajectory is successively to move away from it and to provide the foundations for its abolition. On the issue of gender roles, there is again much greater freedom for, affirmation of, and encouragement for women in leadership roles in the New Testament than in the Old. But in the case of same-sex intercourse, there are no texts anywhere that promote it or even see it as something neutral.[48]

The Gospels and Acts are actually silent about the topic. This means that readers who try to derive principles from them have to use arguments from silence. If Jesus were against same-sex intercourse, surely he would have said so, argues the one side. The other side retorts that because it was uniformly rejected in Judaism, we may assume Jesus the Jew rejected it as well, unless we have accounts of him teaching otherwise. Both wind up arguing from what is *not* said. Both approaches overlook the intentionally selective nature of the narratives, which did not have as their main purpose a comprehensive articulation of Christian ethics but rather sought to provide a representative presentation of who Jesus was and what he did and of how the first generation of his followers lived out his call to take his message to "the ends of the earth" (Acts 1:8). One cannot find any teaching in the Gospels about Jesus's view of circumcision either, which was a huge controversy in the early church (Acts 15:1–29), and about which one really would have expected to learn something.

So we should turn to the Epistles, where we have actual teaching on the topic of same-sex intercourse. In two places, Paul uses the Greek term *arsenokoitēs* in lists of vices that Christians should avoid (1 Cor. 6:9; 1 Tim. 1:10). The word may have been one Paul coined. It is a compound term made up of the words for male and coitus. At root, it means a man who has sex with a man.[49] In the 1 Corinthians passage it comes immediately after a word for "soft" or "effeminate" (*malakos*); together the two words refer to the penetrated and the penetrator, respectively.[50] Because these are nouns in lists with other nouns, it is tempting for translators to use some established term like "homosexual" to render one or both words into English. But the Greek words focus on a specific action, not a person's nature or identity. The same is true for the other nouns in the vice lists in which it appears. So, on the one hand, it is perfectly understandable why scholars create translations like these: "Neither the sexually immoral nor idolaters nor adulterers nor men who have sex with men nor thieves nor the greedy nor drunkards nor slanderers nor swindlers will inherit the kingdom of God" (1 Cor. 6:9b–10); and "We also know that the law is made not for the righteous but for lawbreakers and rebels, the ungodly and sinful, the unholy and irreligious, for those who kill their fathers or mothers, for murderers, for the sexually immoral, for those practicing homosexuality, for slave traders and liars and perjurers—and for whatever else is contrary to the sound doctrine that conforms to the gospel" (1 Tim. 1:9–11a).

On the other hand, few have ever claimed that one or even a handful of instances of any of the sins represented in these lists of nouns disqualify a professing Christian from salvation. It is only when a specific sin so consumes an individual that their entire identity may fairly be described as wrapped up in the practice of a given sin that it becomes impossible to square that identity with a simultaneous claim that they are Christ followers. To drive this point home, one would need to create some overly long translation like, "Those who are characteristically sexually immoral, whose lives are defined by idolatry, who never stop committing adultery, men whose lives are consumed by having sex with other men, those who are constantly stealing something, people who are consistently acquiring material possessions that they do not need, the perennially overindulgent alcoholic, people who routinely lie about others in hurtful ways, and those who unlawfully cheat others out of their money for a living—none of these people can inherit God's kingdom." In other words, their lives are so consumed by sin that any profession of faith they may have made can only be vacuous.[51]

Again, not one of these items refers to a person's "orientation." Heterosexuals routinely lust after opposite-sex partners, money can easily become a god that we dream about, we often want what does not belong to us or what we do not need, we frequently think distorted and evil things about our enemies or those who have hurt us, and on and on. But there is a crucial difference between a desire, a thought, or a longing and acting on those orientations. Window shopping is not the same as going into debt in order to purchase frivolous luxuries. Admiring a person's attractive body is not the same thing as having sex with them. Too often we have not read Jesus's Sermon on the Mount carefully enough, and we make inaccurate claims like "Lust is as bad as adultery." We probably would pause a little longer if we said, "Hate is as bad as murder." I am sure I am not the only person who would vastly prefer someone who harbors hatred in their heart against me but never acts on it to the person who is actually trying to blow my brains out with a shotgun! What Jesus teaches is that all sin places us in danger of judgment (Matt. 5:22), not that all sins are equally bad.[52] Elsewhere he makes it very clear that there are "more important matters of the law" and gives examples with the illustration of the tithe versus justice, mercy, and faithfulness to show what minor versus major legal issues look like (23:23 par.).[53]

Applying this distinction to sexual matters, I may never know if another person, male or female, is lusting after me. Given my age and appearance, I find it unlikely that anyone would, but I don't actually know. But if someone other than my wife were to try to initiate sexual relations with me in some fashion, I would have a big problem.[54] Acting on an orientation and simply having one are two clearly different things. Christians should place no restrictions on how celibate gay and lesbian believers can minister in the church, just as they should not limit the participation of celibate heterosexual singles in any way either. But Christians should not condone same-sex sexual relations, even between committed same-sex partners, even as they should not condone heterosexual singles having sex with someone they live with long term.[55]

I have left the main New Testament passage on our topic for last. In Romans 1:26–27, Paul is in the middle of a section detailing the universal sinfulness of humanity. He has characterized human rebellion against God as idolatry— putting one or more things in place of God and devoting ultimate allegiance to them. At this juncture, Paul writes, "Because of this, God gave them over to shameful lusts. Even their women exchanged natural sexual relations for unnatural ones. In the same way the men also abandoned natural relations with women and were inflamed with lust for one another. Men committed shameful acts with other men, and received in themselves the due penalty for their error." Here is the one place in the New Testament where lesbian as well as gay male behavior is addressed and the two are described in parallel fashion.

There have been a variety of ways in which revisionist interpreters have tried to make this passage address only certain limited forms of gay or lesbian sex. Perhaps this refers only to the "sacred prostitution" that occurred at numerous Greek and Roman temples as part of a worshiper's union with the god or goddess through homo- or heterosexual relations with a priest or priestess of that deity. Perhaps this applies only to the common practice of heterosexual men "practicing" with prepubescent or newly pubescent boys prior to their moving on to taking a wife. Perhaps it refers to other forms of pederasty or to violent or abusive sex. Sometimes it is alleged that the ancients didn't want heterosexuals behaving unnaturally by having homosexual relations (or vice versa), although this should require the acknowledgment that first-century people did have a view of sexual orientation, which proponents of this claim usually deny (though in fact people in the first century did at times have an understanding of sexual orientation).[56] Or else people argue that the proscription refers to excessive lust or to some other form of homosexual behavior without a commitment to an exclusive long-term relationship.[57]

But nothing in the text of Romans itself makes any of these alternative proposals at all probable. When Paul speaks of that which is natural or according to nature (Gk. *physis*), he almost always means according to God's standards, not a human being's natural inclination. He speaks here not of anyone going against their own nature, but merely of them going against nature. Twice the behavior is said to be the product of lust, and twice it is referred to as shameful. Nothing in the terminology or the larger context enables one to narrow down the kind of homosexual sin presented to simply one out of several forms of same-sex behavior.[58]

Of course, the standard complaint is that restricting sex to heterosexual, married couples discriminates against the homosexually oriented person, who may therefore never experience sexual pleasure. At least six replies are in order here. First, a person, heterosexual or homosexual, does not need a partner to experience sexual pleasure, and one does not need to have sex to have an intimate friend that they share life with long term. Second, despite the prejudice and restrictions against reparative therapies today, some (a minority of) homosexually oriented people have successfully led heterosexually married lives.[59] Third, a lot of what people of all orientations are looking for in sex in our sex-crazed world is not met by sex at all but is fulfilled by loving relationships with fellow Christians in churches and extended families or with God himself.[60] Fourth, we are the first entire generation in the history of the world (the last fifty years or so in the West) that has transformed sexual activity from a privilege into a right, and the upshot has been, as a sweeping generalization, more and more dysfunction—in society, in families, and in individuals. Fifth, the gospel is not about getting what we want but about surrendering our desires for the sake of God and others.[61] But in a world that has lost sight of what used to be called the "middle-class value" of delayed gratification, these truths easily fall on deaf ears.[62]

Sixth and finally, and the point that is perhaps most often overlooked, for a gay or lesbian person to argue that a celibate life discriminates against them in ways that heterosexuals never experience overlooks the large number of heterosexual people throughout the history of the world who would have liked to get married but never were able to. Sometimes this has been due to the dearth of eligible people of the opposite sex and around the same age in areas of small populations, or to warfare having decimated a community of many of its young men. Sometimes this is because of unfortunate life circumstances, where a person has been labeled deviant in some way and ostracized. Often it is just because by the standards of the culture someone has been deemed particularly unattractive. Of course, there are plenty of other reasons people have not married and therefore remained celibate as well. What a slap in the face it is to all those heterosexual singles who remained involuntarily celibate (not to mention those who were voluntarily celibate) to claim that life cannot be fulfilling, especially in Christ, without an active sex life! *Our identities run far deeper than our sexuality—a truth that both heterosexuals and homosexuals have often lost sight of.*[63]

Yet there is still one more option for the person who remains unconvinced by everything I have said here. One does not have to reject God or Christianity merely on the basis of its historic convictions about human sexuality. There are churches that are basically evangelical or orthodox in all of their other doctrines and practices while "open and affirming" with respect to the LGBTQ+ community. As strongly as I am persuaded of my convictions on this issue at the moment, there is always the chance that one of the revisionist interpretations of the Bible on homosexual behavior may turn out to be right, should more evidence come to light. As a finite and fallen interpreter, I have to be willing to admit I might be wrong. It would be a tragedy if I made it sound like there were no other options and kept someone from belief in God and following Jesus for that very reason. So I point people to a possible alternative. I do not suggest that they check every "mainline" church that is open and affirming, because many of those congregations have rejected even more central and fundamental Christian doctrines. People may not even hear the true gospel of Jesus Christ in some liberal settings. But in some settings they do, in which case certain individual churches within a given mainline denomination may be another viable alternative for those unconvinced by my remarks.[64]

4

The Meaning of the Miracles

A very different kind of obstacle to belief in the Christian God involves the problem of miracles. It is one thing to accept an ancient historical narrative that only rarely contains miraculous incidents, because one can usually make sense of the story line without them. The Gospels and Acts, however, are steeped in miracles. Take them out and you have to postulate a lot of other changes to the accounts in order to make any sense of them. Of course, Thomas Jefferson famously cut the miracles out of his Bible but still thought he could keep all the rest, and he found the ethics of Jesus inspiring.[1] But Jesus's ethics are so intertwined with his implicit claims about himself that they are ultimately authoritative only if he is who he claims to be, and the miracles play a central role in those claims. The Jesus Seminar in the 1990s excluded the miracles a priori as impossible, with its founder Robert Funk tipping his hat to Jefferson.[2] After they excised numerous other portions, less than 20 percent of the Gospels was left reflecting something that was at all close to what Jesus really said or did. The resulting picture of a laconic sage, an oriental guru, who did little more than utter cryptic parables and proverbs, was a far cry from the Jesus of Christian faith.[3] Without at least a good core of the miracle accounts of the New Testament Gospels being true, a fundamental pillar for belief that Jesus was revealing the one true Creator God of the heavens and earth, the God of the people of Israel, is knocked down. It is not too far from there to disbelief in that God altogether.

Like most of the other topics in this book, the miracles have spawned an enormous literature and seemingly endless debates. *Philosophers* wrestle with the very definition of a miracle. Is it something contrary to the laws of nature, or does that put the cart before the horse as if we knew all the laws of nature?[4] Thoughtful *scientists*, when they are not merely presupposing the antisupernaturalism that someone else taught them is supposed to be part of their practice, have frequently pointed out that science cannot actually adjudicate on miracles at all. Science is the study of what can be reproduced, preferably in the laboratory, by a series of actions that can yield a formula for producing a desired result. Miracles by definition involve events that cannot be reproduced on demand.[5] *Historians of religion* find partial parallels to New Testament miracles in ancient Greco-Roman mythology and wonder whether the biblical counterparts should be deemed legendary.[6] *Theologians* sometimes debate "continuationism" versus "cessationism." If one accepts the biblical miracles as actual events that occurred long ago, might they still occur today? Or has God's miracle-working activity, at least to the extent that it is one of his spiritual gifts that he bestows on some believers, ceased during the centuries after Christianity's inception?[7]

Old Testament scholars set the stage for what I want to do in this chapter, by focusing on the meaning of the biblical miracles in their original contexts. Miracles are not equally common in all parts of Old Testament history but appear in particularly dense clusters to demonstrate Yahweh's power over Pharaoh at the time of the exodus and Elijah's and Elisha's roles as authentic prophets of the Lord in contrast to the major Canaanite deity, Baal. Old Testament miracles regularly demonstrate that Israel's God has authority, power, and sovereignty over precisely those areas of life and the world in which his pagan rivals were alleged to hold the greatest sway. To take just one example, Elisha's raising a sunken ax-head from the bottom of a river (2 Kings 6:1–7) seems both trivial and sensationalist until one realizes that many who heard about the accident of the ax falling into the water would have believed that this meant that Baal, god over the rivers, had greater power than the Lord God of Israel.[8]

Miracles, the Kingdom, and the Messiah

What is left for the New Testament scholar to add? New Testament scholars disagree about many things, but a striking consensus on *the meaning of the miracles* of the Gospels and Acts has emerged in the last fifty or sixty years. Whether or not one is inclined to believe that the miracles happened, the biblical writers included them because they were convinced that the miracles demonstrated the arrival of God's kingdom, or kingly reign. Miracles showed that the long-awaited messianic age had come. If the kingdom had arrived, then God's uniquely anointed king must be present. If the messianic age had begun, there must be a messiah nearby.[9] No other body of ancient literature describing the supernatural activity of a god or the exploits of a famous human being contains the number of miracles attributed to Jesus. No other body of such literature comes even close to containing the homogeneity of themes one finds in the New Testament miracles.[10] Its writers relentlessly link Jesus's miracles to the presence of the kingdom or his messianic identity. This doesn't make their claims correct. Nor does it mean the events happened. But it is an often overlooked major emphasis within the New Testament miracles that one does not find elsewhere in the first-century world.

Six texts demonstrate the link between Jesus and the messianic kingdom in a general, overarching way. The first text is Matthew 4:23, which summarizes the beginning of Jesus's public ministry by explaining that Jesus went about Galilee teaching and preaching about God's kingdom and healing every kind of disease or sickness among the people. Matthew 9:35 repeats these same points in almost identical words, creating an inclusio or literary framework around the Sermon on the Mount (chaps. 5–7) and Jesus's miracle-working ministry (chaps. 8–9). Jesus's great sermon represents the heart of his kingdom teaching; the two chapters of miracles contain many of his most amazing deeds. Apparently, miracle working went hand in hand with the proclamation of the arrival of God's kingship—and both involved unique and God-given authority (7:28–29; 10:1).[11]

In the remaining five texts, Jesus himself suggests that the miracles are a pointer to his identity. In John's Gospel, just before the last and greatest of Jesus's miracles (not counting his own resurrection, which was performed by God), Jesus announces that he is "the resurrection and the life" (John 11:25). To demonstrate the credibility of this astonishing claim, he proceeds to bring Lazarus out of his tomb and back to life after Lazarus has been dead four days (vv. 39–44).[12] The Gospel of John, of course, has been suspected of not being as historical as the Synoptics, so for many this passage would be the weakest link in our case, even if it narrates the most dramatic miracle of all four volumes. But I have devoted an entire book to rehabilitating the historical credibility of John, and research since then has only pushed its plausibility further, even while being ignored by scholars on the "far left."[13]

The third passage is Mark 9:1 and parallels. This saying appears in all three Synoptics but proves no less enigmatic. After talking about his upcoming suffering, death, and subsequent return (8:31–38), Jesus declares auspiciously, "Truly I tell you, some who are standing here will not taste death before they see that the kingdom of God has come with power" (9:1). If this means that some of his disciples alive when he spoke these words would live to see his return, then he was mistaken. But is it just a coincidence that the very next verse begins the narration of the transfiguration experience, in which Peter, James, and John accompany him up a mountain and his appearance now provides a glimpse of his heavenly glory (vv. 2–10)?[14] Since only three of the Twelve went with him, it is appropriate to say that only "some" who were standing there with Jesus got to see this "preview" of his coming splendor. Given that Judas would take his own life only a few months later (Matt. 27:3–10), the statement that only some would "not taste death" (i.e., *live*) to have this kind of experience (which could otherwise equally well refer to Christ's resurrection) also makes good sense. And it is not as if the event happened instantly after Jesus's prediction, which could have made his wording overly melodramatic; Mark says that it occurred after six days (Mark 9:2).[15] The kingdom was arriving throughout Jesus's ministry, but the miracle of Jesus's transfiguration disclosed a sneak preview of its power that one day will be on display for everyone to see.

Mark 2:10–11 and parallels, our fourth passage, move us still closer to the heart of the matter. A paralyzed man has been brought to Jesus, and Jesus tells him his sins are forgiven (vv. 3–5). This is not what the disabled man thought he came for! He would have known how to have sacrificial animals offered on his behalf in the Jerusalem temple; it is Jesus's miracle-working activity that he has heard about. He wants to be healed of his paralysis. The religious leaders in the crowd grumble because Jesus is operating apart from the temple precincts and its sacrifices for forgiveness. Who does he think he is (vv. 6–7)? Jesus responds by employing a classic Jewish "from the greater to the lesser" argument. He asks his critics, Which is easier to say—that the man's sins are forgiven or that he should stand up and walk as a healed person? Of course, literally, either statement is equally easy to utter. But it is easier to *claim* to be able to forgive sins without being proved wrong than it is to claim to physically heal a person. So by healing the man—the more difficult task—he shows he has the authority to forgive sins (vv. 8–10). The whole episode turns out to be even more about Jesus's identity, as one with uniquely divine authority, than about the man's bodily health.[16]

Our fifth passage, Matthew 11:3–6 and parallel, reinforces these observations. After John the Baptist is imprisoned, his followers come and ask Jesus point-blank if he is the Messiah (the Coming One). Jesus does not answer as directly but instructs them to tell their master what they see and hear: "The blind receive sight, the lame walk, those who have leprosy are cleansed, the deaf hear, the dead are raised, and the good news is proclaimed to the poor" (v. 5). Then he adds, "Blessed is anyone who does not stumble on account of me" (v. 6). Jesus is quoting or alluding to Isaiah 35:5–6 and 61:1, which predict the kind of miracles that will accompany the messianic age, the time of the ministry of the Servant of the Lord. Jesus is answering John the Baptist's disciples affirmatively but making them and John come to the logical conclusion for themselves.[17]

Finally, we turn to the clearest text of all. On one occasion when Jesus is exorcising demons from individuals, some of the religious authorities accuse him of being demon-possessed himself (Matt. 12:24). His reply is telling. He exposes the speciousness of their logic: Satan would not cast his own minions out of an individual, because they are doing his bidding by tormenting the person (vv. 25–26). Jesus also acknowledges that there are other legitimate Jewish exorcists and asks his opponents if they would apply the same logic to all such exorcists, knowing that they wouldn't (v. 27). But Jesus's miracle-working activity is quite different from that of his contemporaries. He is the only healer or exorcist in ancient Jewish, Greek, or Roman literature who simply speaks a word to the suffering individual to effect the cure.[18] Jews typically preceded their miracles by invoking God with fervent prayer, and Greco-Roman accounts of healings or exorcisms often involve incantations, use of magical paraphernalia, potions, and other props of various kinds. It seems unlikely that someone would have invented a story without these things and expected it to be credible. Many people didn't even believe the accounts that existed.[19]

It is actually common to find even fairly liberal or skeptical New Testament scholars these days who accept that the historical Jesus cured people of bodily ailments in ways that were believed in his world to be the work of the God of Israel apart from the normal means of bringing physical wholeness to a human being.[20] Not all necessarily ascribe these accomplishments to true miracles, preferring, for example, to think of the healings as psychosomatic and of demon possession as some form of mental illness. They point to other societies and cultures in which holy men, including shamans, have been able to bring about similar kinds of healings fairly instantaneously.[21] However one accounts for it, the point here is to observe the consistent pattern that the Gospels describe: the miracles point to a new stage in God's sovereign working in the world, described as the coming of his reign, in the person of Jesus, who is understood to be the king of God's kingdom.

Explaining More Unique Miracles

Recognizing this pattern helps make sense of quite a few other miracles attributed to Jesus where there are not the same kinds of interpretations in the texts themselves. Turning water into wine (John 2:1–11) is a highly distinctive miracle in Scripture. Some have found its inspiration in stories about the Greek wine god, Bacchus (or his Roman equivalent, Dionysus), but the parallels are fairly remote.[22] The best-known Christian interpretation, still cited in many traditional wedding liturgies, is that this was Jesus's way of blessing the institution of marriage. However, there are many ways he could have shown his approval. Just as he later blessed children who were brought to him (Mark 10:16 pars.), he needn't have even done anything miraculous to simply bless the institution of marriage. The amount of wine provided is enormous—six stone water jars holding about twenty to thirty gallons each (John 2:6)! In a narrative otherwise void of extraneous details, John includes the information that these jars were used for Jewish purification rites. It would seem that this is a key to the meaning of the miracle for Jesus. In the Synoptics, he crafts a little parable or extended metaphor about new wine needing new wineskins (Mark 2:22 pars.). It seems likely that the miracle is teaching something similar: not all of the old ways of Judaism can be contained in the new age of the kingdom.[23] Wine in Israel was often a sign of joy or happiness. The psalmist wrote about God making the "wine that gladdens human hearts" (Ps. 104:15; cf. b. Pesaḥim 109a). The old water jars, representing Jewish purification rites, are inadequate to contain the new wine or blessings of the kingdom age.[24] Now the miracle fits in very well with the main theme of why Jesus works miracles of healing and exorcism throughout the Gospels as well.

Or consider the puzzling account of Jesus cursing the fig tree (Mark 11:12–14, 20–25 par.). It is one of only two miracles of destruction in the New Testament Gospels. Is Jesus behaving like a petulant child, angry that the tree has not satisfied his craving for a breakfast of figs? Some interpreters focus on the tree and argue that the fact that it was in leaf (v. 13a) meant that there should have been at least some of the early figs that often appeared shortly after the tree was in bloom.[25] But Mark prevents us from taking that tack by explicitly adding, "He found nothing but leaves, because it was not the season for figs" (v. 13b). Interestingly, Luke 13:6–9 contains a parable Jesus told about a barren fig tree, in which the tree represents Israel, or at least its leaders, who are threatened with judgment if they do not soon repent. That symbolic meaning also makes very good sense of Jesus cursing this fig tree in Mark.[26] Mark, in fact, regularly employs an ABA sandwich structure, in which he tells one story in two parts sandwiched around a closely related story.[27] He is doing precisely that here, as Mark 11:15–19 intervenes between the two parts of the story about the tree and narrates the temple-clearing incident. It is clear that Mark sees the two episodes as teaching something very similar—impending judgment on the current regime in Israel. The kingdom is arriving, the national and religious leaders for the most part are rejecting it, and God's judgment awaits them as a result. Once again, what at first seems to be a very odd account fits in closely with the Gospels' central theme on why Jesus worked miracles.

A third example involves Jesus's two feeding miracles—first of five thousand and then of four thousand (Mark 6:33–44 pars.; 8:1–10 par.). Only John gives an explicit interpretation of either, when he narrates Jesus's sermon in the Capernaum synagogue about being the Bread of Life (John 6:25–59). Moses had promised that the Lord would raise up a prophet like him (Deut. 18:15–18), and Jews had come to understand this as a messianic prophecy. As a result, the tradition arose that the Messiah would again multiply bread in the wilderness like the manna God provided during Moses's lifetime and the Israelite wanderings.[28] As nice as it was for the crowds to enjoy a good meal while they were a long distance from where they could buy provisions for themselves, the main purpose of these miracles was to demonstrate who Jesus was. He was the new and greater Moses, the eschatological prophet, the Bread of Life.

Fourth, we turn to the walking on water, the very next episode after the feeding of the five thousand in Matthew, Mark, and John (Mark 6:45–52 pars.). Once again, it is easy to imagine trivial reasons that this miracle is unbecoming of Jesus. For example, one could imagine that like his disciples, he was tired after a long day of ministry. Unlike them, however, instead of straining at oars to row a boat against the wind, he draws on his divine powers to frolic across the sea effortlessly! This would indeed be capricious and hardly praiseworthy. Much more likely, this is a theophany—a revelation of Jesus's divinity. The words he speaks that are usually translated as "It is I" (Mark 6:50) are the Greek words *egō eimi*, which can equally well be rendered, "I am." They are the same Greek words used in the Septuagint (the ancient Greek translation of the Old Testament) when God reveals himself to Moses in the burning bush and discloses his name as "I AM WHO I AM" (Exod. 3:14).[29] Mark also prefaces this disclosure with the explanation "He was about to pass by them" (Mark 6:48). It is hard to render this sentence unambiguously in English. The Greek verb comes from the root *parerchomai*, which meant to "pass by" in the sense that contestants in some competition pass by their judges in review. That is to say, they make themselves visible to the others. The word does not mean "pass by" in the sense of escaping notice. Jesus wasn't trying to hide himself from his disciples only to get caught in the process. He was revealing himself to them so they might have glimpses of his divine power and glory.[30] Once again, a miracle discloses something about Jesus's identity.

Fifth, there is the less well-known story of Jesus healing a man in the Decapolis who was deaf and could hardly talk (Mark 7:31–37 par.). The word for "could hardly talk" is *mogilalos*, which appears elsewhere in the Greek Bible only in Isaiah 35:6 in the list we have already noted of miracles that will characterize the messianic age. Given the frequency of illness and disability in the ancient Mediterranean world, this connection seems unlikely to be a coincidence. Jesus could doubtless have selected from many others to demonstrate his healing abilities, but he chose an individual whose healing would have reminded thoughtful Jews of the messianic prophecies in their Scriptures.[31]

Finally, we turn to the remarkable little story in Luke 7:11–17. Found only in Luke, this story is one of three times in the Gospels that Jesus raises a person from death. It takes place at Nain, a small town in Galilee (v. 11). The dead man is the only son of his widowed mother (v. 12). Jesus approaches the grieving mother, who is apparently walking in front of the coffin (v. 14), as was customary in Galilee though not in Judea (where she would have walked behind)—this is an interesting touch that Luke, the Gentile author, was unlikely to have known of, suggesting that he was relying on a factual tradition at this point.[32] Jesus commands the deceased young man to get up (v. 14); the young man does so and begins to speak, confirming that he is well (v. 15)! The miracle would have readily reminded any thoughtful Jew, steeped in the Hebrew Scriptures, of the account of Elisha raising the only son of a woman in Shunem in 2 Kings 4:8–37. All the more striking is the fact that Nain was the closest first-century village to the site of Old Testament Shunem. Not surprisingly, the crowd responds with an acclamation of Jesus as a "great prophet" (Luke 7:16), the same office occupied by Elisha, the eschatological prophet who became synonymous in many people's minds with the Messiah.[33] A new and greater Elisha is here!

The Exception That Proves the Rule?

One passage stands apart from all these examples. A passage unique to Matthew's Gospel (Matt. 17:24–27) begins with a discussion between the collectors of the annual temple tax, levied on all Israelites (for its origin, see Exod. 30:13–16, where it was a one-time payment only), and Jesus's disciple Peter. Jesus was known for his controversial interpretations of the law and for not keeping the Pharisaic oral laws designed to contextualize and supplement the written law of Moses. So it is not surprising that some of the tax collectors ask Peter if Jesus pays this tax (Matt. 17:24). Peter assures them that he does (v. 25a). Jesus appears to be aware of the conversation because he brings up

a topic related to it about whom kings tax—their own children or others
(v. 25b). When Peter gives the obvious answer—"others"—Jesus continues,
"Then the children are exempt" (v. 26). Apparently, he is envisioning a time
when his disciples would no longer pay this tax, especially if he is thinking
of himself, or perhaps God, as the king and his followers as the children.[34]

But then comes the mysterious verse. Jesus adds, "But so that we may not
cause offense, go to the lake and throw out your line. Take the first fish you
catch; open its mouth and you will find a four-drachma coin. Take it and give
it to them for my tax and yours" (v. 27). The tax per person was two drachmas, so four drachmas would cover two persons. That Jesus's purpose for his
instruction is not to cause offense reinforces our surmise that he doesn't think
either he or his disciples should have to pay it. But from what source should
these four drachmas come? Jesus's command to Peter requires a miracle.
No, there is nothing miraculous about coins being found in fish's mouths.
The *musht* to this day likes to scavenge the bottom of the Lake of Galilee for
foreign objects; over the centuries a variety of coins have been found in them
after fishermen have caught them.[35] The miracle would be that Jesus knew
that the first fish Peter would catch would have precisely the needed coin.

But did Peter go to the lake? If so, did he go fishing? If so, did he catch
a fish? If so, did he find a four-drachma coin? Every other miracle we have
looked at—indeed, every other account in the Gospels commonly identified
as a miracle story—ends with a statement of the outcome. Those who have
studied the literary form of miracle stories in the ancient Mediterranean world
have observed that this is a very regular feature of such accounts both inside
and outside of Scripture.[36] Why would a narrator, for example, tell a story in
which Jesus commanded servants to fill jars with water, draw some out, and
take it to the master of ceremonies of a wedding (John 2:7–8), and then end
the story at that point? Everyone would want to know what happened. Even if
Jesus had added something like "and he will discover it has turned to wine,"
listeners and readers would all the more want some closure. Could such a
miracle really occur? Did it happen as Jesus predicted? Or consider the healing
of the paralyzed man in Mark 2:1–12. There Jesus actually implies the outcome
in his command, "Get up, take your mat and go home" (v. 11). If Mark had
stopped his narration at that point, everyone would be clamoring to know if
the man actually received the ability to stand on his previously atrophied legs.
Was he able to walk as well? Verse 12 assures us that he could and that he did.

So one cannot just assume that Peter went to the lake and did as Jesus
told him to in Matthew 17:27. Maybe he did; maybe he didn't. We simply
have no way of knowing, and those who claim that if Jesus gave Peter a command, he must have obeyed it, are ignoring Peter's very spotty track record

of discipleship prior to Jesus's resurrection and are not seriously asking why Matthew in this one passage, out of all the miracle stories in the Gospels, chose not to tell us anything about what finally happened. Is it because all that matters is that we understand the principle that in the age of the new covenant Christians should be free from spiritual taxation?[37] Is it because Jesus and Peter at this point in the ministry are so poor that they cannot afford to pay the tax?[38] If so, would Matthew prefer not to draw any more attention to this fact than necessary? Is it because Jesus is not speaking literally but using some kind of metaphorical or parabolic speech in verse 27? Might he mean that Peter should catch a fish and sell it for four drachmas to pay the tax, so that metaphorically it is as if he found the coin in its mouth?[39] Did Peter just walk away shaking his head and not do anything? Is there some other reason for Matthew not telling us the outcome that we may never know about and that doesn't matter? I am unaware of any way of answering these questions with any degree of confidence; those who do so must by the very nature of the matter go beyond the text for their answers.[40]

But what about the skeptic who lampoons this little passage in Matthew because the miracle that it narrates is so frivolous? There is nothing here about demonstrating the arrival of the kingdom or the presence of the Messiah. No prophecy is fulfilled; there is not even a dire need met. Nothing is said about miraculously provided money for the other eleven disciples or whether they shared a common treasury (John 12:6). If their resources were very low, presumably they would have divided them up and then each man would have had to find a little more somehow. If they did not function in a completely egalitarian fashion, then surely Jesus as the master and Peter as the leader of the Twelve would have gotten their taxes paid for and some others would have had to roust up the resources elsewhere. But if no actual miracle took place—and again I stress that the text itself never tells us that one did—then the passage cannot be charged with disclosing a frivolous use of Jesus's miracle-working powers. If such a fish was caught with the necessary coin in its mouth, then at least obliquely Jesus is implying something about the arrangements for the new covenant, which is equivalent to the kingdom age, so even then it is not entirely fanciful. We may never know, but we need to leave all these options open.[41]

Other Reasons for Jesus's Miracles

I do not want to leave the impression that disclosing Jesus's identity and the presence of the new age he came to inaugurate are the only reasons he worked miracles. Of course, he had *compassion* for hurting people. But it is interesting how comparatively rarely such concern is explicitly mentioned in the context of a Gospel miracle. In Mark 8:2 and parallel, Jesus has compassion for the four thousand who have been with him in a desolate place for three days and have exhausted their food supplies.[42] In Matthew 20:34, Jesus takes pity on two blind men and restores their sight.[43] But that is it! Jesus does have compassion on the crowds *before* he goes with them in the wilderness and multiplies the loaves and fishes for the five thousand, but it is because they are "harassed and helpless, like sheep without a shepherd" (Matt. 9:36; cf. Mark 6:34), a commentary on the failure of the nation's leadership in Jesus's day. Perhaps we are meant to assume that Jesus takes pity on the man whose son is demon-possessed (Mark 9:22) or on the ten lepers (Luke 17:13), but in each of those cases it is others who request pity, while Jesus, even though working the requested miracles, moves the conversation in different directions. In the former instance, he turns it into a lesson about faith and prayer (Mark 9:23–29); in the latter, into one about faith and giving thanks (Luke 17:15–19).

The typically best and most reliable New Testament manuscripts render Mark 1:41 as Jesus having compassion on the leper who comes to him for a cure. Yet several reasonably important and early manuscripts have him being indignant instead (particularly Codex Bezae but also old Italic manuscripts). It is so hard to imagine scribes changing "compassion" to "indignant," with all the questions that would raise, and so very easy to imagine them toning things down by changing "indignant" to "compassion" that perhaps "indignant" was original.[44] Why should Jesus not have been indignant, especially if it was at the damage the horrible disease of leprosy had inflicted on the man? A similar debate surrounds John 11:33, only this time it is not a textual variant but a translation of a single Greek word. Translations often read that when Mary and her friends are weeping outside Lazarus's tomb, Jesus "was deeply moved in spirit and troubled." But the Greek for "deeply moved in spirit" comes from the verb *embrimaomai*, which has the etymology of meaning "to snort like a horse." The HCSB translates, "He was angry in His spirit"; the NAB that "he became perturbed." The NLT has "a deep anger welled up within him"; while the NRSV gives "greatly disturbed in spirit." Of course, Jesus cared deeply about Lazarus, but mere compassion or pity does not seem to be his main motive here either.

In a number of passages Jesus uses a miracle or its absence to teach about *faith*. In Mark 5:34, after Jesus has healed the woman with the flow of blood, he explains, perhaps precisely to debunk any superstitious idea that touching his clothes automatically guaranteed a miracle (v. 28), "Your faith has healed you." In this instance, the faith led to what bordered on magic, so

Jesus is quick to clarify the true source.[45] Not long afterward, he tells Jairus, whose daughter has just died, "Don't be afraid; just believe" (v. 36). The dead girl obviously couldn't exercise any faith on her own behalf, but her father could.[46] Yet when Jesus comes to Nazareth, Mark tells us that Jesus "could not do any miracles there, except lay his hands on a few sick people and heal them" (6:5) and that "he was amazed at their lack of faith" (v. 6a). The two sentences are connected only with an "and" (Gk. *kai*), but Mark regularly uses this conjunction when tighter connections between clauses are implied.[47] Given the context, it seems natural enough to understand the people's lack of faith as part of the reason Jesus could work only a few miracles there. Of course, this doesn't mean he couldn't have chosen to do more, but simply that on this occasion he has decided to limit himself to what the people are able to believe.[48]

Reinforcing this conclusion is the observation that on other occasions, Jesus works a miracle where there is little or no faith in order to instill some or help what is present to grow. In Mark 4:40, after Jesus stills the storm, he turns to the disciples and asks, "Why are you so afraid? Do you still have no faith?" Matthew edits Mark's "no faith" and turns it into "you of little faith" (Matt. 8:26). But despite celebrated attempts to argue that Jesus's disciples in Matthew have significantly more faith than in Mark,[49] this is still not intended as a compliment, and Matthew just like Mark has Jesus ask, "Why are you so afraid?"[50] In both Gospels the miracle was intended to produce greater faith than it actually did. Or consider John 2:11. After Jesus turned water into wine, which John terms as that which "revealed his glory," we read that his disciples believe in him. Here the sign at least brings initial faith. Finally, in John 4:48, Jesus seemingly berates the crowds (at least a little) for needing to see signs in order to believe.[51] But he goes on and heals the nobleman's son anyway, and John says that it has produced faith at least in that whole family. Several more examples could be given, both of faith leading to a miracle or of a miracle leading to faith. What is important to observe, however, is that even if we put all of these together, not even half of all of Jesus's miracles are said to have something to do with faith, one way or the other. Of those that do, about half are in response to faith and about half are to instill faith, so there is no demonstrable pattern one way or the other.[52]

Another subordinate motive in the Gospel miracle stories is to *challenge the Pharisees* and their additions to the laws of Moses. The number of times cannot be coincidental that Jesus works a miracle on the Sabbath that is perceived as him doing work and therefore violating the commandment to rest. What is even more intriguing is that not a single person who is healed on a Sabbath has had an emergency. No one's life is in danger on that very day.

Sometimes the Gospel writers seem to go out of their way to stress how long a problem of some kind has persisted. John 5:5 provides the most extreme example. A man has been disabled for thirty-eight years! Just a little empathy with the Pharisees could imagine them saying, "Jesus, look how long this man has coped; one more day won't hurt him any worse. Heal him tomorrow and everyone will love you and God will be glorified!"[53] But no, Jesus insists on doing good on the Sabbath (Matt. 12:12). Similar dynamics are at work in the Sabbath healings in Luke 13:10–17 and 14:1–6.[54] Jesus also challenges the status quo when he heals a Gentile centurion's servant from a distance and rubs it in the bystanders' faces, as it were, by declaring that he has never seen such faith in Israel (Matt. 8:10). Worse still, from an orthodox Jewish perspective, verses 11–12 go on to teach that many Gentiles will join faithful Jews in the kingdom while some of the "subjects of the kingdom" (ethnic Jews) will be thrown outside.[55]

The flip side of challenging the powerful and respected in Israelite society is Jesus's disproportionate *help for the dispossessed and marginalized*. It is also no coincidence that Jesus is never once depicted as healing or working any other kind of miracle for one of the religious leaders or wealthy Jewish individuals within Israel.[56] Given the frequency with which most people in the ancient Mediterranean world were sick, sometimes acutely so, this cannot be because he never encountered any of these people needing his help.[57] He must be going out of his way to stress his ministry to the least, last, and lost. One thinks of his willingness to touch lepers and make the unclean clean rather than incurring their uncleanness himself (Mark 1:41 pars.).[58] Or when ten lepers come for cleansing, only a Samaritan, not the nine Jews, receives spiritual wholeness as well (Luke 17:16). Perhaps the best example of all is the healing of the Syrophoenician woman's daughter in Mark 7:24–30 and parallel. Whatever else one makes of Jesus's seeming rudeness and ethnocentrism at the beginning of his conversation with her, he succeeds in drawing out her faith in a way that might otherwise not have been visible, and he provides an important lesson for his disciples, who are actually telling Jesus to send her away.[59]

A final theme may be termed *links with sin*. This is probably the least common of all, but two passages in John put the matter about as pointedly as possible. Jesus first heals the paralyzed man by the side of the pool of Bethesda and later tells him, "See, you are well again. Stop sinning or something worse may happen to you" (John 5:14). In other words, at least in his case, something about his affliction appears to have been related to his own sinful behavior.[60] Four chapters later, nevertheless, another disabled person, this time due to blindness, is involved with another pool in Jerusalem—the pool of Siloam,

where he is to wash his eyes and be cured. The disciples undoubtedly are trying to apply the lesson that they thought they have learned from the previous
healing. This man has been blind from birth (9:1). So they ask Jesus if the
blindness was due to his parents' sin, as often in the Old Testament, when the
sins of the parents are visited on subsequent generations of family members,
or if the man himself has sinned—presumably *in utero* (v. 2). Surprisingly,
Jesus replies, in essence, that it was neither of the above. Rather, it was so
that the works of God might be displayed in the healed man (v. 3).[61] So while
an *individual's* sin might on occasion be the cause of *that person's* physical
affliction, often it has nothing to do with it.

Conclusion

What does all this have to do with the credibility of the New Testament miracles? It shows that there are recurrent, discernible, worthy patterns behind
Jesus's miracle-working behavior. When one turns to the later Christian apoc-
rypha or to Jewish and Greco-Roman "parallels" from the years immediately
before and after Jesus's ministry, no such patterns emerge. In fact, no one else
has more than a handful of miracles ever attributed to them. In apocryphal
texts, later Christians are fancifully imagining what Jesus, the "boy wonder,"
might have been like, and filling in other perceived gaps in the earliest Gospels.[62]
The Greco-Roman parallels more often than not are myths about the cycle of
the seasons, from the new birth of plant life each spring to its seeming death
the following winter.[63] The closest parallels come in ancient Judaism and, of
course, before that in the Old Testament. But even there, miracles are at most
a harbinger of the messianic age to come. In none of these bodies of literature,
apart from the Old Testament, do the individuals treated act in a consistently
coherent and meaningful fashion. And even the Old Testament miracles are
considerably more diverse than the New Testament ones.[64] On occasion, an
alleged miracle may be used to point to a person's supposed postmortem deification.[65] But nowhere do we have anything like the claim that a shift in the two
main stages of human history has come, from the age of prophecy to the age
of fulfillment, from the old to the new age, or from the premessianic to the
messianic age. Nowhere is there even the claim that a god's kingly reign has
arrived but only partially and that the rest of what has been predicted about
him awaits a future coming.

None of this demonstrates the veracity of the New Testament miracles
beyond any reasonable doubt. I have not even had the space to discuss the
miracles in Acts and the Epistles, but a fair generalization is that they very

closely parallel Jesus's miracles in their nature and purpose, except that they are done in his name, often accompanied by prayer, so as to make it clear that they are derived from his ultimate power that the disciples are at times permitted to utilize rather than from their own power.[66] Perhaps more so than with some of the other topics in this book, it is often the philosophical issues that ultimately prove determinative in whether someone will believe the biblical accounts. But for a book emphasizing the distinctive contributions of the New Testament to the issues discussed, my purpose in this chapter has been to show the consistent and credible patterns of miracle-working activity in the life of Jesus as portrayed in the canonical Gospels and thus to debunk charges that they are random, flippant, unworthy of deity, simply borrowed from other sources, and so on. The next chapter will include some of the supposedly closer parallels to the New Testament miracles from outside the Christian world and show how far removed in form and substance they actually are.

Weren't the Stories of Jesus Made Up from Greco-Roman Myths?

A hundred years ago, the history-of-religions school of biblical studies had already started to be eclipsed by other, better-grounded approaches to interpretation.[1] Nevertheless, particularly due to the influence of Wilhelm Bousset's *Kyrios Christos*,[2] there were still many scholars who believed that the New Testament's portraits of Jesus went through a slow period of evolutionary growth, with the high Christology (the exalted views of Jesus as more than a man) due largely to a late first-century transformation of the Christian faith based on Greco-Roman religion. Fifty years later, it was almost universally recognized that this perspective could not withstand careful scrutiny and that one had to speak of at least three phases of development: what occurred in Palestinian Jewish Christianity, what emerged in Hellenistic Jewish Christianity, and finally, what purely Hellenistic Christianity contributed.[3]

All that has changed further from the 1980s to the present, as the field of "divine identity" Christology has been growing with every few years.[4] To use the expression of Larry Hurtado, himself a key contributor to the movement, Christianity's growth was "revolutionary" rather than "evolutionary."[5] At the earliest stages of Christian history, in every decade, we find signs that people were worshiping Jesus in ways that Greeks and Romans would find appropriate only for a god and that Jews would view as appropriate only for Yahweh, the one God and Lord of the universe.[6] First Corinthians 8:6, in an undisputed letter of the apostle Paul written no later than about AD 55, a scant twenty-five years after Jesus's death, illustrates this phenomenon well. Having just alluded to the clarion call of Jewish monotheism, the Shema of Deuteronomy 6:4, that "there is no God but one" (1 Cor. 8:4), and having then explained that though there are "so-called gods" in other religions, for Christians just as for Jews "there is but one God, the Father, from whom all things came and for whom we live," Paul immediately adds, "and there is but one Lord, Jesus Christ, through whom all things came and through whom we live" (vv. 5–6). In other words, Paul affirms almost the identical role for Jesus as for God, with both existing before the creation of the universe, even in the same breath as he affirms that there is only one God.[7] This is not yet explicit trinitarianism, but it is binitarianism (belief in the Father and the Son), and it does not rely on the use of any particularly exalted titles for Jesus. It is also not Paul's main point, which is about how Christians deal with weaker spiritual siblings who do not eat food sacrificed to idols (8:1–13). Therefore, it is even more striking that Paul can acknowledge the deity of Jesus as a point of common knowledge and agreement with the Corinthians on this otherwise divisive issue.[8]

In quite different circles, nevertheless, a handful of biblical scholars, along with certain researchers in other disciplines who sometimes try their hand at biblical studies, have been reviving the old history-of-religions school.[9] At times the more skeptical authors appeal to hundred-year-old sources, long since superseded, seemingly without realizing that scholars have learned so much more in the intervening years.[10] Various claims are cited, not always accurately, often second- and thirdhand, about the contents of ancient Greek and Roman literature.[11] The results then make it appear to the uninitiated that there is a credible case for Greco-Roman mythology as the source of most of the New Testament's convictions about Jesus. As with the other chapters in this book, I can only scratch the surface of the topic because this approach has emerged in so many different arenas, but in the notes I point readers to more extensive and detailed studies to confirm and also nuance my generalizations.

The Virginal Conception

To read some writers' grandiose claims, one might think that stories of human children being conceived by women who had never had sexual relations with anyone were widespread in the ancient Mediterranean world.[12] Often this is because the expression "virgin birth" (which, with reference to Jesus, is more precisely a virginal conception) is used whenever there are any unusual circumstances surrounding the story of someone's birth—a far cry from what the words actually mean.[13] In some instances, there are Greek or Roman myths about a god or goddess being born apart from two divine parents, as with Athena springing fully grown from Zeus's head. But here we are not talking about human conception at all, nor was Zeus, the father of countless gods or demigods, a virgin by any means even in the myths about him. In some cases, a god comes to earth in the appearance of a man and has sexual relations with a human woman to produce what our world today would probably call a superhero. Whether or not the woman has previously engaged in sexual relations is usually irrelevant, and often she has. In any event, the hero is still born as a result of a sexual relationship. There are actually *no* examples of nonsexual supernatural conceptions similar to Luke's account of the virgin Mary becoming pregnant merely "through the creative power of the Holy Spirit" (cf. Luke 1:35).[14]

Plutarch, in his *Life of Alexander*, writes this about Alexander's parents, King Philip of Macedon and Olympias:

> Well, then, the night before that on which the marriage was consummated, the bride dreamed that there was a peal of thunder and that a thunder-bolt fell upon her womb, and that thereby much fire was kindled, which broke into flames that travelled all about, and then was extinguished. At a later time, too, after the marriage, Philip dreamed that he was putting a seal upon his wife's womb; and the device of the seal, as he thought, was the figure of a lion. The other seers, now, were led by the vision to suspect that Philip needed to put a closer watch upon his marriage relations; but Aristander of Telmessus said that the woman was pregnant, since no seal was put upon what was empty, and pregnant of a son whose nature would be bold and lion-like. Moreover, a serpent was once seen lying stretched out by the side of Olympias as she slept, and we are told that this, more than anything else, dulled the ardour of Philip's attentions to his wife, so that he no longer came often to sleep by her side, either because he feared that some spells and enchantments might be practised upon him by her, or because he shrank from her embraces in the conviction that she was the partner of a superior being. (2.3–6)[15]

One looks in vain for Olympias's virginity here, or even for a miraculous conception, when she conceived Alexander!

In the case of Augustus, there were reports of omens and dreams that portended the birth of a great king, including unusual celestial phenomena. The closest one can get to a virginal conception is the account of Augustus's mother falling asleep while in the service of Apollo. A serpent, one of the forms Apollo took, glided past her while she slept. "When she awoke, she purified herself, as if after the embraces of her husband, and at once there appeared on her body a mark in colours like a serpent, and she could never get rid of it; so that presently she ceased ever to go to the public baths." In the tenth month after that Augustus was born and was therefore regarded as the son of Apollo (Suetonius, *Life of Augustus* 94.4).[16] But Augustus's mother is already married and most decidedly not a virgin, while the indelible mark suggests divine impregnation via a very crass form of bestiality.

Plutarch recounts several very different stories of the conception of Romulus and Remus, the twins who helped found Rome. In what he agrees is the least credible, the mother was a slave girl who replaced her mistress when she refused to unite with a divine phallus that emerged on their hearth (Plutarch, *Life of Romulus* 2.3–4). The account he says most people give credence to is that the twins' mother was originally to have been a vestal virgin but was found pregnant and narrowly escaped execution for it (3.1–3). In order to get a narrative of an actual virginal conception, one has to conflate the two stories that Plutarch finds incompatible. To make this new version relevant to Jesus's life, one has to assume both that it once actually existed in this conflated form and then that it predated Plutarch's early second-century setting, without any actual evidence for either assumption.

Partial parallels also exist in Jewish literature,[17] but Judaism's most famous story related to an unusual birth is in the Hebrew Scriptures: Pharaoh's stepdaughter rescues Moses, who has been placed in a basket in the river to save his life, since Pharaoh has commanded the midwives to kill all the male Hebrew babies (Exod. 2:1–10). There is absolutely nothing here about Moses's mother being a virgin, since she was already married, nor is there anything out of the ordinary about Moses's conception. Whether it is due to simple lack of awareness either of what these supposed parallels to the virgin birth contain or of the details of the New Testament, or whether it is intentional duplicity, authors of claims about how common virginal conceptions were in the ancient Middle East are flatly mistaken. There simply is no known parallel to the Gospel accounts of a human woman becoming pregnant before she has ever had sex with anyone, and with fatherhood attributed to an invisible deity.[18] It is also notable that no sexual relations are recounted in the Gospel accounts of Jesus's conception. The most the Gospels ever allege is that the angel Gabriel spoke to Mary, telling her, "The Holy Spirit will come on you, and the power of the Most High will overshadow you. So the holy one to be born will be called the Son of God" (Luke 1:35). The contrast with the vulgar details of the Greco-Roman myths could hardly be greater. That the Christian account circulated perhaps even during Mary's lifetime and at least within the lifetimes of some of those who knew her makes it all the more unparalleled.[19]

Jesus's Proclamation of the Kingdom

Countless myths and legends in world history describe a hero on a quest to gain a kingdom. Often, after many obstacles, including wars with opponents, they succeed. If they are noble heroes, they may rescue a certain land from previous evil rulers; if evil themselves, they may bring new terrors to a country.[20] The central theme of the historical Jesus's teaching, by almost all accounts, was the arrival of the kingdom of God. As the Gospel accounts unfold, it becomes progressively clearer that Jesus envisions himself as the king of God's kingdom. Does this suggest a mythical origin for this part of the Gospels' plotline? Hardly.

The New Testament story of Jesus is not one of a hero on a quest for a kingdom. Rather, it is about the public ministry of a Jewish teacher announcing that God is becoming king in a new and decisive way. The story line is steeped in Old Testament and Jewish backgrounds. Israel has had a theocratic kingdom whenever they have had their independence; that is to say, God has been their ultimate king, providing checks and balances on their human kings through his word and his prophets. From the time of Nathan's promises to David onward (2 Sam. 7:12–16), Israel has been told that one day a descendant of David would rule on his throne and his kingdom would have no end. This had never literally happened by the time of the first century, and Jesus over and again rejects the notion of reigning as an earthly king. John 6:15 puts it most pointedly. Just after the feeding of the five thousand occurs, we read, "Jesus, knowing that they intended to come and make him king by force, withdrew again to a mountain by himself."[21]

But couldn't the idea of gaining a kingdom, even if spiritual in nature, still have been borrowed from Greco-Roman mythology? It is highly unlikely, because while "kingdom of God" (or "kingdom of heaven") language dominates the Synoptic Gospels, it is comparatively rare elsewhere in the New Testament. Counting parallels, it occurs about 120 times in the Synoptics, three times in John, eight times in Acts, fourteen times in all of Paul's Letters, twice in Hebrews, once in James, once in 2 Peter, and seven times in Revelation. This is most readily explained by the fact that the Gentile world, which forms the predominant audience for these other books, was not nearly as familiar with the story of Israel's theocratic kingship and promises about a messianic king, so other language and teaching were primarily used in order to expound the gospel to them.[22] The Synoptics, on the other hand, preserve the teaching of Jesus much more in his own idiom. "Kingdom" language with Jesus is Jewish, not Hellenistic, in background, and it is the fulfillment of divine prophecy, not a quest for human grandeur, that Jesus undertakes and the Gospels narrate.[23]

A similarly striking observation may be made about Jesus's parables, which were the rhetorical form that he utilized most in illustrating God's kingdom. One can ransack Greco-Roman literature and find allegories, riddles, and anecdotes of many different kinds. Perhaps the most famous illustrative stories are Aesop's fables, complete with talking animals.[24] The Greek word *parabolē*, which has a broad semantic range, was even discussed by Aristotle (*Rhetoric* 2.20). But not one single narrative parable *of the form Jesus employed* has ever come to light in Greco-Roman literature. That is to say, nowhere are there very brief stories of a paragraph or two in length, with a master figure and one or more contrasting subordinates, where a central theme illustrated by two, three, or four points derives from each main character.[25] Yet there are over two hundred such parables in the earliest centuries of the rabbinic movement alone, and by the time one canvasses nearly a millennium of all the rabbinic literature, over nine hundred parables just involving a king as the unifying figure emerge. Few of these are perfectly identical in form to Jesus's parables, but they are much closer than anything in Greek or Roman thought and far briefer and more tightly structured than its mythology. Where Jesus differs from the rabbis is largely in his use of parables to illustrate God's kingdom rather than to help in exegeting Scripture.[26] The closest match in form, structure, and dynamic is actually in the Old Testament, with Nathan's parable of the ewe lamb in 2 Samuel 12:1–12, further reinforcing the Israelite origins of this form of teaching.

Miracles

At the end of the previous chapter, I promised to return to the question of supposed parallels to Jesus's miracles in Greco-Roman mythology. Probably the most important observation to make is that the vast majority of miracles in this literature have no bearing on the New Testament at all. Instead, one tends to find "humans talking with the animals and birds, and even transforming themselves into other creatures, charming rocks and trees with their music, appearing and disappearing, or appearing in two places at the same time, travelling the world without eating, or sending their souls on journeys while their bodies remained at home."[27] Of course, one does find healings and exorcisms, but as a broad generalization, the closer the parallel, the more likely the story emanates from post-Christian times.[28] This means that the Greco-Roman myths could not have influenced the Gospels, but the Gospels might have influenced the later Greco-Roman myths.

The most dramatic example of this is no doubt the resurrection of a young woman attributed to Apollonius of Tyana (a late first-century healer) by Philostratus (his third-century biographer). She has just died in the hour of her marriage, and while she is being carried in funeral procession on her bier, Apollonius comes to her, bends over and whispers to her and touches her at the same time, at which point she comes back to life (*Life of Apollonius* 4.45). The similarities with Jesus's raising of the son of the widow of Nain in Luke 7:11–17 are patent. But the dates of Apollonius's life and Philostratus's writing make it impossible for Luke (or Jesus) to have been imitating these Greek figures.[29] Moreover, there is an even closer parallel in 1 Kings 17:17–24. There, the prophet Elijah raises the son of a widow in Zarephath: the son has just died, so Elijah stretches himself across the bier and prays fervently for the boy's recovery, and then God brings the son back to life. Luke indicates that the Jewish crowd in Nain in Jesus's day recognized the parallel when they exclaim, "A great prophet has appeared among us" (Luke 7:16).[30]

A pre-Christian parallel of sorts involves Asclepius. Numerous miracles were attributed to him, especially of physical healing, leading to the establishment of the shrine at Epidaurus, where priests were said to interpret sick people's dreams and prescribe treatments for them on that basis. But we know next to nothing about Asclepius. Sometimes he was referred to as one of the many gods in the Greek pantheon and not as a human being at all. Yet in the eighth century BC, Homer, in the *Iliad*, spoke of him solely as a skilled human physician and not as a god.[31] Again, closer parallels to Jesus's physical healings appear in the miracles of Elisha in the Old Testament (esp. 2 Kings 5).

More occultic practices surrounded the ancient Greco-Roman world of exorcisms. Characteristic of the accounts of these supposed miracles are elaborate incantations, the use of magical paraphernalia, and protracted battles with the evil powers.[32] Nothing like this appears in the New Testament, where Jesus commands and demons flee, and where the apostles similarly command in Jesus's name but again without spells, charms, incantations, or drawn-out spiritual warfare. The closest parallels are again Jewish, with such Second Temple figures as Hanina ben-Dosa and Honi the Circle-Drawer, though even here prayer to Yahweh was necessary.[33] No one was said to be able to do what Jesus did: he simply commanded the demons to come out of the person they were possessing and experienced immediate success.

Examples could be multiplied, but these are the strongest cases for Christian derivation from pagan mythology, and they are not at all compelling.

Others prove weaker still.[34] More significantly, the miracles of Jesus clearly fulfill Isaiah's prophecy, "Then will the eyes of the blind be opened and the ears of the deaf unstopped. Then will the lame leap like a deer, and the mute tongue shout for joy" (Isa. 35:5–6). It is no coincidence that a considerable number of Jesus's miracles (unlike those in the Old Testament) involve giving sight to the blind, hearing to the deaf, the ability to walk and jump to the crippled, and the ability to speak to the mute.

Christological Titles

One of the areas to which Bousset devoted considerable attention was the Gospels' use of christological titles for Jesus. It was not just miracles but the most spectacular titles used by and about Jesus to explain his identity that were frequently supposed to have been derived from pagan parallels. In the century since Bousset, the four most common titles in the Gospels—"Son of Man," "Christ," "Lord," and "Son of God"—have continued to receive huge amounts of attention. "Son of Man" almost certainly derives from a Jewish milieu. Some scholars continue to defend the idea that it meant only a "mere mortal," as frequently in Ezekiel, in which God often addresses the prophet as "son of man."[35] But a strong case for seeing Daniel 7:13–14 as the most important background is accepted by an ever-increasing number of researchers. Here one who appears to be a human being ("one like a son of man") is ushered into the presence of the Ancient of Days (another name for God) to receive an eternal kingdom and everlasting dominion over all the peoples of the world. This is no "mere mortal"![36] At any rate, "son of man" in Greco-Roman circles would have meant a person whose father was a human male—that is, any human being, and nothing else. Jewish backgrounds are entirely decisive for understanding this title that is Jesus's unique and characteristic way of referring to himself.

"Christ/Messiah" is a second title that would have little meaning for the person not steeped in Jewish backgrounds. One commentator remarks that because *Christos* means "anointed," to use "Christ" as a virtual last name for Jesus would strike the average Greek or Roman just like calling a person "Smeared" for a name today! One just didn't use the word as a title or label for someone.[37] In the Jewish milieu, however, especially by the time of the first century, it had become the stock expression for the coming deliverer figure within Israel, usually accompanied by the belief that this deliverance would arrive in the form of a political and militaristic ruler who would lead the Israelite troops into battle to overwhelm the occupying imperial forces.[38]

"Lord" was the standard term used to refer to a whole range of human and divine masters or authorities in both Greek and Roman societies. Its Greek form (*kyrios*) is also by far the most common word that the Septuagint uses when translating the sacred tetragrammaton (YHWH). Roman, Greek, and Jewish usage all pointed to someone as an exalted authority, God/god, or both. Because "Lord" was so universally and similarly used throughout the ancient Mediterranean worlds, its frequency in the New Testament proves nothing about its origin. Countering the idea that it developed from other Greco-Roman religious usage is the telling observation that its Aramaic form, *Mar*, survives in the New Testament word *Maranatha* ("Come, Lord!" [1 Cor. 16:22]).[39]

The one title that at first glance might plausibly have originated in Hellenistic religion is "Son of God." Greeks and Romans often used the term "sons of God" for human beings (especially emperors) whom they believed were deified after their deaths. An older era of scholarship argued that there was a divine-man Christology in first-century Rome that influenced the New Testament development of the meaning of "Son of God." More careful scrutiny, however, has led to widespread scholarly rejection of this hypothesis or at least of the idea that it was old enough to have influenced the use of the title in the canonical Gospels.[40] The Dead Sea Scrolls famously show how "son of God" could refer to a purely human messiah figure right within Judaism. Still, a handful of scholars have tried to revive the old history-of-religions school of thought that "Son of God" shows indebtedness to the Hellenistic concept of a divine man.[41] This can also be tied up with the issues of baptism and the Lord's Supper, to which we turn next.

Ritual Washings and Meals

Baptism and the Lord's Supper have long proved fertile ground for those engaging in "parallelomania," to use the famous term that Jewish scholar Samuel Sandmel coined a generation ago.[42] The Greek and Roman myths, especially within the so-called mystery religions, had a plethora of ritual washing ceremonies and sacred meals of various kinds; for that matter, most religions do. The more common the ritual, the harder it is to defend the claim that one form of it is dependent on another form of it unless there is compelling evidence of close proximity in time and space between the two and a shared religious ethos. The Cybele cult had a new high priest stand in a pit that was dug for his "baptismal" ceremony. A bull was brought and tied to wooden latticework placed across the opening of the pit, a spear was plunged deep into its heart, and the fresh, hot blood disgorged through the openings in the wood slats into the pit below, raining its ghastly dew all over the initiate.[43] Clearly, Christian baptism must have derived from such a ritual—not!

Or take the next-most-popular new religion in the ancient Roman world after Christianity—Mithraism. It too had its sacred washings. In fact, many of their ritual objects for their secret services were sprinkled with water to purify them, though we don't actually know of people being sprinkled by the water. They also regularly practiced a sacred meal before their worship liturgies.[44] Now we have the potential background for both baptism and the Lord's Table, we are told![45] Never mind that because they worshiped in secret, no one actually knows what went on at this meal; all we have are carved and painted pictures that have been preserved of people eating together. We do have one document that reflects a Mithraic liturgy of a much later time, but there is dispute as to how representative it is. Mithraism was an all-male cult, often made up of retired military personnel, and very warlike in its philosophy. Its creation myth has Mithras springing from a rock (touted by some as a virgin birth!); he establishes his primacy at the time of creation by slaughtering a powerful bull. Claims that Mithras was crucified and resurrected are entirely fictional.[46] One wonders how desperate some people must be to try to discredit Christianity when they claim seriously to believe that the origins of Christian baptism and the Eucharist lie in these directions.

All this is made even more astounding when the true origins of the Christian rituals lie ready to hand: Judaism and the Hebrew Scriptures. Jews baptized proselytes when they converted to the Jewish religion. Temple worshipers in Jerusalem had to submerge themselves in one of the many *mikvaot*, or immersion pools, before ascending the Temple Mount for the sake of ritual purification. The Essenes at Qumran immersed themselves daily to symbolize their repeated purification. John the Baptist, as described by Josephus in a passage of undisputed authenticity, preached baptism to symbolize Jewish repentance of sin and God's subsequent forgiveness (Josephus, *Jewish Antiquities* 18.117). Christian baptism came directly out of Judaism. No one needs to posit any other origin, nor are any other ancient sources nearly as close in how baptism was practiced and in what it meant.[47]

The origins of the Last Supper of Jesus with his disciples are even more transparent. All the Gospels explicitly set it in the context of the annual Passover celebration (Matt. 26:17–19; Mark 14:12–16; Luke 22:7–15; John 13:1–2). This was the festival that commemorated the exodus and the deliverance of the children of Israel from Egypt (Exod. 12). Jesus took the bread and the wine that formed staples of that Jewish family ceremony and invested them with new significance as pointing to his soon-to-be-broken body and -spilled blood in his crucifixion.[48] We should not be surprised that other religious traditions have sacred meals; eating together has been meaningful for almost every human community and subgroup.[49] But we cannot legitimately claim any origin of the Lord's Supper apart from the Jewish Passover ceremony.

Indeed, recent studies of the best-known Greco-Roman ritual meal—the symposium—have given us much greater insight into that practice of the well-to-do in the Hellenistic world, showing just how different it was from Jesus's meals in Israel. Although it began with the ancient Greek philosophers, by New Testament times more often than not it had devolved into a fairly debauched festivity. An elaborate feast was served to a host and his elite male guests, who reclined around a triclinium—a three-sided collection of couches, allowing slaves to attend to them by serving food and drink in the middle. A libation to one or more gods marked the shift from the mealtime to the after-dinner entertainment. What was once an opportunity for philosophical discussion became more commonly an opportunity for triter conversation, complete with plenty of wine, games, and at times female courtesans for the sexual pleasure of the participants.[50] While the symposium possibly illustrates the seating arrangements for the practice of the Lord's Supper in house churches in some Hellenistic communities, very few other parallels emerge, other than perhaps with what the rich in Corinth were starting to make the ritual resemble through their greed (1 Cor. 11:20–22)![51]

Crucifixion and Resurrection

Those who would derive the Christian gospel from Hellenistic mythology often equivocate on the meaning of the terms "crucifixion" and "resurrection," using them as if they mean nothing more than "execution" and "deification." To be sure, Jesus was hardly the only person the Romans ever crucified— nailed to a wooden pair of crossbeams with a small, elevated footrest and left to die one of the most agonizing deaths humanity has ever invented. The victim would finally expire due not to the blood loss or the pain but to the inability to pull oneself up sufficiently to continue to breathe. Of course, thousands of individuals were crucified during the centuries of Roman rule in the ancient Mediterranean world, but not a single human being anywhere other than Jesus was even alleged to have started a new religious movement of any kind after death by crucifixion.[52] And death on a cross does not figure into Greco-Roman mythology at all; it was much too new a practice for that.

In a culture of honor and shame, the degradation of having one's naked (or barely clothed) body hung on a cross, being tortured by birds pecking at one's eyes, and eventually being unable to control one's bladder or bowels, made even the Romans exempt their citizens from such cruelty. In Jewish circles, it had already been decided that this manner of execution was similar enough to hanging from a tree that the curse in Deuteronomy 21:23 applied to crucifixion as well. That God had forsaken Jesus and that he was a convicted criminal and accursed by his heavenly Father were the only logical conclusions that any normal Jew could deduce.[53] Yet, it was precisely in that Jewish environment that the first followers of Jesus, all Jews themselves, came to the conviction that he was their divine Messiah. When one reads the ancient noncanonical accounts of the executions of various other would-be messianic figures, in every instance the death of the founder of the "rebellion" led either to the group's extinction or to the passing of leadership to a brother or son.[54] In the case of fledgling Christianity, neither happened. Jesus was believed to have been raised from death and to have ascended into heaven, and thus he was still guiding the community as its true leader.

That brings us to resurrection. Here the biggest problem of the revived history-of-religions school is the inability or unwillingness to distinguish a person's living on in some disembodied form from their bodily resurrection.[55] With a handful of exceptions, Greeks and Romans, if they anticipated any form of life after death, envisioned the immortality of the soul apart from the body. Of course, they often thought a soul (or spirit) could take various forms and be temporarily visible. So there are plenty of stories of the appearances of individuals, especially from a distance, perhaps as part of an ascension to heaven, often in conjunction with a famous person's apotheosis—becoming a god. Deification after a person's death was a well-known concept. None of those phenomena, however, provides conceptual parallels to the Jewish notion of bodily resurrection, which was so focused on a restored body that it some-times resembled the revivification of a corpse to be reunified with the soul.[56]

The vast majority of so-called resurrections in ancient mythology are thus actually the postmortem appearances of someone's spirit. Of course, the older the myth, the harder it sometimes is to know what was being claimed about a legendary figure. There *are* beliefs in embodied life in the next world in antiquity; witness the lavish material provisions that the Egyptians left in their Pharaohs' tombs for them, but such life remains in the underworld.[57] There are many stories of gods and goddesses returning from the underworld annually, corresponding to the reawakening of life each spring, but these are not human beings.[58] What makes the New Testament accounts of Jesus's resurrection utterly unique in the ancient world is that no other accounts ever claimed a *bodily* resurrection, of someone known to have lived as a human being, by people whose lives overlapped with (or were even just closely associated with) that individual. However, Jews did distinctively look for the bodily resurrection of all people at the end of this age. What makes the story of a resurrected Messiah unique, as Tom Wright has frequently stressed, is not the concept of bodily resurrection by itself but the fact that it happened to the Messiah without the general resurrection of all humanity closely following suit.[59] None of this *proves* the Christian resurrection accounts to be true, but it does make them unique and moves them out of the realm of Hellenistic religion almost entirely.[60]

The Romulus Myth and Other Supposed Patterns

Richard Carrier is a contemporary atheist who has written a lot to question the credibility of Christian faith, the biblical witness, and even the existence of a historical Jesus.[61] Although he is not a biblical scholar, his grasp of the literature in the field is noticeably better than most outsiders to the guild who try to pontificate as if they had the proper educational background to do so. Carrier appeals to numerous Greco-Roman mythological parallels in his discussions of various dimensions of the New Testament accounts of Jesus's life. At the end of the day, though, what he has no explanation for is where the notion of this new savior god, Jesus, came from in the first place. If Jesus were believed to be a celestial deity whose career was enhanced by the accounts of his incarnation, life, death, and resurrection, as Carrier argues,[62] who invented this Jesus in the first place and why? Who was the true genius behind the teachings and accounts that have inspired and motivated more people in the history of the world than any other religion? Communities do not invent religions; anonymous individuals do not inspire major world movements. Charismatic figures with powerful personalities who really lived and whose lives can often be sketched in some detail (Confucius, the Buddha, Muhammad, Lao-tze, Moses, Joseph Smith, and many more) start new religions (or offshoots of existing religions). One can debate who Jesus really was, but it is irrational to question his existence.[63]

There is still more that is wrong with Carrier's attempts to account for the rise of Christianity. Like various others in the new history-of-religions school do, he generalizes about details of the ancient stories of humans and gods to make them appear to be much more similar than they actually are. Citing a study by Richard Miller, Carrier thinks the clearest example of a Greek or Roman myth that is so parallel to the accounts of the death and resurrection of Jesus that they must be of the same fictional genre is the story of Romulus.[64] The fullest account is found in Plutarch's *Lives*, already an admittedly stylized version of the subjects he treats because he is pairing his short biographies to highlight parallels among the individuals paired. The relevant parts of the *Life of Romulus* are sections 27–28. Like Dionysius of Halicarnassus, who provides the next-fullest account (*Roman Antiquities* 2.56.2–6; 2.63.3–4), Plutarch notes three differing versions of Romulus's death. One that he doubts is that Romulus had been caught up into heaven to become a god. The other two that he finds plausible both involve the fact that the day on which the death occurred was punctuated by a huge thunderstorm with great winds, making the sky turn dark, during which time Romulus was murdered by some of his leading citizens and the body hidden or cut up into pieces and carried away. But some of the senators, who may have been responsible for the murder, convinced the gullible townspeople that Romulus had been taken up into heaven, as the son of the god Mars, and a certain trustworthy patrician entered the forum and solemnly swore that he had seen Romulus on the road arrayed for battle in bright and shining armor. Romulus told the patrician to tell the Romans to practice self-restraint and valor and thereby attain the heights of human power, and he added that he would be their propitious god Quirinius. In Livy's much shorter account the message is that Rome is to be the capital of the world as it prepares for ever-more war.

One scarcely can deny that the Gospel writers employed literary forms and genres with partial parallels in Greco-Roman historiography and biography.[65] Final commissioning narratives were commonplace in the Jewish world as well, and the belief in the deification of great mortals was so widespread in the ancient Roman world that stories that narrate how a person's soul went to heaven and how a great human became a god should cause no surprise. Since Miller does not actually recount the stories so that his readers can see the differences as well as the similarities, his list of twenty details that the "translations" to heaven of Romulus and Jesus have in common can easily deceive. He lists (1) "missing body," (2) "prodigies," (3) "darkness over the land," (4) "mountaintop speech," (5) "great commission," (6) "ascension," (7) "son of god," (8) "meeting on the road," (9) "eyewitness testimony," (10) "taken away in a cloud," (11) "dubious alternative accounts," (12) "immortal/heavenly body," (13) "outside of the city," (14) "the people flee," (15) "deification," (16) "belief, homage and rejoicing," (17) "bright and shining appearance," (18) "frightened subjects," (19) "all in sorrow over loss," and (20) "inspired message of translation."[66]

Of course, this is a fairly artificial construct. As his biblical references demonstrate, Miller has combined the various transfiguration, passion, resurrection, and ascension narratives from the four Gospels and Acts along with theological interpretations found in the Epistles. He has also made the list of "parallels" seem longer than it actually is. With the *Life of Romulus*, there are no prodigious events other than the horrible weather and darkness, just as ascension, deification, and being called a son of god are all really just three ways of saying the same thing (since there is no account of Romulus actually ascending). A mountaintop speech appears only in the Gospels, and there is no reference to a cloud that takes Romulus away; both of these items are merely inferred from the Greek and Roman accounts without ever being stated. The Romulan "great commission" is a command to prepare for war and pursue valor, not a mandate to evangelize the world. Responses of sorrow and fear but also belief and homage are common at the deaths of many great people, real and legendary. The people who flee in the Romulus stories are, first of all, the murderers themselves, while there are no dubious alternate accounts to the Gospels about Jesus's death, just the fear that the disciples will come and steal his body. One by one the remarkable number of occurrences, to which Carrier applies sophisticated statistical techniques never designed for use with historical (or mythical!) narrative,[67] dissipates. There are some interesting similarities, to be sure, but nothing requiring any literary dependence or common historical (or nonhistorical) origin between the accounts of the ends of Jesus's and Romulus's lives. Moreover, by his own admission, this is the *best* example Carrier can cite.[68] Above all, the Romulus tale is a classic example of precisely what Jews and the earliest Christians did *not* believe in—mere immortality of the soul *rather than* a bodily resurrection.[69]

The Gospels and Homer (or Other Epic Narratives)

If it is easy to overstate how similar pairs of individual stories are, as regularly occurs when the New Testament Gospels are compared to Greco-Roman myths, it is also easy to overstate how similar entire books are, especially when there is very little actual verbal parallelism. Dennis MacDonald has spent much of his career authoring works about how the Gospel writers were Christianizing the tomes of classic Greek or Roman authors. Mark, he is convinced, was telling Jesus's story in a way that would make his readers think of Homer's epics. Luke was then indebted to Vergil, while John was later imitating Euripides.[70] MacDonald *is* a bona fide New Testament scholar who has discovered various fascinating parallels, mostly at a fairly abstract and conceptual level, and he is well aware of the dangers of seeing more similarities than the original authors intended or were even aware of. Like many scholars engaging in such comparisons, he has found some parallels that convince him the Gospel writers knew the classical authors in question, and then he has become persuaded to various degrees that other similarities must have been consciously intended as well. To his credit, in order to make his theory of the origins of John's Gospel plausible, he postulates multiple stages of composition, with only the earliest imitating Euripides; the influence is found only in select parts of the final version of the Gospel, because later additions don't contain the same type of imitation.[71]

The case is stronger for Mark's awareness of Homer overall. When examined one at a time, however, the supposed parallels are of quite varying degrees of probability. Taking an example almost at random, we may analyze how Mac-Donald compares Mark 5:1–20 with *Odyssey* 9–10. He observes that Odysseus and his crew sail to the land of the Cyclopes, where countless goats graze. Going ashore, they discover a savage giant, Polyphemus, living in a cave and usually nude. Polyphemus asks Odysseus if he has come to harm him, and he asks Odysseus his name, to which Odysseus replies, "Nobody." Odysseus then proceeds to subdue the giant with trickery. A nearby shepherd calls to his neighbors, who come to ask about Polyphemus's sheep and goats. Odysseus and his crew board their ship, telling the giant to report to others what has happened to him. The giant asks Odysseus to return, but he refuses and sails away.[72]

MacDonald notes that Byzantine-era poets saw parallels with the demonized man from Gadara and adds, "Mark wanted his readers to note that Jesus was a better and more powerful hero than Homer's. Whereas Odysseus blinded a monster, Jesus made a monster sane." As he is consistently in the Gospels, "Jesus is a hero of compassion."[73] Here and elsewhere, how convincing one finds these parallels varies from one reader to the next.[74] But nothing would have prevented Mark from taking real events in the life of the historical Jesus and stylizing them in a way to bring out some of these potential similarities, so the parallels, even if present, do not necessarily discredit the foundational Christian story, even if MacDonald frequently uses them as putative support for fiction in the Gospels.

Judaism, the Old Testament, and the Historicization of Prophecy

If we had no other options, finding origins of various parts of the Gospel stories in Greco-Roman mythology, at least to a limited degree, might be a little more plausible. Yet, as I have noted just in the sampling of topics that this chapter has introduced, the origins in Judaism, and foundationally in the Old Testament, are far clearer in every instance. But we may go further. Allusions to and echoes of the Old Testament permeate almost every passage in the four Gospels. Consult almost any detailed, well-documented commentary on the Greek text of any one of the Gospels, and you'll see references to many of these Old Testament texts. Craig Keener's commentaries on Matthew and John have particularly copious lists.[75] There is little need to debate extensively the closest parallels to the Gospel accounts when time and again the answer is found in ancient Jewish sources that were well known.

All this raises a different question. Perhaps the Gospel accounts (or at least a significant number of them) represent prophecy historicized.[76] In other words, precisely because there are so many Old Testament passages that are allegedly fulfilled in the life of Jesus, maybe overeager followers of this man from Nazareth used those very prophecies to invent what they depicted the Messiah doing. Interestingly, the biggest cluster of fulfillment texts appears in the infancy and passion narratives of the Gospels, exactly those areas where the history-of-religions school has often claimed the greatest amount of creativity by the Gospel writers. Take Matthew 1:18–2:23, for example.[77] Isaiah 7:14 prophesied that the Messiah would be born of a virgin, Micah 5:2 predicted that he would be born in Bethlehem, and Hosea 11:1 said that he would come out of Egypt. Then Jeremiah 31:15 spoke of mothers in Israel near Bethlehem weeping for their children because they were no more, while still other passages declared centuries ahead of time that Jesus would be called a Nazarene. So Matthew simply composed a narrative and fleshed out the details so that each of these prophecies would appear to have been fulfilled (Matt. 1:18–25; 2:1–12, 13–15, 16–18, 19–23).[78]

The problem with this approach is that a significant majority of the Old Testament quotations in the Gospels were not predictive prophecies in their original contexts. Yes, Micah did foretell the Messiah's birthplace. That part of Matthew's story could have been made up, theoretically, based on Micah's prophecy. But the "virgin" of Isaiah 7:14 was first of all a young woman born in Isaiah's day, whose son would not even be old enough to tell good from evil before the two kings of the north (Rezin and Pekah, in Aram and Israel) would no longer be threatening Judah (vv. 15–16). Hosea 11:1 is not even a prophecy but rather is a past-tense statement about how God led his "son," Israel, out of Egypt at the time of the exodus (see Hosea 11:3–8). Jeremiah 31:15 is about mothers near Bethlehem at the time of the fall of Judah to Babylonia in the sixth century BC (cf. vv. 16–18). Above all, there is no Old Testament text that even says, "He would be called a Nazarene," as Matthew 2:23 claims.[79] So why would any first-century person steeped in Judaism construct a fictional narrative of the birth and earliest years of the Messiah based on these last four texts?

One can, of course, explain their choice after the fact. Once Matthew has learned about Jesus's earliest days, which he narrates in his opening two chapters, then he might well think of the Old Testament texts he comes to cite. Employing the well-known practice of typology, he reasons as a monotheist who believes that God is sovereignly orchestrating the events of world history. It is thus too "coincidental" for all of these details of Jesus's life to have happened *even partially resembling* their Old Testament counterparts without it being a sign of God's providential hand in guiding Israel's history.[80] Nevertheless, the parallels are not close enough for Matthew to think of all of them as part of messianic prophecy in their own right and therefore as grist for the mill of a fictional author wanting to turn Jesus into a credible messianic candidate.[81] The same principles can be illustrated for the uses of the Old Testament in the passion narratives and, for that matter, in any major part of the Gospel accounts.[82]

Conclusion

There are probably places where one or more of the New Testament Gospel writers drew on certain aspects of the way Greeks and Romans tended to tell stories about their legendary heroes. It is even likely that Jesus was aware of what forms the lives of sages in his world took and in places deliberately conformed to those models.[83] But these need not call into question the historicity of the essential core of each passage in question, whether in the Synoptics or in John. On the other hand, many of the supposed parallels prove doubtful after they have been more closely scrutinized.[84] What keeps them from playing too large a role even when they are most likely described accurately is the whole host of very close Jewish parallels we have throughout all four Gospels (and indeed throughout almost all of the New Testament). Here lies the real origin of Jesus's stories. Multivolume works have been published on the amount of rabbinic literature we have that impinges on the life and career of Jesus as possible historical background.[85] Normally, we need look no further afield. Far from calling into question the historicity of the Gospels' accounts of Jesus, the Jewish background reinforces it.

This is the first chapter so far where it might be alleged that there is nothing about my positions that reflects a distinctively "New Testament" perspective. But that would be mistaken. It cannot be coincidental that there is a revival of interest in Greco-Roman mythology even as there is an increase in biblical illiteracy. Throughout much of Western church history, education has focused much more both on the Bible and on the Greek and Latin classics, including their myths. When one knows the contents of both bodies of literature well, it is the dissimilarities more than the similarities that stand out. When one reads only excerpts of each piecemeal or, even more commonly, just accepts the reports of others second- or thirdhand, the parallels that do exist will seem more prominent and significant than they actually are. We need to regain a deep familiarity with the contents of the New Testament and understand how they fit in the context of the grand narrative of Scripture. Then we will be able more accurately to weigh the extent and importance of its similarities to other bodies of literature.

6

How Should We Respond to All the Violence in the Bible?

This chapter at first glance might seem like a strange one to include in a book on *New Testament* answers to difficult questions for those who would believe in God. After all, the majority of the scenes of violence in Scripture occur in the Old Testament. It is there we read about the near-extinction of human life at the time of the flood (Gen. 6–8), the unparalleled wickedness of Sodom and Gomorrah and their destruction (Gen. 19), horrible instances of rape (e.g., Gen. 34; Judg. 19; 2 Sam. 13:1–22), the issue of apparent attempts at genocide in the conquest of the land of Canaan at the time of Joshua (Josh. 1–12), ongoing warfare between Israel and the Philistines (esp. throughout 1–2 Samuel), the defeat of the Northern Kingdom and its exile to Assyria (2 Kings 18:9–12), and the defeat of the Southern Kingdom with its exile to Babylon (2 Kings 24–25). And those are just the highlights or, perhaps better put, lowlights!

Numerous good studies by *Old Testament scholars*, nevertheless, have helped make some sense of those narratives in their original contexts.[1] The war with the Canaanites recorded in the book of Joshua is the only one that Israel actually started. Various passages show that the Israelites in no way were trying to obliterate everyone in Canaan (see esp. Josh. 13:1–7, along with the presence of other peoples in the land in the years immediately following). In many places, the language that speaks of killing every last woman, child, and even animal (e.g., Josh. 6:21; 8:26) is hyperbolic and conventional in

85

ancient warfare reports for a lopsided victory. Locations that were attacked were often more like military encampments than complete cities, especially at Jericho and Ai. Archaeology and ancient literature attest to the extreme immorality of these Canaanite cultures, especially with respect to child sacrifice. Even with that, Genesis 15:16 speaks of God allowing the sins of the Amalekites to go unpunished for over four centuries until they had reached "full measure." The Gibeonites' ruse (Josh. 9) demonstrates that there was at least one option that was open to anyone who wanted their lives spared. Much better, however, is Rahab's option of seeking mercy through serving the God of Israel, especially as she notes how everyone in the land has heard of him and his exploits on behalf of the Israelites (Josh. 2, see esp. vv. 9–11).[2]

Philosophers and *ethicists* have also made good contributions to these topics, as we noted they did on the issues treated in previous chapters.[3] Precisely what have not received enough attention are distinctively New Testament perspectives on violence and warfare. As with all the chapters in this volume, I can merely scratch the surface of the topic, but I can at least point in fruitful directions for how *Christians* and those analyzing Christian belief should understand the faith. If, like Orthodox Judaism, Christianity were subject solely to the Hebrew Bible, a different kind of discussion would be needed. But Christians filter the Old Testament through the grid of its fulfillment in the New.[4] The upshot is that it is hardly the case that we have to reject God just because of the violence of his people in the Old Testament. In stark contrast, one looks in vain for examples of Christians acting violently in the New Testament. Instead, believers in the time of Jesus and the apostles routinely have to absorb the hostility and violence of others. Imagery of military warfare no longer deals with human armies and their battles but is applied to spiritual warfare. Precisely because perfect justice and perfect grace have met at the cross of Christ, believers can trust that God will one day right all wrongs rather than think that they are responsible for avenging evil now.

The Absence of Violent Christians in the New Testament

Scarcely have we been introduced to the ministry of Jesus when the Gospel of Matthew presents his famous Sermon on the Mount (Matt. 5–7). Here appear some of the most important texts to which Christian pacifists have appealed.[5] In the Beatitudes with which the Sermon begins we read, "Blessed are the peacemakers, for they will be called children of God" (5:9). Glen Stassen, a Christian ethicist unusually conversant with New Testament scholarship, spent much of his career highlighting the importance of proactive peacemaking, particularly from Jesus's great sermon, as a strategy that could be embraced both by pacifists and by just-war theorists. The more one can calm down the kinds of conflicts that sometimes end in war, the more likely one can avoid having to decide if a certain war is righteous in the first place.[6]

Jesus ups the ante when he contrasts his teaching with standard interpretations of the Old Testament in the so-called antitheses in Matthew 5:21–48. In verses 38–39, he declares, "You have heard that it was said, 'Eye for eye, and tooth for tooth.' But I tell you, do not resist an evil person. If anyone slaps you on the right cheek, turn to them the other cheek also." Unfortunately, this has often been misinterpreted as requiring that persons repeatedly put themselves in harm's way, especially in situations of domestic abuse. Yet a typically right-handed person in Jesus's world could not strike an aggressor's blow on another person's right cheek; it would have to be a backhanded slap, which was a characteristic Jewish insult of an authority to a subordinate. Jesus is more likely calling on people not to retaliate by trading insults.[7]

The stakes become higher still in verses 43–44: "You have heard that it was said, 'Love your neighbor and hate your enemy.' But I tell you, love your enemies and pray for those who persecute you." It is often pointed out that, whereas the first five antitheses all quote an actual Old Testament passage ("You shall not murder" [v. 21]; "You shall not commit adultery" [v. 27]; etc.), there is no Old Testament text that commands hatred of one's enemy. This, in turn, is seen as supporting the approach that understands that even where Scripture *is* quoted, Jesus's expression "you have heard" (rather than "you have read") means that he is contrasting an errant with an accurate interpretation of the Hebrew Bible.[8] On the other hand, the commands in Joshua and elsewhere to fight against the Canaanites certainly appear to reflect hatred for one's enemies. Moreover, Jesus's immediately preceding commands in the Sermon on the Mount call for the complete abolition of oath taking (vv. 33–37), which is more than just correcting a misinterpretation of the law. It actually anticipates a change in God's will for his people more broadly.[9]

Indeed, Jesus's fulfillment of the law (Matt. 5:17) does mean that his followers need not observe certain Old Testament commands, at least in any literal sense. The clearest examples involve all of the many laws of animal sacrifice (Lev. 1–9), which are now rendered unnecessary by the once-for-all sacrifice of Jesus for the sins of humanity (cf. Heb. 7–9). Almost as clear are the abolition of the dietary laws (Mark 7:19; Acts 10:9–16) and the need for circumcision (Gal. 5:6). So while God does not change in his essence or character (Num. 23:19; Heb. 13:8), he does at times alter certain stipulations for human behavior from one age of history to another.

Are warfare and violence among such stipulations? As we flip through the Gospels, we see Jesus sending out both the Twelve and the seventy(-two) without even adequate provisions for their own sustenance, much less protection from bodily harm (Mark 6:8–10 pars.; Luke 10:3–4). Worse still, he predicts that others will persecute them and reject them, while they are simply to imitate Jesus's own model throughout his ministry of withdrawing from hostile locations and moving on to other people and places (Mark 6:11 pars.; Luke 10:5–12). On one such occasion (see Matt. 12:17–21), after Jesus has left a place of opposition, Matthew quotes Isaiah 42:1–4, in order to identify Jesus as God's chosen servant, who "will not quarrel or cry out" (v. 19). He adds, "A bruised reed he will not break, and a smoldering wick he will not snuff out" (v. 20). Whatever else Matthew may be implying, at the very least he is highlighting Jesus's typically gentle character, as one who will not treat the already bruised of the world with any kind of antagonism or violence.[10]

One chapter later, Jesus explains, in interpreting his parable of the wheat and the tares, that his disciples should not try to weed evil out of God's kingdom (Matt. 13:28–30). Ever since Augustine mistakenly equated the kingdom and the church, expositors have often taken Jesus to mean that one should not try to separate believers from unbelievers within God's household. Jesus, on the other hand, explicitly states that his field, over which he exercises his kingly rule, is the *world* (v. 38). Precisely because judgment day will right all wrongs and punish the unrepentant wicked, God's people do not need to take vengeance into their own hands and try aggressively or coercively to uproot evil from the world in this age.[11]

It is true that on one occasion, Jesus promises to bring a "sword" rather than peace (Matt. 10:34 par.). Yet the context of family members pitted against one another clarifies that he is talking about the inevitable hostility of some kind that non-Christians will exhibit toward believers (vv. 35–36). When Peter actually brandishes a sword in the garden of Gethsemane, Jesus rebukes him, tells him to put it away, and explains that the Son of Man must be crucified (John 18:10–11).[12] Indeed, he has already admonished the Twelve that they must take up their own crosses and die daily for his sake and for the kingdom (Mark 8:34–38 pars.). The parable of the good Samaritan (Luke 10:29–37) is not merely about imitating one man's compassion but about loving one's enemy, since Jews and Samaritans regularly despised one another.[13] When Pilate asks Christ if he is indeed a king, he replies that the origin of his kingdom is not from this world; otherwise he would fight back (John 18:36).

Jesus's temple-clearing incidents (Mark 11:15–19 pars.; John 2:13–22) are too often exaggerated in ways the text of Scripture does not require. Nothing in the text points to more than a token protest in one corner of the vast temple precincts; presumably even the money changers and animal vendors who are affected would be back at their stalls the next day.[14] Jesus's use of a whip (John 2:15) is to drive out sheep and cattle, not humans,[15] in the manner to which they are already accustomed. Of course, Jesus is wholly righteous in his indignation, a characteristic that sinful humans often desire and even claim to imitate, but one in which they rarely succeed. Whereas Jesus regularly calls on his followers to imitate him in suffering and weakness, singularly absent from the temple-clearing narratives are any similar calls to act like he does there.

Moving beyond the Gospels, we find nothing that changes the pattern that Jesus has already established. The only significant passages that could potentially support Christians behaving violently, and then only in state-sponsored violence, are Romans 13:1–7 and 1 Peter 2:13–17. The passage in Romans is the better known of the two, and some Christians act as if it were the only text in the entire Bible relevant to the relationship between believers and governments. In it, Paul writes,

> Let everyone be subject to the governing authorities, for there is no authority except that which God has established. The authorities that exist have been established by God. Consequently, whoever rebels against the authority is rebelling against what God has instituted, and those who do so will bring judgment on themselves. For rulers hold no terror for those who do right, but for those who do wrong. Do you want to be free from fear of the one in authority? Then do what is right and you will be commended. For the one in authority is God's servant for your good. But if you do wrong, be afraid, for rulers do not bear the sword for no reason. They are God's servants, agents of wrath to bring punishment on the wrongdoer. Therefore, it is necessary to submit to the authorities, not only because of possible punishment but also as a matter of conscience. (Rom. 13:1–5)

Does this mean that every time a government declares war on another country, its citizens must participate? Does it mean that Christians must obey every governmental mandate? As we noted in the discussion of slavery, Paul obviously knew the Old Testament instances when God's people had to disobey the authorities of the lands in which they were living because they were being asked to contravene God's will—especially the midwives at the time of Moses's birth (Exod. 1:15–21) and Daniel and his companions in Babylon (Dan. 3; 6). Paul would almost certainly have also known about the occasions on which Peter and the Twelve had to tell the Jewish supreme court (the Sanhedrin) that they had to obey God rather than men, even though those men were their most powerful religious leaders (Acts 4:19–20; 5:29).[16] As a result, believers who adopt just-war theory must still determine if any war in which they might be called to serve meets the historic criteria for being "just."[17] Pacifists, on the other hand, remain conscientious objectors to all wars. Both approaches have a long and respected place in Christian history; what cannot be squared with authentic Christianity is the mentality that *glorifies* violence by human beings against one another.[18]

Returning to Romans 13, we must note that it is crucial to understand that "being subject" or "submitting" to someone (v. 1) is not necessarily the same as obeying them.[19] It is ironic that those who promote civil disobedience to object to a war (or any other state-mandated obligation they deem unjust) sometimes themselves resort to violence. The most Christian way to submit to governments even when one believes one has to disobey them is to do so as nonviolently and even as courteously as possible, accepting arrest and even incarceration if there is no peaceful alternative. Likewise, verse 2 cannot mean that anyone who ever breaks a law or disobeys a public official's order is thereby living in sin, if the law they are disobeying is itself against biblical directives. In verses 3–4 Paul generalizes, preferring government to anarchy, but it is hardly true in all times and places that "rulers hold no terror for those who do right." As we have just seen, Paul himself would have known about exceptions. So when he speaks of "the authorities" (CEB, NLT), he may well mean the specific Roman authorities (and any others like them) as they were functioning around AD 57, before Nero initiated the first state-sponsored persecution of Christians seven years later.[20] This would then also explain verses 6–7, on paying one's taxes, because this was a period of several Roman tax revolts, which were antagonizing the emperor and polarizing the people.[21] But would Paul have written the identical words seven years later, after Nero unleashed his pogrom against Christians in 64? It is hard to know.

It is also crucial to observe the context of Romans 13:1–7. In the immediately preceding passage, Paul reveals his awareness of the oral tradition about Jesus's teaching, as he alludes to his Savior's words about enemy love (12:19–21).[22] Whatever a given Christian may determine is their responsibility as the citizen of a nation (especially in times of war), the church must live separately enough from every government so that believers can be seen corporately to function as peacemakers. This is easier for pacifists to do, but even supporters of just war who enlist in military forces or encourage others to do so can simultaneously work to offer relief and humanitarian aid to the countless noncombatant victims of every form of armed conflict. It is not a little ironic that American Christians often recognize this principle only when the political parties or leaders whom they have *not* supported are in power and then glibly cite only Romans 13:1–5 when people they have supported get elected.

Something similar can be said about 1 Peter 2:13–17. In the phrase "Submit
. . . to every human authority" (v. 13a CSB, NIV; cf. NLT), the object could just
as easily be rendered as "every human institution" (CEB, ESV, NAB, NASB,
NET). The Greek word is *ktisis*, which normally means simply "creature"
or "creation."[23] The most common translation of verse 13b, referring to the
king or emperor as "supreme," seems a bit misleading, since the adjectival
participle is simply *hyperechonti*—being above something, in this case other
humans.[24] "Supreme" is a superlative form that is best reserved for God. The
NASB translates it just as "the one in authority," and the NLT, more freely,
as "head of state." It is striking at the end of the paragraph that God is to
be feared whereas the emperor is only to be honored (*timaō*), the same verb
that is used of "everyone," even though translated there as "show respect" in
the NIV (v. 17).[25] Even the honor due the governing authorities comes from
the fact that their role is to "punish those who do wrong" and "commend
those who do right" (v. 14 [recall Rom. 13:3–4]), and Peter says nothing about
what to do when governments punish the innocent and protect the wicked.[26]
Indeed, the motive clause in 1 Peter 2 is explicitly to "silence the ignorant talk
of foolish people" (v. 15)—those who maligned believers as threats to the state
when in fact they were not. Revelation 13, however, shows what can happen
when the state becomes demonic and not divine, and Christians must never
submit to the overtly diabolical.[27]

The Consistent Pattern of Human Violence against Christians

This last observation reflects a broader generalization that is true throughout the New Testament. Jesus's followers only rarely initiate violence but
regularly are treated violently through persecution and even martyrdom. Of
course, Jesus himself gives his life for the sins of the world. The hostility he
experiences throughout his ministry sets the stage for the climactic violence
inflicted on him at his crucifixion. Yet he predicts that his followers will
experience similar hostility (Matt. 10:17–39; John 15:18–25; 16:1–3), even
if it does not occur until after Jesus's resurrection (see throughout Acts).
Indeed, he tells them that whoever wants to follow him must carry their
own cross (Mark 8:34 pars.), a call to utter self-renunciation to the point
of martyrdom, should it come to that.[28] John the Baptist, Jesus's forerun-
ner, is beheaded (Mark 6:14–29); and Stephen, one of the first additional
church leaders beyond the twelve apostles, is stoned to death (Acts 7:57–8:1).
Later in Acts, the apostle James, brother of John, is martyred by Herod
Agrippa I (12:1–2).

The apostle Paul doubtless holds the record in the first generation of Christianity for the amount of personal injury inflicted on him because of his faith and his bold testimony about it. Acts gives us periodic references to his persecution (e.g., 13:50; 14:5, 19; 16:19–24), but 2 Corinthians 11:23b–28 gives a much fuller catalogue. Some of these hardships reflect simply the rigor of an itinerant ministry in the ancient Mediterranean world, but Paul endured many of them precisely because of his Christian commitment.[29] In a rare text outside of the Gospels where the risen Lord speaks directly enough to someone for modern translators to put his words in quotation marks (and sometimes in red letters), Jesus replies to Paul's repeated prayers for removal of his mysterious thorn in the flesh by explaining, "My grace is sufficient for you, for my power is made perfect in weakness" (2 Cor. 12:9).[30] It is the height of irony that any Christians ever developed the reputation, deserved or undeserved, for being violent themselves. Prior to Constantine becoming the first Christian emperor, almost all Christians were pacifists and refused to serve in the Roman military.[31] That the ownership and use of private firearms should be so bound up with certain forms of contemporary American Christianity would have been almost inconceivable in the first three centuries of the church's history. It is equally difficult to fathom the love affair that some American Christians have with weapons of self-defense (unlike most of the rest of the English-speaking Christian world), as if the preservation of physical life were the highest good of all.[32] In stark contrast, Jesus proclaims, "For whoever wants to save their life will lose it, but whoever loses their life for me and for the gospel will save it" (Mark 8:35).

First Peter 4:12–16 typifies the early Christian approach to hostility from unbelievers:

> Dear friends, do not be surprised at the fiery ordeal that has come on you to test you, as though something strange were happening to you. But rejoice inasmuch as you participate in the sufferings of Christ, so that you may be overjoyed when his glory is revealed. If you are insulted because of the name of Christ, you are blessed, for the Spirit of glory and of God rests on you. If you suffer, it should not be as a murderer or thief or any other kind of criminal, or even as a meddler. However, if you suffer as a Christian, do not be ashamed, but praise God that you bear that name.

There is no place here for a military-crusader mentality. For those convinced by just-war theory, Christian entry into armed conflict should be done with great sorrow, recognizing all peacemaking overtures as having been exhausted, and not as something glamorous, exhilarating, or to be celebrated.[33] A Rambo-like spirit may be one of American culture's icons, but it should be allowed no place in the Christian church.

Turning Physical Warfare into Spiritual Warfare

One of the reasons so little physical violence is endorsed in the New Testament is that it has been turned into spiritual battle. Indeed, it is too infrequently observed that the New Testament consistently takes the imagery of physical warfare from the Old Testament and transposes it to the concept of spiritual warfare.[34] Instead of a Roman legion of armies, Jesus confronts a demon-possessed man whose inhabitants refer to themselves as "Legion," because there are many of them (Mark 5:9 par.).[35] Jesus's exorcisms rid human beings of the evil powers that have overtaken them in the same ways that military troops try to rid lands of wicked enemy forces. After the seventy(-two) return triumphant over demonic powers in their mission, Jesus declares, "I saw Satan fall like lightning from heaven" (Luke 10:18). Like a vanquished ruler in battle, Satan can no longer remain in God's direct presence but must do his dirty work exclusively on earth.

Jesus's followers after his death and resurrection are also empowered to cast out demons from the people they inhabit (e.g., Acts 16:16–18). After an exorcism, the person's wholeness is restored. Humans alone are created in the image of God, so he shows unique concern for their well-being. Neither animals nor angelic/demonic beings merit the same level of concern, because neither bears God's image. If there is a story in Acts that would have made Jew and Gentile alike chuckle, it is the aftermath of the failed attempt by the seven sons of Sceva to cast out demons "in the name of the Jesus whom Paul preaches," when they have had no relationship with that Jesus himself. Not only does their failure show that the name of Jesus is no talisman, but also the demons turn and attack the men, causing them to flee their domicile naked (19:13–16)![36]

Paul's Letters make clear that humanity's warfare is "not against flesh and blood [i.e., other human beings], but against the rulers, against the authorities, against the powers of this dark world and against the spiritual forces of evil in the heavenly realms" (Eph. 6:12). Paul then goes on to unpack the concept of spiritual warfare by itemizing the various pieces of armor that a soldier in this kind of combat must wear: truth, righteousness, the gospel of peace, salvation, and the word of God (vv. 14–17), all undergirded by prayer (vv. 18–20). Only in this way can we stand in the day of evil (v. 13). While some have tried to match each character trait with the part of the body protected by the metaphorical armor used to represent it (belt of truth, breastplate of righteousness, helmet of salvation, etc.), the use of several of these military metaphors with different traits in Isaiah 59:17 suggests that it is the whole package of protection on which we should focus.[37] It *may* be significant that the only offensive weapon is the sword of the Spirit, which is identified as God's word, though even here it is hard to be sure.[38] What is crystal clear, however, is that Paul is not saying a word about fighting evil people through human warfare but is stressing the power of a godly, faith-filled life devoted to Jesus through the power of the Spirit as the key to opposing the spiritual powers that inevitably lurk behind the worst of the world's evil.[39]

Spiritual warfare comes to its biblical climax in the book of Revelation. We are so used to taking our teaching from popular Christian novels and dooms-day scenarios rather than carefully studying Scripture for ourselves that it is easy to miss what John actually teaches in this last book of Scripture. Exiled on Patmos for his faith, and probably for being a prominent Christian leader, he receives a remarkable series of God-given visions about both the world in his day and the end of the age. Revelation 4–5 provides the key to John's theology of warfare. No one in the universe is qualified to open the scroll on which God has written his coming judgments until Christ appears as the Lion who is also the slain Lamb (5:5–6). The King of creation has to suffer and die rather than fight back against his opponents in order to be resurrected, exalted, and glorified. Only then is he qualified to function as Ruler and Judge.[40] Believers must imitate him in this experience, not because our deaths contribute to pay-ing the price for the world's sins, but because in God's upside-down kingdom we triumph when we don't fight back but instead allow God to fight for us. Spiritual warfare appears explicitly in chapter 9, where John sees a vision of grotesque locusts ascending from the Abyss, the very home of the devil (vv. 1–11). In the next phase, horses with soldiers are described in very similar imagery, and there are two hundred million such mounted troops (v. 16; liter-ally "two myriads of myriads," with a myriad, when it equaled ten thousand, functioning as the largest named numeral in ancient Greek), so these are also most likely demonic hordes rather than human warriors.[41] As a result, when we are then told that a third of humankind is killed by the plagues that these mounted troops have released, it is most likely that God is revealing to John these people's spiritual rather than physical deaths.[42]

The famous battle of Armageddon provides perhaps the greatest contrast of all between what the Bible actually teaches and popular imagination and folklore. In Revelation 16:14 demonic spirits prompt "the kings of the whole world" to gather together "for the battle on the great day of God Almighty." Verse 16 then explains that the place where they gather is in Hebrew called

Armageddon. The underlying Hebrew that is implied, *har-magedon*, most likely means the Mount of Megiddo, which is a hill that rises about seventy feet above the Jezreel Valley in the southwest of Galilee.[43] Still, just as we often talk about someone meeting their "Waterloo" as a cipher for a war-ending defeat in battle, because that is where Napoleon met his downfall two hundred years ago in what was then part of the Netherlands, so also the mount overlooking the valley where the kings of Israel and Judah often did battle in Old Testament times is likely just a reference to the fateful place of this final battle, wherever on earth it may actually occur.[44] John does not immediately proceed to tell us any more about this warfare, though, but reflects in chapters 17–18 on the fall of the great, evil end-times empire, so reminiscent of Rome in the New Testament and Babylon in the Old. When he does resume the story in 19:19, with all the players in place and ready to fight the returning Christ and his army, the battle is over before it begins, so to speak. Verse 20a proceeds to explain almost matter-of-factly that "the beast was captured, and with it the false prophet who had performed the signs on its behalf." The two are thrown into "the fiery lake of burning sulfur," while Christ and his armies slay the kings' armies poised to attack him (vv. 20b–21). Nothing is said about Christians alive on earth at that time using a single weapon of human warfare or experiencing a single casualty.[45]

Divine Judgment

One might well summarize this scene in Revelation 19 with the recurring biblical refrain, "Vengeance is mine, I will repay, says the Lord" (Rom. 12:19 NRSV, ESV, quoting Deut. 32:35). Precisely because we know God will right all wrongs in the end, we don't have to take judgment into our own hands. Sooner or later, humans invariably kill innocent people and let the guilty go unpunished, even if only by mistake. The parable of the wheat and the weeds in Matthew 13:24–30, 36–43 puts it as strikingly as any passage does. I have already mentioned one aspect of it above, but not its overall message. In this parable, Jesus tells the story of a farmer defying the agricultural logic of the day by refusing to have his hired hands weed his fields. In what was an ancient equivalent to what we might call "bioterrorism," the farmer's enemy has deliberately but clandestinely sowed a kind of weed that looks very much like wheat right in the midst of all the wheat plants. Common sense would dictate that he is going to have a bad harvest, but at least the workers should weed out what they can. This farmer, however, replies that they are not to attempt any weeding, because they would invariably pull up many of the wheat plants as well—both because their root systems are intermingled and because the two kinds of plants are not always clearly distinguishable.[46]

The parable is teaching that God's people are not to try to prematurely uproot evil unbelievers from the world in this life. If Christians, for example, through some bizarre set of circumstances, were allowed to perform a citizen's arrest of every particularly undesirable non-Christian in the world so that each might be imprisoned for a long time, we would doubtless select some who were genuine Christians (but just not *our kind* of Christian!). We would also surely fail to go after many unbelievers who were truly wicked and dangerous but didn't appear so on the outside. What is more, many of the greatest Christians in history at one point in their lives were among the gospel's most hardened opponents, so the whole hypothetical scenario becomes ludicrous. God assures the farmer in Jesus's parable that there will be enough fruit-bearing seed to provide a harvest and that he will judge all humanity fairly (and graciously) at the end of the age.[47]

This one passage alone should give pause to any Christian who remains overly eager about starting a war or inciting any kind of violence against others. If it doesn't rule out Christian participation in all warfare and violence (and it just might), it at least means that we opt for such only as a counsel of despair after all less extreme measures have been tried, and only for the very clearest and most righteous of causes. The same is true with other state-sponsored violence, including capital punishment.[48] Jesus's parables, in fact, frequently depict final judgment, by means of the imagery of imprisonment, death, extreme grief, fire, or outer darkness (Matt. 13:30, 42, 50; 18:34; 22:13; 24:51; 25:30; Mark 12:9; Luke 13:28; 16:24). As we saw earlier in the discussion of hell in chapter 2, an overly literal interpretation of these metaphors can create logically contradictory pictures. But the point to make here is that it is no mere mortal but only Jesus who is a completely righteous judge. Only he can be guaranteed never to treat people in ways they do not deserve. Amazingly, he often treats them far more graciously than they could ever merit (Matt. 20:1–16).[49]

It is simply false, therefore, to claim that the actions of God in the Old Testament are primarily those of a harsh judge, whereas the God who revealed himself in Jesus Christ is solely a loving Father. Both mercy and judgment permeate both Testaments. What *does* change from the Old to the New Testament is that, in the New, God nowhere commands anyone to go to war, or even to defend themselves against others who incite hostilities against them. Jesus models flight when possible (Mark 3:7 par.; Matt. 14:13; John 11:54), and Paul undertakes nonviolent protest on occasion (Acts 16:37; 22:25). It remains quite unclear whether a theory of just war could have been derived from the New Testament alone.[50]

In addition, there clearly are various differences in God's commands to his people in the two Testaments. The objector often asks at this point, "So, does God change?" In his fundamental character, in his faithfulness to his promises, the answer in both Testaments of course is no, which is what we have seen in passages like Numbers 23:19 and Hebrews 13:8. But if we believe there is any point to prayer, we have to admit in virtually the same breath that God *does* change with respect to his temporal purposes for humanity. Perhaps a better way of putting it is that he has willed that some things will occur if and only if his people ask him for those things (James 4:2). They are part of what theologians often call God's conditional rather than his unconditional will.[51] Yet if we acknowledge even this much, then it follows that God's will on a certain issue at one point in time *can* be different than what it is at a later point. That is true on a much broader scale as one moves from the Old Testament era to the New. Because Jesus fulfilled the entire Hebrew Scriptures, we no longer have to obey all of the commands of the Mosaic law, at least not literally. We do not offer animal sacrifices, we need not observe the dietary laws, and we don't have to circumcise our baby boys as a religious requirement. What Christians have often referred to as the civil and ceremonial law (as opposed to the moral law) extends the catalogue of changes considerably further. Still other changes include the penalties for violating even some of the moral laws. We are not called on to stone to death the most egregious of lawbreakers, even while the behaviors that once led to their being put to death are still considered sinful.[52]

As a result, it may well be that the Old Testament commands for literal, physical holy war are completely fulfilled in the New Testament analogues for spiritual warfare. It may be that part of Christ's work on the cross, paying fully for the sins of humanity, which animal sacrifices never could accomplish, means that no other human being ever again should face the death penalty because of their sins. It may be that Genesis 9:6, with its call for a "life for a life," is overturned by Jesus's rejection of the law of retaliation (an "eye for an eye") in his teaching in the Sermon on the Mount (Matt. 5:38–42).[53] This is not because Christians do not care about justice but because we care so deeply about it that we want it to be implemented ultimately by the only Judge who will never make a mistake.

At the same time, we dare not claim that all human acts of judgment are wrong or misguided. It is always interesting to have a discussion with someone who talks as though they object to all forms of judging other people. Sooner or later, when that person has been dealt an injustice, especially a very serious one, they decide they do want justice for themselves. And that requires that someone hold the perpetrator of the injustice accountable—which is the very heart of the concept of judgment! The otherwise fairly liberal commentator Ulrich Luz insightfully comments on Matthew's parable of the ten bridesmaids, observing that "there is also the question whether a story of God's pure love [such as an ending without judgment would suggest] would not cause people to depend on the love in their own calculations and thus not take the holy God seriously. That is indeed what the foolish women have done."[54] Put differently, if I ever think there is a gross injustice in the world that needs correcting, I have to be prepared to allow the same kind of correction to occur in my life.

What, then, do we do with the text that various pundits have been saying for some time has replaced John 3:16 as the best-known verse in the Bible: "Do not judge, or you too will be judged" (Matt. 7:1)? As with every other verse, we read it in context. Jesus immediately goes on to criticize hypocritical judging—the person who wants to take the speck out of a fellow believer's eye without taking the log out of their own. But as we address our own sins, we are still called on to deal with others' issues (vv. 2–5; cf. Gal. 6:1). Deciding when it is inappropriate to continue to subject the gospel simply to rejection and violence, which is the point of the next verse in Matthew 7, also requires thoughtful judgment (v. 6).[55] When we recognize that the Greek verb for "judge" here (krinō) can mean not only to analyze or declare something wrong but also to condemn or punish harshly, we realize that it must be the latter meanings that Matthew 7:1 intends.[56] Responsible Christians will always seek to explain to other believers with whom they have built healthy relationships that certain actions transgress the boundaries of God's will, especially if they have good reason to think that the other persons aren't even aware of that fact.

Many times, however, it is reasonably clear that others know God's word and will, but they are simply choosing to rebel against it, thumbing their nose in his face, as it were. In these situations, it often seems counterproductive to keep harping on their sins. While someone is living in rebellion, whether against a parent, a spouse, or even God, constantly stressing that fact tends to push them further and further away. Moreover, as Paul clarifies in 1 Corinthians 5:9, 12–13, it is not our responsibility at all to confront those who are not believers in the first place.[57] We can refrain precisely because we trust that God will avenge all the wrongs of the world, including those we have perpetrated ourselves, in a wholly righteous way that we could never fully replicate. Of course, we still must do all we can to bring about justice for others, especially for those who have the least ability to bring it about for themselves.[58] But we must be very careful in our pursuits of justice, especially if the only beneficiary is ourselves, lest in winning a skirmish we lose the war—which is ultimately the struggle for the salvation of as many people as possible for all eternity. This greatest of all goods should make us think long and hard before ever doing anything that could forever prevent or even seriously hinder a person from coming to Christ—whether by repeatedly berating others, sentencing someone to death, or bombing them into oblivion through the "collateral damage" that seems to be a constant feature of modern warfare.

Conclusion

We have covered a lot of ground all too briefly in addressing distinctive New Testament perspectives on violence in the Bible. But it is a huge issue, and sometimes broad-brush overviews are more helpful than detailed studies of just one or two parts of the topic. What is particularly striking is that the New Testament simply contains nothing at all like the divinely sanctioned use of violence by God's people that appears scattered throughout the Old Testament. The New Testament has no descriptions of it and no prescriptions to undertake it. Christ has absorbed that violence and defeated death on the cross. The New Testament, therefore, consciously contrasts its ethics with previous biblical models and principles of retaliation. The human race may well have not been able to handle more at an earlier stage in its history; it scarcely seems prepared to countenance New Testament ethics even today, even at times in the church!

What we *do* see in the New Testament is the promise that the world will exercise hostility and violence against believers and think that it is justified in doing so. When possible, we should flee from harm's way. When nonviolent protest holds out hope for redressing injustice, we may choose this option. We look in vain, though, for Christians violently defending themselves anywhere in the New Testament. If Christ's suffering provided the ultimate redemption for the sins of the world, believers are called to imitate that suffering for a host of less ultimate but still spiritually crucial reasons. Where we do see the language of warfare, it is transmuted entirely to the spiritual plane, with our struggle against the dark forces of the demonic realms. We successfully stand our ground through righteousness, faith, truth, and peace; we advance by the Spirit-filled sword that is God's word; and we accomplish it all by relying on the Triune God in prayer. Above all, the main reason we need not resort to violence ourselves is that God will have the last word and make all things right. He will vanquish his enemies entirely. But if even final judgment offends us, we need to recall that without *judgment* there can never be the *justice* that we so strongly crave. The same biblical word groups lie behind both concepts. At any rate, nothing in the biblical teaching on the subject, rightly understood, counts against belief in God. Such belief is part and parcel of our only hope for ultimate justice.

7

The Problems of Prayer
and Predestination

A friend of mine who has been an atheist since he was a teenager talks about the realization that came to him one evening as he was saying the bedtime prayers that he had been taught to recite as a child: he was just speaking to the ceiling. No one was really there to hear him, much less to answer those prayers.[1] Of course, what he speaks of as a realization is no more objective than the believer's "realization" that there is a God who does respond. Both are interpretations of the subjective thoughts and feelings that people experience, combined with the extent to which those individuals value other forms of alleged revelation that testify to God's existence. But even if what my friend should say, in order to be more precise, is that he came to believe that no one was there, he speaks for many people who have had similar experiences. Even Christians, after praying fervently over a long period of time for something they have every reason to believe is a good thing for someone else, can become disillusioned. Francis Schaeffer wrote a best-selling book a generation ago, *He Is There and He Is Not Silent*,[2] but others dispute both of those assertions.

If some people think that the Christian God doesn't directly cause enough to happen for us to believe he exists, others think that he is alleged to cause too much to be credible. I am not returning to the problem of evil here; we explored that in chapter 1. Rather, I am thinking of people's rejection of the form of Christianity that attributes so much direct causation to God that it would appear that human freedom is denied. Nowhere does this issue become more acute than in the understanding of a person's eternal destiny. Many people think that the concept of predestination found in the Bible leaves human beings with no meaningful choice as to whether or not they become believers. God elects some to be saved, and he chooses others to be lost, and that's that. We can be eternally grateful if we find ourselves within the first group, but we have no recourse if we turn out to be in the second. Most trained theologians would cringe at this way of putting things, but I have met a remarkable number of present or past churchgoers who describe their understanding of the Christian message in precisely this kind of language.[3] A few have stayed in the church and retained those beliefs, which they try valiantly to defend. Many have remained Christians but tempered their views on this topic over time. Sadly, still others have given up the faith because, from their perspective, even more restrained explanations of predestination or election violate the human free will that they "know" they have. Or, if it turns out they really don't have that kind of freedom, then they decide that it's pointless to worry about the question, because God will save them or damn them regardless of their preferences.

What both of these issues have in common is the topic of agency. Who or what causes things to happen when human beings are involved? Is there a divine agent who at some level causes everything that happens in the world? Are there different levels of causation or multiple agents behind some or all events? Is permitting something to happen significantly different from causing it, or does it really amount to the same thing if the agent permitting it had the ability to change the course of events? If God responds to people's prayers, does that mean his plans change? Or that *he* changes? What is the point of prayer in the first place if God has promised to do what is his will and only what is his will? These and related questions, like all of those in this book, have been well dealt with from *philosophical*, *historical*, and *theological* perspectives.[4] Old Testament passages and episodes about God relenting from a promised course of action and changing his mind, but also being the direct agent behind what looks for all the world like something evil, have all received extensive discussion.[5] But there are a series of *New Testament* passages that seem not to get the attention they deserve or to be interpreted completely fairly when they do get that attention. In some small way, I would like to begin to rectify that in this chapter.

What Is the Point of Prayer?

A number of key passages in the New Testament are regularly paraded by the so-called prosperity gospel as if they were blank checks enabling us to get anything we want from God. Of course, even prosperity preachers know about all the times when prayer appears not to work, so they usually fall back on explanations that allege a person simply hasn't had enough faith or obedience when God doesn't give them what they ask for. If a person believes that kind of explanation, it can produce enormous amounts of false guilt in them. If they don't believe it, it can lead them to embrace deism at best (there is a God, but he doesn't interact directly with people) or atheism at worst (there is no God, and the few times prayers appear to be answered can be adequately explained in other ways).[6]

A big part of the problem of rightly understanding prayer is the pervasive practice of citing and even memorizing Bible verses with no knowledge of the contexts in which they appear. It is telling to observe how consistently the passages that seem to offer carte blanche guarantees of answered prayer have important qualifiers in their larger contexts. Matthew 7:7 (par. Luke 11:9) offers a classic example. Here Jesus declares, "Ask and it will be given to you; seek and you will find; knock and the door will be opened to you." In case his audience wasn't listening carefully enough, he repeats himself in the next verse: "For everyone who asks receives; the one who seeks finds; and to the one who knocks, the door will be opened" (v. 8). After two short illustrations, he concludes this little unit of thought with a rhetorical question: "If you, then, though you are evil, know how to give good gifts to your children, how much more will your Father in heaven give good gifts to those who ask him!" (v. 11). What could be clearer? No caveats or provisos appear anywhere nearby. Still, at least as Matthew has arranged Jesus's Sermon on the Mount, only one chapter earlier Jesus was teaching people what has come to be called "the Lord's Prayer," in which one of the central petitions is, "May *your will* be done on earth, as it is in heaven" (6:10 NLT, italics added). It would be extraordinary if Jesus had not intended that key qualifier to carry over to other prayers for good things in his teaching one chapter afterwards.[7]

Later in the same Gospel, Jesus teaches his followers about the power of faith. He has cursed a fig tree as an object lesson about the coming judgment on Israel and its leaders if they do not repent (Matt. 21:18–19).[8] The disciples marvel at how quickly the tree has withered (v. 20), and Jesus declares, "Truly I tell you, if you have faith and do not doubt, not only can you do what was done to the fig tree, but also you can say to this mountain, 'Go, throw yourself into the sea,' and it will be done" (v. 21). But this is not a proverbial statement about faith moving mountains as, for example, in 1 Corinthians 13:2. Jesus is referring to one particular mountain when he uses the demonstrative adjective ("this"). Depending on where the conversation occurs in their walk from Bethany to Jerusalem (Matt. 21:17), he is pointing to either the Mount of Olives from its eastern slope or the Temple Mount, Mount Zion, from the top or the western slope of the Mount of Olives.[9]

Both mountains have great eschatological significance. About the Mount of Olives, Zechariah 14:4–5 prophesied that the Lord (presumably through his Messiah) would stand on it and it would "be split in two from east to west, forming a great valley," in which the Israelites would flee as from an earthquake. "Then the LORD my God will come, and all the holy ones with him." In other words, God is metaphorically turning the world upside down as this current age is coming to an end. And, of course, it wouldn't be long before Jesus would sit on the slopes of the mount overlooking the temple and prophesy its coming destruction in a context in which the disciples could only assume the end of the world was arriving (Matt. 24:3).[10] It is in this context— desiring the coming of the age when all God's promises will be fulfilled—that Jesus proceeds to declare, "If you believe, you will receive whatever you ask for in prayer" (21:22). Matthew will not have forgotten the Lord's Prayer even this many chapters later, nor will the first listeners, who probably heard the entire Gospel read aloud from start to finish. This cannot be a blank check any more than 7:7 was. Disciples must still pray "your will be done" (6:10).[11]

Readers of the parallel passage in Mark 11:20–25, however, cannot fall back on a previous account that instructs the disciples to pray in this fashion. Moreover, in Mark's Gospel Jesus promises, "Whatever you ask for in prayer, believe that you have received it, and it will be yours" (v. 24). Taken out of context, this has led to the bizarre practice in certain brands of the prosperity gospel not only of people being guaranteed physical healing contingent on sufficient faith but also of requiring them to believe that their bodies are already healed after they or others pray for them, even if they feel absolutely nothing different.[12] Taken in context, it is much more likely that Jesus is talking about how his followers should confront the centers of power in their world that are opposed to God's kingdom. As Ronald Kernaghan puts it, the word "whatever" in this verse "should be taken in the sense of no matter how formidable, rather than in the sense of anything and everything."[13] The past tense ("you have received") reflects a Semitic construction, found in Greek as well, even if not as commonly, in which the future is so certain that it can be spoken of as past. We are not meant to deny reality and claim something has literally occurred that has not.[14]

John 14:14 offers another wonderful, seemingly unlimited promise until we explore it more carefully. Here Jesus tells his disciples in the upper room, "You may ask me for anything in my name, and I will do it." In fact, he has just made the same promise in only slightly different words in the immediately preceding verse: "I will do whatever you ask in my name" (v. 13). Is it time to take our wish lists off Amazon and just start demanding everything in prayer? No, that would certainly be premature. Here, the key question is what "in my name" means. In ancient culture, one's name carried great significance and was often viewed as a key to one's identity or character. More importantly, a person's name represented their power or authority.[15] Asking for something in Jesus's name invoked his inexhaustible divine resources, making the fulfillment of any request theoretically possible. But it also meant that the request had to be in keeping with Jesus's character, identity, and will.[16] Verse 15 immediately reminds us of this with Jesus's conditional statement, "If you love me, keep my commands." Those who do so will have their priorities straight and their prayers properly motivated.

The very next chapter in John confirms this interpretation. Here Jesus is teaching about the need to remain in him, just as branches must remain in a vine to receive nourishment (15:4–6). Verse 7, then, which reads, "If you remain in me and my words remain in you, ask whatever you wish, and it will be done for you," must be taken in this same context. Jesus wants every follower to stay connected to him so that they receive the spiritual nourishment that enables them to bear fruit.[17] Verse 8 follows immediately with the assertion, "This is to my Father's glory, that you bear much fruit, showing yourselves to be my disciples." Thus, there are two contextual qualifications to the apparent blanket promise of verse 7. First, one has to be connected to Christ, which means living according to his will and therefore praying according to it. Second, "whatever you wish" means "whatever will lead a person to bear much fruit for Jesus."[18] Debates about what specific produce Jesus has in mind are fruitless, because nothing in the context suggests he is referring to anything delimited. Whatever lines up with God's purposes for the world, and with believers' exercise of the spiritual gifts they have been given, can qualify. But there is nothing here promising us material or physical blessings of any kind, even though God graciously gives many of us abundant resources in exactly these areas.

Before we leave the Gospels, it is important to recall the most important example of unanswered prayer in the way the person praying it desired: Jesus in the garden of Gethsemane. If the divine Son of God in his human nature could request of his heavenly Father that he not have to suffer the astonishing agony of the crucifixion, but not receive what he asked for (Mark 14:36 pars.), we must never claim that God owes us, or has promised us, more than what he gave Jesus.[19] Nevertheless, if under such horrific circumstances Christ could still pray that his Father's will be done even if it were different from his own most natural of all human desires, how dare we ever maintain that there are certain kinds of requests that we must simply name and claim without any caveats like "if it be your will, Lord"![20] To be sure, Hebrews 5:7 teaches that Jesus "offered up prayers and petitions with fervent cries and tears to the one who could save him from death, and he was heard because of his reverent submission." Yet it is equally clear that the author of Hebrews, like every other early Christian, knew that Jesus died. The very next verse, in fact, alludes to that death (v. 8), as it speaks of the obedience Christ learned from his suffering. So it can be only the resurrection to which the author is referring. Jesus was saved from *permanent* death; he was rescued on the third day out of the realm of the dead.[21]

Looking at prayer in Acts, we see the believers implementing Jesus's encouragement to request things in his name. Sometimes that includes miraculous healing (e.g., Acts 3:6), often it involves preaching and declaring the gospel and baptizing those who believe (e.g., 2:38), and sometimes it involves suffering (e.g., 5:41). Yet nowhere do we find anything to suggest that the disciples used Jesus's name indiscriminately or in any self-serving kind of way. When onlookers are tempted to give them credit or glorify them in some fashion, they always deflect attention from themselves and point people to God (e.g., 14:11–15), now manifesting himself through Jesus (e.g., 4:7–12). When the Sanhedrin attempts to silence them so that they no longer speak in Jesus's name (4:17–18), they refuse and then pray with thanksgiving for the privilege of suffering for the name and for strength to continue to speak boldly (4:24–31).[22]

The letters of Paul show him praying in all circumstances and encouraging others to do the same (1 Thess. 5:17–18). Philippians 4:6 is particularly well known: "Do not be anxious about anything, but in every situation, by prayer and petition, with thanksgiving, present your requests to God." But here Paul does not even sound like he could be saying God will give his people everything they ask for. Instead, he promises that "the peace of God, which transcends all understanding, will guard your hearts and your minds in Christ Jesus" (v. 7). Given the propensity for human anxiety, this is a greater gift than most we could request.[23] Of course, Philippians 4:13 is on virtually every website of most-abused Bible verses. A fairly formally equivalent translation may read, "I can do all things through him who strengthens me" (ESV, NASB, NRSV). Yet the context makes clear that Paul is not claiming he can leap tall buildings in a single bound. Rather, he has learned how to be content in all circumstances, whether in plenty or in poverty (v. 12). An optimally equivalent translation proves less misleading: "I can do all *this* through him who gives me strength" (NIV, italics added) or "I can endure all *these things* through the power of the one who gives me strength" (CEB, italics added).[24]

First Timothy 6:17b is a wonderful verse, but not in the sense some use it. It speaks of God richly providing us "with everything for our enjoyment."

But it is sandwiched between two explicit commands not to put our hope in wealth but to be generous in doing good and sharing with those in need (vv. 17a, 18). Once we have established patterns of generous giving, however, Paul makes it clear that we do not have to become ascetics; God does want us to enjoy the material possessions that remain. It is precisely because he wants everyone to have a chance to enjoy such possessions that he calls on those with surplus to share from that bounty rather than to hoard it all (cf. esp. 2 Cor. 8:13–15).[25]

Paul did not have a Gethsemane experience per se, but what he describes in 2 Corinthians 12:7b–10 remains powerful enough. Balancing out indescribable revelations and possibly out-of-the-body glimpses of heaven, he explains that he was given a "thorn" in his "flesh" (v. 7). He adds that he pleaded with the Lord three times that it be taken from him (v. 8), but Jesus's reply was "My grace is sufficient for you, for my power is made perfect in weakness" (v. 9). All kinds of improbable suggestions have been made about this thorn in order to avoid the implications that God often may not want to heal someone. Some have argued that this was some recurring sin or temptation to sin, but the whole of Scripture is univocal in desiring that people not sin or yield to temptation. God could hardly say that his power is perfected in our *sinful* weaknesses! Others focus on Paul's expression that the thorn was "a messenger of Satan" (v. 7) to argue that Paul repeatedly experienced some kind of demonic oppression or that the thorn was a person who was a particularly annoying and persistent opponent. The first of these approaches would fall victim to the same kind of criticism as the previous view, while the second reads too much into the words for both "messenger" and "Satan." All that such an expression necessarily means is that the devil had something to do with sending this "thorn," whatever it was. Given that the only other common meaning for "flesh" besides "sinful nature" was "body," and that the word for "thorn" meant "stake" (which inflicts a bodily wound), Paul's malady was almost certainly a recurring physical problem of some kind.[26] Suggestions have been adequately rehearsed elsewhere; the sole important point here is that the Lord's response is that his power is perfected in people who aren't enjoying unbroken good health and physical vigor. So even prayers that are as well intended as "Please make me well enough to be able to use my spiritual gifts to the fullest for your kingdom and glory" may have a skewed view of what God thinks are the most important purposes for a given person to fulfill.[27]

When we turn to the rest of the New Testament, perhaps no prayer-related promise stands out more strikingly than James 5:14–15: "Is anyone among you sick? Let them call the elders of the church to pray over them and anoint them with oil in the name of the Lord. And the prayer offered in faith will make the sick person well; the Lord will raise them up. If they have sinned, they will be forgiven." In the 1990s and 2000s, for nearly eight years, I served almost two complete terms as an elder in a church that believed in obeying James's injunction, and we anointed and prayed for probably about seventy or eighty seriously ill people during that period of time.[28] In two instances, we saw individuals whose confirmed cancerous tumors vanished from follow-up MRIs the week after our prayers. In several other instances, people with less readily demonstrable problems reported feeling better immediately afterward. In a couple dozen instances, people claimed to have improved over time at a faster rate than they were expected to. In the rest of the cases, nothing even slightly supernatural was perceived to have occurred, though most of the people did eventually improve. In a few terminal cases, nevertheless, the individuals died.

However one explains what happened, it certainly seemed that our prayers and obedience to James's specific instructions were worth the time and effort. Certainly, no one was harmed by them, and we always prayed, "If it is your will, Lord." This is James's explanation also, it would seem, for the times when someone did not improve: it was simply not God's will. In 4:13–17, James has already rebuked those who plan without leaving room for the Lord's will to override theirs (see esp. v. 15). And if God's power is perfected in weakness (2 Cor. 12:9), then we should not have expected miraculous healing in all or even a majority of the instances. Still, weakness does not have to be physical, and there are enough examples of people whom God has supernaturally healed to make it worth the effort to pray and ask for healing.[29] Indeed, James 4 also gives us perhaps the best biblical incentive anywhere for petitionary prayer more generally, when James tells his congregations, "You do not have because you do not ask God" (v. 2). Sometimes, moreover, when we ask, we do not ask properly. But notice that what James deems proper is not a certain amount of faith but rather the proper motives: "When you ask, you do not receive, because you ask with wrong motives, that you may spend what you get on your pleasures" (v. 3).[30] Douglas Moo is almost certainly right, then, when he explains that "the prayer of faith" (5:15 ESV, NRSV) is by definition not a prayer of presumption that claims to know God's will but is the prayer that leaves room for God's will to be different from ours.[31]

Still, there are plenty of other situations in life when God delights in giving us good gifts in response to our prayers, including at times our perseverance in prayer and our involving others in praying with us.[32] That alone is a more than adequate motive for making prayer a priority. Does this mean, then, that prayer changes God's mind? That all depends on how we understand a change of mind. It is certainly possible that what looks like a change is simply God being faithful to his already determined plans to bless his people with certain things if and only if they pray for them. But this, in turn, raises the other concern this chapter needs to address: God's sovereign freedom to initiate the chain of events among his creatures to bring some people to himself. Unanswered prayer may create a crisis of faith or an unwillingness to come to faith in some people, even if we can give good answers to their questions. Yet others don't have this problem with prayer, and they would have no problem speaking about prayer changing God's mind. *Their* difficulties come with topics like God's electing or predestining people to an eternal destiny. No matter how others try to reassure them, they simply can't see how this doesn't fundamentally compromise human freedom, because everything seems predetermined from the outset.

Can We Make Sense of Predestination?

Even more so than with the topic of prayer, limited space requires me to engage only the most important New Testament texts on predestination. But one of the first things that must be said is that the New Testament, as already the Old Testament, holds God's sovereignty and human responsibility together in ways most of us find difficult to imitate or preserve.[33] We are forever falling off one side of the balance beam or the other. Philippians 2:12–13 affords as good an example as any New Testament text. Here Paul exhorts his fellow Christians to "continue to work out [their] salvation with fear and trembling" (v. 12b). Yet he immediately adds as his rationale for the command, "for it is God who works in you to will and to act in order to fulfill his good purpose" (v. 13). Our finite and fallen minds cry out, "Well, Paul, which is it? Do we work out our salvation or does God work it out in us?" And he calmly answers, "Yes." It is both![34] In this text, one may argue that God's activity is prior—only *because* it is his will does our obedience to his commands make any difference.[35] In other texts, especially with respect to granting our requests in prayer, one might insist that human activity is prior.

Genesis 50:20 forms the oldest scriptural backdrop for all texts like these, when Joseph has been reunited with his brothers in Egypt but now their father, Jacob, is dead. They fear that Joseph may want revenge on them for originally having sold him into slavery. Joseph reassures them, however, that everything is fine, and he explains, "You intended to harm me, but God intended it for good to accomplish what is now being done, the saving of many lives." What is most striking about this text is that it does not say God decided that all this should happen at some previous time, so that humans were just his pawns to bring things about. But neither does it say that the brothers' purposes were either logically or chronologically prior to God's. Divine and human purposes ran on parallel tracks, neither stated as initiating or producing the other and neither canceling out the other.[36]

If we reflect on this phenomenon as it applies to the debate over the role of predestination with respect to salvation and damnation, we have three logical possibilities: either God predestines no one individually, either to salvation or to damnation; or he predestines only those who are saved but not the lost; or he predestines both saved and lost. While it is easy to sympathize with those on either end of the spectrum who say that the middle option seems illogical, it does appear as if the New Testament teaches what theologians have called "single predestination."[37] Simply put, this concept means that anyone who is saved has to thank God for taking the initiative in moving toward them; those who are lost have only themselves to blame.

Of course, it is possible to argue for only "corporate election"—that God chooses groups of people, not individuals.[38] In the Old Testament, he elected Israel and those who attached themselves to the Israelite religion; in the New Testament, he elects the multiethnic church of Jew and Gentile alike. The analogy is sometimes made to a new sports franchise. For example, the Colorado Rockies professional baseball team came into existence in the early 1990s when Major League Baseball owners voted that Denver could have an expansion team, and a name was selected for it. But then began a process of recruiting managers, players, and all the other personnel needed to run a team. The team as a corporate entity or group was elected, but people voluntarily associated themselves with it.[39] If that is all the Bible means by election or predestination, then the solution is straightforward. God elected the church, as those who would serve his elect Son, Jesus Christ, but he did not elect individual believers in the same way. A passage that can be read in this way is Ephesians 1:4, in which God chose us *in Christ* to be his adopted children.[40]

The most extensive chapter on this topic in the New Testament, Romans 9, starts out in a fashion very much in keeping with this approach. God elects Abraham to be the progenitor of Israel, but the elect line goes through his son Isaac rather than his other son, Ishmael (v. 7). Then it goes through Isaac's son Jacob rather than Esau (vv. 11–13). This approach can work throughout Paul's discussion all the way through verse 18. But then he switches to speaking about individuals, using the second-person singular verb form: "You will say to me then, 'Why does he still find fault? For who has ever resisted his will?'" (v. 19 NET). Of course, this could be due to the standard diatribe form that Paul turns to here, and this could also explain verse 20a: "But who are you, O man, to answer back to God?" (ESV).[41] But Paul continues to use singular rather than plural examples when he speaks of the pot not speaking back to the potter as an illustration of how an individual person should not complain to God about how he or she has been made (v. 20b). And the Greek continues with singular forms as verse 21 goes on to insist that God, as creator, has the right to make individuals however he likes.[42]

Returning to the example of the baseball team, one can in theory speak about an elect group—a new franchise—before anyone has joined it. Nevertheless, unless at some point people do agree to coach and to play for the team, it won't really exist. It's all well and good to say the church is the elect people of God who accept Jesus, but unless God can guarantee there is at least one church member (and for all he says about the church he probably has to guarantee at least one small congregation), there never is any real ecclesiastical entity. On the other hand, arguing that God chooses some for salvation does not require one to say the same thing about those he passes over. It is intriguing to watch Paul's discussion continue to unfold in Romans 9:22–23. A very formally equivalent translation of verse 22 reads, "What if God, although willing to demonstrate His wrath and to make His power known, endured with much patience vessels of wrath prepared for destruction?" (NASB). The word for "prepared" (*katērtismena*) is a perfect middle or passive participle. If it is a middle, it means something like "prepared themselves"; if it is passive, "having been prepared" (by some unspecified outside agency, presumably God). Second Timothy 2:20–21 returns to this topic as Paul reuses much of the same imagery he introduced in Romans 9—particularly "vessels for honor" and "for dishonor."

The next verse in our passage in Romans helps us decide between these two options: "And *He did so* to make known the riches of His glory upon vessels of mercy, which He prepared beforehand for glory" (v. 23 NASB, italics original). Here Paul uses a verb for "prepared" that is in the active voice (*proētoimasen*). It also is a compound verb, with the prepositional prefix meaning "before" or "pre-" combined with the aorist (or simple past) tense of *hetoimazō*. If Paul envisioned God working symmetrically with respect to both lost and saved people, one would have expected him to use the active form of *proetoimazō* in both instances. Rather, only the second statement refers explicitly to God (and he appears as the agent), and only the second statement has God's actions occur in advance. This suggests that "prepared" in verse 22 means not that God prepared the lost but that they prepared themselves for their fate.[43]

While personal experience should never be the first or even second criterion for truth, Gordon Lewis and Bruce Demarest are correct in their systematic theology to list "existential viability" as a third-tier criterion.[44] If an attempt to formulate Christian doctrine from Scripture fits exegetical and systematic analysis best (equivalent to their first two criteria of correspondence and coherence) *and* it rings most true to life experience, then it is almost certainly correct. Believers can never say that they chose their birth parents or the places where they grew up during their earliest years. There are always people who come into their lives and circumstances that occur over which they had no control whatsoever. And these people, places, and circumstances have significant influence in shaping each of us to become the person that we become in adulthood. To that degree, no two people are ever exactly equal in their opportunities to become Christians. On the other hand, discounting the coerced conversions of some past eras, none of us today can legitimately say that we were forced against our will to follow Jesus (or to reject him). At least as adults, we freely chose to love and serve him. So God gets all the glory for those who are saved, but we cannot blame him when we choose to go our separate ways. This is single predestination.

The philosophical theory of middle knowledge goes beyond what exegesis can derive from Romans 9 by itself or from any other text or combination of texts in Scripture that address the tension between divine sovereignty and human responsibility. But it appears to be completely in sync with such exegesis. This is the view that takes a cue from the sequence of activities Paul outlines in Romans 8:29–30: "For those God foreknew he also predestined to be conformed to the image of his Son, that he might be the firstborn among many brothers and sisters. And those he predestined, he also called; those he called, he also justified; those he justified, he also glorified." Predestination here is not the first element in the chain of the *ordo salutis* (order of salvation) but the second. Predestination comes after and is based on "foreknowledge." While the simple verb "to know" often has the stronger meaning of "to choose," the compound verb "foreknow" does not demonstrate any consistent pattern of usage that would tilt the scales in this direction.[45] It is better to conclude that God's predestining activity of those who will subsequently be called, justified, and glorified is based on his knowing from eternity past who would and wouldn't choose him.[46] How, then, does this avoid giving humanity all the credit and "one-upping" God in the salvific process? Middle knowledge answers this question by claiming that God's omniscience is so great that it extends not merely to every actually created being and how they would act in every actual circumstance they would ever find themselves in. Rather, it insists that God is able to know every response to every possible circumstance that every person who could possibly be created would ever make. Yet since he has only actualized a finite number of human beings, his sovereign freedom to create whomever he wanted is still thoroughly intact. But because he knows how we will act in the finite number of circumstances we will find ourselves in but does not cause us to act in those ways, our human freedom and responsibility remain intact.[47]

Many other texts could be discussed, but hopefully these are sufficient to suggest that the New Testament teaching on election or predestination need not be an obstacle to keep people from Christian faith. There *are* unfortunate ways that this teaching has been represented (or, rather, misrepresented) that understandably do keep some people from the faith. In those formulations, determinism seems inescapable. In addition, when predestination to damnation is presented as entirely symmetrical with predestination to salvation, the apparent determinism seems all the more objectionable.[48]

At the opposite end of the theological spectrum there are those who so limit God's foreknowledge that they say it is impossible for him to know the future, freely chosen actions of human agents—a view that has come to be known as open theism.[49] But when I think of how well I know certain very predictable human beings and often know exactly how they will respond to a variety of situations, it is not hard to imagine an infinite and omniscient being who can always correctly predict what people will do in all possible situations, without in any way causing their behavior. It may at first seem more comforting to think of God as not even anticipating that people will plan evil things and yet allowing them the freedom to carry out their intentions. It may seem reassuring to claim merely that God is the perfect first responder once he sees what people actually do. But his omnipotence then has to be so compromised that one wonders if he can be worth worshiping or even liking.

Put another way, it is very important to translate Romans 8:28 correctly, with the NIV, and recognize that it claims that "in all things God works for the good of those who love him, who have been called according to his purpose" (cf. RSV, "in everything God works for good").[50] Paul does *not* say that "all things work together for good" (KJV, ESV, NRSV), which is more pantheistic than Christian. Nor does he say that "God works all things together for good" (CEB) or "causes all things to work together for good" (NASB), because he patently does not. But he is present *in all things*, accomplishing his good purposes. On the other hand, this also means that God is more than merely responding to everything; he has foreknown it all, and in whatever ways do not overly compromise human freedom and accountability, he is present in the midst of evil circumstances, bringing out some kind of good for those who love him. And middle knowledge avoids the Calvinist charge that election based on foreknowledge overly compromises God's sovereignty. God did not have to create any one of us in the first place. That he chose to create you and me but not an infinite number of other beings who could possibly have been created, human or otherwise, who also would have had free agency, preserves his initiative-taking role.[51]

Conclusion

Neither prayer nor predestination, then, need prove to be a stumbling block to Christian belief in God. Certain ways in which these two doctrines can be misunderstood may well become such obstacles, but they are neither the only ways to interpret them nor even what the biblical writers most likely intended. Prayer is not a blank check. God's will is so often so different from ours that unanswered prayers (in the ways we *wish* they would be answered) should cause no surprise. But there are enough times that his will and ours coincide and do not require overriding anyone else's freedom that prayer is still well worth undertaking. In his inscrutable wisdom, he has determined that there are many good things that he will give to people if and only if they pray, and sometimes if and only if they continue to pray over a period of time or involve others in praying as well. A responsible articulation of the biblical teaching on predestination will likewise preserve God's sovereignty, without making it arbitrary or overriding free agency. It is based on his foreknowledge, but that foreknowledge is not limited, as in open theism. It is in fact magnificently expansive, encompassing all possible actions of all possibly created beings (middle knowledge). As long as God has created only a subset of that set of all possibly created beings, his initiative-taking action still outstrips our genuine human freedom in the same way that all infinite sets vastly exceed in size even the biggest finite sets in comparison, however large they may be in their own right.

8

What about All the Apparent Contradictions in the Gospels?

Some people put forward, as a reason for not believing in God, all the contradictions they perceive in the Gospels.[1] Of course, for this to make any sense there have to be a number of implied but unstated premises. To begin with, either these individuals have already written off the God or gods of all other religions besides Christianity or they are speaking just of the God and Father of Jesus Christ. Second, they must recognize the central role of the Gospels in all of biblical teaching. Of course, some people protest that the whole Bible is filled with contradictions, but it is interesting that many are much more interested in the accounts of Jesus than any other portion of Scripture. They recognize that Jesus is at the heart of Christian faith. Third, it would appear that these critics have imbibed an all-or-nothing approach to history. Either the Gospels' accounts of Jesus are without any error or contradiction or nothing about them can be believed. Tragically, some conservative Christians have championed this position as well,[2] even though no responsible historian would approach any other historical or biographical work in this fashion. Even the very liberal and antisupernatural findings of the infamous Jesus Seminar in the 1990s accepted about 20 percent of the Gospels as supplying relatively accurate information about Jesus and another 30 percent or so as bearing at least some similarity to the Jesus of history. They may not have concluded that Jesus was God, but they certainly recognized that he, like almost all other Jews of his day, believed in God.[3]

Nevertheless, there is a potentially logical connection between finding the Gospels riddled with contradictions and rejecting the Christian message as implausible. Some people have produced websites with long lists of all the so-called contradictions they have found.[4] Usually, however, these are crafted without any sensitivity to, or possibly even awareness of, the contexts in which the cited verses occur. It is true, for example, that Jesus in one and the same Sermon on the Mount tells his followers to let their light shine before others (Matt. 5:16) but soon afterward instructs them not to practice their acts of righteousness in front of others (6:1). But if one reads the complete sentences in which these commands appear, the tension immediately resolves itself. Matthew 5:16 explains that shining one's light is so that others will see one's good deeds and glorify God, who is their heavenly Father, whereas 6:1 is prohibiting acts designed to draw attention to oneself.[5] Or perhaps the "contradiction" highlighted will be between or among parallel accounts of the same episode. Whom did the women who discovered the tomb on Easter Sunday morning see: "a young man dressed in a white robe" (Mark 16:5), "an angel of the Lord" (Matt. 28:2), or "two men in clothes that gleamed like lightning" (Luke 24:4)? A straightforward harmonization is easy: there were two angels dressed in gleaming white, but Matthew mentions only one, while Mark and Luke describe their appearance like men.[6] But isn't such a harmonization just some kind of desperate expedient by evangelical scholars who wouldn't acknowledge a true contradiction if one hit them squarely in the face?

Other supposed discrepancies calling the trustworthiness into question involve chronological differences among parallel accounts, dramatic abbreviations or expansions of episodes, highly distinctive theological emphases, apparent doublets (one writer duplicating a real event to create a similar fictitious one), and specific pieces of information within what are otherwise clear parallels that just don't seem to match. I have written elsewhere about a large number of the most well-known examples of these supposed discrepancies, both within the Synoptics and between the Synoptics and John, and my intention is not simply to repeat myself here.[7] I have also reconfigured that discussion in a different work and added issues that come into play when one compares Acts and Paul's Letters, along with further questions from all parts of the New Testament.[8] Still, even after one surveys these supposed contradictions, a sizable majority of the canonical Gospels remains unaffected. Other critics reject the Gospels overall because of the pervasiveness of miracles or supposed parallels to Greco-Roman legends and myths, and I have already addressed each of these claims in earlier chapters.

The only way to charge the majority of the Gospels with contradictions is to impugn them in almost every place where they do not simply repeat verbatim what another account contains. But there would be no point in multiple accounts of the life of Christ if all they did was repeat one another. The issue that too often remains unaddressed is what makes a difference from one Gospel to another an actual contradiction. When is it not appropriate to combine information from all accounts of an event and create a larger whole? When does one writer recount the same information so differently that he is not just putting a different slant on things but inventing them? Putting it another way, the problem with both the charges of contradictions and many attempted resolutions is that they rarely ask what would have been considered a contradiction or error in biblical times.[9] For example, we read today in one Gospel that something happened "immediately" and then discover a lapse of time in another Gospel and think that both can't be true. However, we fail to realize that in an age of great selectivity in historical and biographical writing, and when considering the entire span of a person's life, what was described as happening immediately after a certain event was often not thought of as necessarily occurring the same day or even within a few days.[10] Likewise, topical or thematic arrangement of passages was extremely common, so one must not envision chronological connections unless the text makes them explicit.[11] Even then, it may not be enough to read in an English Bible the words "then" or "now," because their Greek equivalents (*tote* and *nyn*) could often be logical rather than chronological connectives (just as in English we might say, "Now, the point of this is . . ." or "The upshot, then, is . . ."). Finally, in the world of the Gospels—a world without quotation marks or any felt need for them—we certainly must not expect to find a verbatim transcript of someone's words. Accurately reporting their gist was normally deemed adequate.[12] Indeed, in a world before footnotes or bibliographies, one of the ways to acknowledge sources was to quote them verbatim, while one of the ways to make work genuinely one's own was to introduce freedom and variation in quotations.[13]

What about the kind of harmonization that follows the logic of "if there were two, then there was one"? Of course, it is logically true and sometimes transparently obvious. A TV news announcer who knows that the network has several reporters plus a filming crew at a sporting event may still say, "Wendy is live with us from the stadium." The announcer means simply that Wendy will be the next voice one will hear on the air. We know that from years of experience with television and sporting events. If the announcer then turns to a different report and reads from the teleprompter, "In other news, the superintendent of schools, Jonathan Hollingsworth, was shocked last night to find that his home had been vandalized," we may be less confident about assuming that other people were with him when he made that discovery. Such break-ins usually happen when the residents are not home, we may not know if Jonathan even has a wife or children, and even if he does, we don't know if they were around. Still, if it turned out that both Jonathan and his wife walked into the house together to see the mess, we wouldn't normally think of accusing the reporter of lying because Linda Hollingsworth wasn't mentioned by name.

What were the conventions in the ancient Mediterranean world? Michael Licona has recently produced a hugely important volume addressing precisely these kinds of questions based on the numerous places in Plutarch's *Lives of the Noble Greeks and Romans* where the biographies of the people he wrote about overlap in the events they discuss. What did Plutarch himself consider acceptable variation in the telling of the same story from one *Life* to another? Licona highlights numerous features that mirror, to one degree or another, differences among parallel accounts in the New Testament.[14] The vast majority of minor differences from one account to the next were just par for the course; no one would have called them errors or mistakes. Even slightly bigger differences were commonplace. One of the clearest and most common examples is the spotlighting of a single spokesperson within a group of two or more people, so that one of Plutarch's *Lives* mentions only one character functioning in a certain way, while the parallel contains two or more.[15] Still, not every convention that Plutarch adopts is necessarily paralleled in the New Testament, nor would every one of his conventions have been considered good history writing by all of his contemporaries.

In a study I published early in my scholarly career, "The Legitimacy and Limits of Harmonization," I also used Plutarch as a model but compared him with his near-contemporary Arrian (both writing in the late first through early second centuries), on the life of Alexander the Great. I also consulted Josephus (late first century) when he narrated some of the same incidents or episodes in his *Jewish Antiquities* and *Jewish War*, and I compared a variety of the Old Testament accounts paralleled in Kings and Chronicles. In each case, I discovered reasonable parallels to about seven different categories of alleged contradictions in the Gospels that classical historians didn't necessarily consider to be problems. In each case, they were well within the range of what the ancients considered accurate history or biography.[16]

This book is narrower in its focus, however, as we are looking for distinctive *New Testament* answers to thorny questions. Yet there is not a hint anywhere in the New Testament of a theory of the composition of historical or biographical works. No statement declares how round a round number can be and still be considered reliable. No chapter and verse discusses at what point two stories are just too different for one to plausibly harmonize them. Why in the world, then, would I envision a chapter in *this* book on such a topic? The answer lies in the fact that on three occasions the book of Acts narrates a particular event three times. First, in Acts 9:1–19, Luke tells the account of the conversion of Saul of Tarsus, thanks to his encounter with the risen Lord on the Damascus road. Then, in 22:3–16, Luke narrates how this same man, now going by the name Paul, after his third missionary journey speaks to a crowd in Jerusalem, recounting this same conversion story. Finally, in 26:2–23, Luke depicts Paul testifying before Herod Agrippa II in Caesarea Maritima, recounting some of the same story a third time.

The second episode that Luke narrates three times in Acts is the conversion of Cornelius. The lengthiest version is the first, which occupies all forty-eight verses of chapter 10. But 11:1–18 immediately follows this account with Peter's fairly detailed retelling of what he experienced to the other church leaders back in Jerusalem. Finally, and much more briefly, 15:7–11 quotes Peter highlighting the gist of what happened when the apostolic council convened in Jerusalem to discuss the matter of those who were requiring circumcision for salvation.

The third and final event that Acts reports three times is the result of that council. The participants conclude that they should not make it difficult for Gentiles to turn to God, and so they impose only four restrictions on Gentile behavior in 15:19–21. They determine to write a letter to the churches of Syria and Cilicia articulating this decision, which Paul and Barnabas will deliver to the believers in Syrian Antioch, and then Luke narrates the key contents of that letter, repeating all four stipulations again, in verses 22–29. When Paul is back in Jerusalem years later, the apostles there again refer to the heart of that letter and its four restrictions, in 21:25.

A look at the similarities and differences among the three accounts of each of these three episodes proves highly instructive. *It is evidence from within the New Testament of what one author, one who also wrote one of the Gospels, understood to be acceptable diversity in retelling a story more than once.* One does not need to believe that Luke was divinely inspired to take his prologues (Luke 1:1–4 and Acts 1:1–3) seriously as representing his conviction that he has provided accurate information about the lives of Jesus and the early church.[17] Nevertheless, as one compares these multiple accounts in Acts with one another, one finds a fascinating combination of some verbatim parallelism with a lot of internal variety of details. The results of these comparisons, in turn, strikingly resemble the similarities and differences from one Gospel writer to another, suggesting that many of what some scholars call contradictions would not have been viewed as such in the first-century Roman Empire.[18]

Learning from Acts: The Conversion of Saul

Luke introduces the character of Saul of Tarsus for the first time in Acts 7:58b–8:3. Here Luke relates only that Saul was a "young man" at whose feet the witnesses at Stephen's hearing laid their coats (7:58). Presumably, he had some official, legal role, however minor, in Stephen's stoning.[19] In 8:1, Luke adds that Saul approved of this execution, while in 8:3, after the great persecution against Christians had broken out, he reports, "Saul began to destroy the church. Going from house to house, he dragged off both men and women and put them in prison." All of this serves as a literary foreshadowing of the dramatically contrasting role that Saul would play after his conversion.[20]

Saul became a follower of Jesus shortly afterward, and 9:1–19 narrates that conversion. Picking up where he left off, Luke begins chapter 9, explaining that Saul is "still breathing out murderous threats against the Lord's disciples." Saul goes to the high priest and asks him for "letters to the synagogues in Damascus" (vv. 1–2a), which would give him the right to take those he arrested to Jerusalem (v. 2b). As he nears Damascus, suddenly he sees a flashing heavenly light, which causes him to fall to the ground (vv. 3–4a). He then hears a voice ask him, "Saul, Saul, why do you persecute me?" (v. 4b). Obviously using "Lord" at first just as a term of respect for a superior authority, Saul asks the person who has appeared to him who he is (v. 5a). The voice replies, "I am Jesus, whom you are persecuting" (v. 5b). The voice then commands him to go into Damascus and await further instructions (v. 6). Luke notes that those traveling with Saul "heard the sound but did not see anyone" (v. 7). Paul himself is blinded by this experience for three days, during which time he fasts (vv. 8–9).

The scene changes as Luke takes us to the home of a Christian named Ananias in Damascus (v. 10). Jesus speaks to him in a vision as well, telling him to go to the home of Judas on Straight Street, ask for Saul, lay hands on him, and restore his sight (vv. 11–12). Ananias balks because he knows who Saul is and what he has come to do (vv. 13–14). But the Lord replies, "Go! This man is my chosen instrument to proclaim my name to the Gentiles and their kings and to the people of Israel. I will show him how much he must suffer for my name" (vv. 15–16). So Ananias does as he is told and goes to heal Saul, at which points Saul stops fasting, is filled with the Holy Spirit, and is baptized (vv. 17–19).

It is intriguing to compare and contrast this account with the two Luke records later in Acts in which Paul, now a Christian defending himself before fellow Jews, tells his story. In Acts 22, he is speaking to the crowd in Jerusalem that has just beaten him until the Roman soldiers arrest him to spare his life. But they quiet down and listen when Paul addresses them in their native tongue of Aramaic (vv. 1–2). After he briefly describes his upbringing (v. 3), his narrative begins to overlap with details from earlier in Acts. For the most part, Luke does not use the identical forms of the same Greek words in the same order, but he does use the same root words in various places. Verse 4 speaks of throwing both men and women into prison, as does Acts 8:3. Acts 22:5 refers to obtaining letters from the high priest in order to bring people to Jerusalem, as does 9:1–2. Acts 22:6 contains a few identical words ("suddenly," "from heaven") that could not have been inflected in any other way and confirms 9:3, where a bright light shines near him as he approaches Damascus. More extensive and significant verbatim parallelism begins, not surprisingly, with the central and climactic dialogue between Jesus and Saul. "Saul, Saul, why do you persecute me?"; "Who are you, Lord?"; and "I am Jesus, whom you are persecuting" are identical in both 22:7–8 and 9:4–5, except that Acts 22:8 adds "of Nazareth" after "Jesus."

As both narratives continue, no longer quoting any direct speech from Paul's experience on the Damascus road, the most famous apparent contradiction between the two accounts emerges. In Acts 9:7, Luke writes that Paul's companions heard the voice but saw no one (*akouontes men tēs phōnēs mēdena de theōrountes*). In 22:9, Paul says that "they saw the light, but they did not understand the voice [*tēn de phōnēn ouk ēkousan*] of him who was speaking to me." The NIV is the only major translation not to use "voice" in both verses, saying rather that they heard the "sound," but there is a grammatical reason for the change in translation. Classically, *akouō* with a genitive direct object meant "to hear without understanding," while *akouō* with an accusative direct object meant "to hear with understanding."[21] Thus the expression in 9:7 with the genitive could easily mean they heard the voice without understanding, and one way that could have occurred was that they heard a sound but didn't distinguish words. Then in 22:9, Luke would understand Paul's words in Aramaic, whatever they were, to have meant that the companions did not hear the voice/sound with understanding, which amounts to the same thing. The main objection to this harmonization is that this classical distinction was breaking down in first-century Greek and doesn't always apply elsewhere in the New Testament, including Luke. But that doesn't mean it couldn't apply in these specific contexts, and it is hard to understand why Luke would vary the case if he didn't intend some distinction.[22]

The remainder of Paul's address in Acts 22 adds a lot of information not found in Acts 9, though in no way in tension with it. Verbal similarities to Acts 9, without much significant verbatim repetition, occur only in 22:11 (Saul being led by the hand into Damascus due to being blinded), verses 12–13 (Ananias enabling Saul immediately to regain his sight, and he is called "brother Saul" in both texts), verse 16 (Saul getting up and being baptized), and verse 21 (him being sent to the Gentiles). Otherwise we learn about the Lord also instructing Saul to continue to Damascus to discover everything that he is being assigned to do (22:10), numerous details about Ananias and his actions (vv. 12–13), Ananias's explanation of God's choice of Saul and his mission (vv. 14–15), a call for purification and forgiveness (v. 16), and what happens to Saul when he returns to Jerusalem (vv. 17–20).[23]

Acts 26, Paul's appearance before Agrippa II, presents fewer verbal parallels with either Acts 9 or Acts 22 but still contains plenty of conceptual parallels. "Chief priests," "prison," and "synagogue" reappear as Paul rehearses his former persecution of Christians (26:10–11). A bright "light," "falling" down, a "voice," and the identical question, "Saul, Saul, why do you persecute me?" recur when Christ appears (vv. 12–14). Paul asks the same question, "Who are you, Lord?" and is again told, "I am Jesus, whom you are persecuting," and he is sent to the Gentiles (vv. 15–18). Otherwise, Luke does not have Paul exactly repeat what he said to the Jerusalem crowds, yet it is clear he is telling the same story of his conversion without any conflicting details. Supplementary information includes more detail about Saul's pre-Christian persecuting activity (vv. 9–11) and about his encounter with Jesus on the Damascus road (vv. 12–14), most notably that the voice spoke to Saul in Aramaic and added the observation, "It is hard for you to kick against the goads" (v. 14). Verses 16–18, finally, give additional detail about his commission to preach the gospel to the Gentiles.

What would account for the variations in these three narratives in Acts? It is actually the second that is the longest. Given how much was on the line with Paul addressing the angry mob in Jerusalem, it makes sense that Luke would want to stress Paul's innocence by including the most amount of detail here.[24] The first narrative, in Acts 9, is simply Luke's narrative account of Saul's conversion to set the stage for him becoming the main human character or protagonist in the book from chapter 13 onward. What seems like a contradiction at first about what Saul's companions did or did not see and hear becomes clearer too. When Luke tells the story the first time more dispassionately, he does not need to say anything about the light and can just refer to the companions hearing a noise of some kind. When Paul is on trial, he wants to make the best possible case for his character and the genuineness of his encounter with the Lord, and so he stresses that his companions did see the light and may have recognized that a voice was speaking to Paul even though they couldn't understand it.[25] Then the third time Luke includes Paul's story, in Acts 26, he can afford to have Paul tell it in a significantly abbreviated form because he has just had him tell it once, only four chapters earlier.[26]

A Sample Passage in Gospel Parallels: Jesus Walking on the Water

It is striking to compare all these similarities and differences among the three accounts in Acts that narrate Saul's conversion with the typical similarities and differences that one discovers in passages that are paralleled in more than one Gospel. An excellent example involves the three versions of Jesus walking on the water (Matt. 14:22–33; Mark 6:45–52; John 6:16–24). This is a good example particularly because Luke does not have a version, so we can compare what Luke does in Acts with what the *other* three Gospel writers do, and not have our comparisons complicated by the fact that Luke is in each set of texts. There are very few places, however, where John parallels both Matthew and Mark but not Luke, so this is a felicitous exception.

Many of the details in Matthew and Mark match one another. As in the Acts passages, the closest and most consistent verbatim parallelism comes with direct speech, particularly Jesus's words, which form the central focus of the text: "Take courage! It is I. Don't be afraid" (Matt. 14:27; Mark 6:50).[27] But some of the same Greek words appear in the language of Jesus making the disciples get in the boat and go on ahead of him (Matt. 14:22; Mark 6:45), going up the mountainside to pray alone (Matt. 14:23; Mark 6:46), and coming to the disciples in their boat shortly before dawn (Matt. 14:25; Mark 6:48), and of the wind dying down when he climbed into the boat (Matt. 14:32; Mark 6:51). There is little doubt that one of these two Gospel writers used the other as a source, and the standard conclusion is that Matthew used Mark. Returning to the Acts accounts, Luke certainly could have reread what he dictated in Acts 9 when he came to narrate Paul's addresses in chapters 22 and 26, but he may well have been familiar enough with what he wrote earlier that he didn't need to, and that could also account for the smaller amount of verbatim parallelism. Above all, Acts 22 "is adapted to the Jewish audience to which it is addressed."[28]

Resuming the story of Jesus walking on the water, we see that there are striking differences between Matthew and Mark as well. The biggest one is Matthew's inclusion of the episode of Peter trying to imitate Jesus by walking on the water himself, only to start quickly sinking (Matt. 14:28–31). This certainly fits Matthew's increased interest in Peter in the middle of his Gospel.[29] This little narrative is one of five places where Matthew adds to one of Mark's passages a reference to something Peter did or said. More seemingly contradictory are the two endings of the pericopes. In Matthew, the disciples worship Jesus and acclaim him as the Son of God (14:33). In Mark, however, they are amazed and fail to understand because their hearts are hardened

(6:51–52). Even just a moment of empathetic thought, however, helps one to realize that if such an event really happened, then those who experienced it would surely have mingled fear, awe, and confusion in their reactions. Who *could* have understood this theophany, but who would *not* have been inclined to show some form of devotion as to a deity? That Matthew is not claiming that the disciples understood more than Mark says they did is shown by the fact that two chapters later Matthew can record Peter's confession of Jesus as the Christ but note, uniquely, that Jesus attributed this insight to a new stage of divinely revealed understanding (Matt. 16:17). They clearly didn't "get it" very much back in chapter 14. Why, then, do the two evangelists end their accounts so differently? Just as with the two accounts of Paul's conversion, theological emphases contribute to an explanation. Mark is the Gospel that most stresses the fear and failure of the disciples, whereas Matthew consistently tempers Mark's negative view of discipleship and has a heightened Son-of-God Christology.[30]

John's account of the water-walking miracle is noticeably the shortest of the three, just as the account of Paul's conversion in Acts 26 is noticeably the shortest of those three versions. Apart from the central pronouncement by Jesus that it is he, and that the disciples should not be afraid, there is very little close verbal parallelism, not least due to the significant abbreviation. But John arguably has the strangest difference from Mark by claiming that the disciples were heading across the lake to Capernaum (John 6:17), whereas Mark has them set off for Bethsaida (Mark 6:45). When one looks at a map of the area around the Sea of Galilee, however, one realizes that the most likely remote location for the feeding of the five thousand, which took place earlier that day, would be northeast or even east-northeast of the lake. From there one can chart a course to Capernaum that almost goes through Bethsaida. On a stormy night, travelers would not deliberately put their boats out in the open sea but rather would hug the coastline. They might have been satisfied if they got as far as Bethsaida if the weather remained bad. Thus another potential problem can be resolved.[31] What is interesting is that the narratives of Saul's conversion in Acts also contain geographical differences. Only in Acts 9:11 do we read that the Lord commands Saul to "go to the house of Judas on Straight Street and ask for a man from Tarsus named Saul." In Acts 22:12, all that Paul says is that a man named Ananias came to him, but there is no indication where Paul was staying. Still, one can easily see how both accounts can be true at the same time. Acts 9 narrates with greater specificity and chronology what Acts 22 depicts more piecemeal, just like heading first for Bethsaida offers more detail than just saying they go into the region of Capernaum.[32]

Learning from Acts: Peter and Cornelius

The same pattern of Luke narrating an important event followed by the main character in that episode retelling his experience twice characterizes the three versions of God supernaturally orchestrating a meeting between Peter and Cornelius that leads to the latter's conversion. The main difference is that the second retelling is extremely brief. Most of our comparisons, therefore, will have to be made between Luke's narrative in Acts 10 and Peter's telling the other apostles in Jerusalem about his experience in 11:1–18. The respective lengths of these two accounts also means that much of the detail in the first will be omitted in the second. Acts 10:1–48 contains Luke's third-person narrative of Peter's experiences that led him to go to the home of a God-fearing Gentile centurion. Here the fullest narrative comes first. Not surprisingly, when Peter immediately turns around and recounts his experience to the apostles and other believers in Jerusalem in 11:1–18, the narrative is noticeably shorter, though still not just summarizing. Finally, in 15:7–9 Peter again refers back to these events, but extremely briefly.[33]

The details of Acts 10 that are repeated in some form later include Cornelius seeing an angel, who tells him to send to Joppa for a man named Simon, also called Peter. Meanwhile Peter, in a trance, is having a vision of something like a large sheet let down from heaven by its four corners, containing animals, reptiles, and birds. A voice three times tells Peter to get up, kill, and eat, and not to call anything impure that God has cleansed, before the sheet is pulled back up to heaven. At first, Peter protests by replying, "Surely not, Lord!" (v. 14) and that he has never eaten anything impure or unclean. Right after this, the messengers from Cornelius arrive where Peter is staying, so Peter does not hesitate to go with them to Caesarea, and they go into Cornelius's house ready to hear a message from Peter. So he proclaims the way of salvation, the Holy Spirit falls on the Gentiles present there, and Peter deduces that it is appropriate to baptize these new believers. Luke narrates these points at times with the exact words he used in his first, fuller account, while sometimes he just uses other words similar enough to what he used before to show that he is highlighting the identical events once again.[34]

Within the first account itself, it is interesting to see how Luke repeatedly refers to the angel who appeared to Cornelius (Acts 10:3, 4, 7; cf. 11:13) only to have Cornelius himself refer to how "suddenly a man in shining clothes stood before me" (10:30).[35] This reminds us of the classic "contradictions" at the beginnings of the Synoptic resurrection narratives, as we noted at the beginning of the chapter. Was there a young man in a white robe (Mark 16:5), an angel (Matt. 28:2), or two men in gleaming clothes (Luke 24:4)? It is clear from Acts that Luke believed that such men were angels, as obviously Matthew did also.[36] It is also fascinating how initially Luke refers simply to Peter taking "some of the believers from Joppa" (Acts 10:23) along with him to Caesarea. Later he specifies that they were "circumcised believers who had come with Peter" (v. 45). And when Peter himself recounts the event, he refers to "these six brothers" who "also went with me" (11:12). This style of adding extra details when retelling stories, even while abbreviating the stories overall, was commonplace in the historical and biographical literature of the day.[37] Thus, Luke's treatment of the "angel/man" in the Cornelius narrative makes his addition in his Gospel of a second man looking like an angel at the empty tomb less surprising and more credible.

In Acts 15:7–9, the third version of Peter's experience with Cornelius becomes extremely brief. Explaining his embracing of a law-free gospel, Peter reminds the Jerusalem Council, "You know that some time ago God made a choice among you that the Gentiles might hear from my lips the message of the gospel and believe. God, who knows the heart, showed that he accepted them by giving the Holy Spirit to them, just as he did to us. He did not discriminate between us and them, for he purified their hearts by faith." While for the most part this is a summary statement without verbal parallels to either of the earlier accounts, some echoes of the original wording remain. The language of God accepting Gentiles and not discriminating recalls 10:34–35 on God showing no favoritism and accepting people from every nation. Giving them the Holy Spirit, "just as he did to us," parallels 10:47 ("They have received the Holy Spirit just as we have") and 11:15 ("The Holy Spirit came on them as he had come on us at the beginning"). It fits, then, that Peter should later stress the similarities of the Jewish and Gentile believers' experiences in arguing against the requirement of circumcision for salvation (15:1). Finally, the role of faith harks back to Peter's own sermon when he referred to "everyone who believes" as receiving forgiveness of sins (10:43).[38]

Learning from Acts: The Apostolic Decree

Our third example from Acts is much shorter, so my comments will be briefer also. In the account of the apostolic council, James ends the proceedings with these words: "It is my judgment, therefore, that we should not make it difficult for the Gentiles who are turning to God. Instead we should write to them, telling them to abstain from food polluted by idols, from sexual immorality, from the meat of strangled animals and from blood. For the law of Moses has been preached in every city from the earliest times and is read in the synagogues on every Sabbath" (Acts 15:19–21). They proceed to write the letter, and it is longer than what Luke records James saying initially (vv. 24–29). But that is because it summarizes how the whole council developed and how they decided to send this letter by means of Barnabas, Saul, Judas, and Silas, as well as the contents of the four restrictions. What was previously James's "judgment" is now attributed "to the Holy Spirit and to us" (v. 28), and what could have seemed like a set of absolute prohibitions is presented simply as that which the readers "will do well to avoid" (v. 29).[39] On the other hand, not all of James's original words are repeated. Most notably, the letter does not contain James's rationale for the inclusion of the four restrictions, that Jewish scruples are well known throughout the empire (v. 21).

Those inclined to look for inconsistencies could charge the letter with flatly contradicting James's original intent. In 15:19, James declares, "We should not trouble those of the Gentiles who turn to God" (ESV). That is why the "decree" imposes only the four fairly minimal restrictions of prohibiting the eating of food sacrificed to idols, meat of strangled animals, and blood, along with sexual immorality (v. 20). James wants Gentiles who are considering becoming Christians to realize that they do not have to adopt all of the Jewish law, especially circumcision. In the actual letter, however, the addressees are "the brothers who are of the Gentiles" (v. 23 ESV). Now the recipients are already Christians. Of course, seeing the differences as contradictions would be ridiculous since James is among those who write the letter, and Luke narrates James's verdict and the letter in back-to-back passages. The Greek of verse 19, especially given the present-tense participle, can just as easily mean, "We should not make it difficult for Gentiles *who are turning* to God" (NIV, italics added).[40] The Jerusalem apostles could very easily have in mind both those considering Christianity and those who have recently become Christians. If such a commonsense harmonization works where we have every reason to think that the same author, quoting the same speaker, in closely juxtaposed passages means the same thing despite variation in wording, we should be open to identical kinds of harmonization when different Gospel writers quote the same people saying similar things, even with some interesting variation.

The third and final passage about the apostolic decree appears in Acts 21:25 when Paul returns to Jerusalem after being away for several years. The Christians there want to defuse false rumors about Paul and show the law-abiding Jewish believers there that Paul still keeps the law (v. 24).[41] Verse 25 refers to the Gentiles *who have believed* (ESV, NASB; cf. NRSV, "who have become believers"), employing the Greek perfect tense with the participle. This confirms that both those who have believed and those who are in the process of believing are in view, and that our harmonization was no desperate expedient. Other than that, all that verse 25 contains is the listing of the four prohibitions—exactly what we should expect, because this is the essence of the decision that was made. Interestingly, the order of the four elements changes from the first to the second passages that list them (15:20, 29), but the order remains the same from the second passage to this third one (21:25). Luke apparently recognized that referring to the contents of the written letter required more formality and consistency of wording than when James initially rendered his oral verdict.[42]

Conclusion

These examples from Acts do not contain similarities to everything that comes into play in comparing Gospel parallels. But they do introduce a striking number of the major issues: (1) considerable difference in length and detail included in parallel narratives; (2) verbatim parallelism at the theological or literary heart of the passage and/or when speakers in the accounts make decisive pronouncements; (3) looser conceptual parallelism among the next-most-important parts; and (4) a fair amount of freedom to add or expand, delete or abbreviate, from one account to the next in full knowledge of the possibilities of saying either more or less. In addition, (5) distinctive theologies account for some of the differences; (6) considerable freedom occurs with describing certain individuals or events without creating any contradictions; and (7) order and sequence of detail can easily vary as well.

All of these features are commonplace in ancient historical and biographical writing more generally. On their own, none would have impugned the care and credibility of the narratives' authors or led readers to think that the writers had made mistakes or had contradicted one another. One hardly need presuppose the inspiration of the text to give careful writers the benefit of the doubt in matters like these. Conversely, the presence of this variety in narration in no way undermines the case for the inspiration of the text. Because of this, then none of the so-called contradictions in the Gospels excludes their divine origin, which in turn presupposes the existence of God. Neither do any of these phenomena suggest that one should reject Christianity or the Christian understanding of God that accompanies it. But what about the errors introduced in copying these texts? Aren't they more damaging to the case for Christ? Our next chapter turns to that question.

Hasn't the Church Played Fast and Loose with Copying and Translating the New Testament?

When I was engaged in my doctoral studies in the early 1980s, New Testament scholars of all stripes could agree on one thing. Textual criticism (the art and science of determining the earliest attainable text from the multiplicity of copies) was a "safe" place to do research, because the ideological presuppositions that divided conservative and liberal interpreters played almost no role in the discipline.[1] Scholars uniformly recognized the incredible wealth of data available for reconstructing the New Testament text. The United Bible Societies (UBS) and Nestle-Aland editions of the Greek New Testament, the two most respected and widely used editions, had already standardized their texts, so that all that differed was the textual apparatus in their footnotes.[2] In fact, some textual critics were so confident that they had gotten back to the very original wording of every book that scholarly articles had to warn against treating the text of these Greek New Testaments as a new *textus receptus*, or "received text," akin to the way some fundamentalists so idolized the King James Version of the Bible.[3]

Unwarranted Doubt

All this has changed in a generation. In fact, most of the change has come within the last twenty-five years. In 1993, Bart Ehrman published the first edition of his technical volume called *The Orthodox Corruption of Scripture*.[4] In it, he analyzes in detail what textual critics have long known. Pious scribes, possibly thinking that the text of a New Testament manuscript they were copying was slightly defective, would turn a simple reference to "Jesus" or "Christ" into "Jesus Christ" or "Christ Jesus." Texts that already had both the name and the title might become "the Lord Jesus Christ," to honor him all the more. Gospel parallels that clearly had the same wording but differed in some minor way were often harmonized, to bring them even more closely in line with one another. More so than previous textual critics had done, Ehrman suggests that at times even readings that are very poorly attested in terms of age and numbers of manuscripts might nevertheless reflect the original reading, if the dominant variant is one that is easier to bring into line with Christian orthodoxy.[5]

An example that became widely discussed was Mark 1:41. A woodenly literal translation of the UBS and Nestle-Aland texts of this verse, describing what happens after a leper approaches Jesus and asks to be cleansed, reads, "And having had compassion, having extended his hand, he touched [him], and he says to him, 'I will; be cleansed.'" The disputed word is *splanchnistheis* ("having had compassion"). While the vast majority of all the ancient manuscripts read *splanchnistheis*, including those usually deemed most reliable, and cutting across the major text-types and families of manuscripts, a few have *orgistheis* ("having become indignant"). These include Codex Bezae (D), the best representative of the so-called Western text-type (manuscripts that circulated in Italy or the western half of the Roman Empire) and dating to the fifth century. Various Old Italic (Latin) manuscripts, some dating to as far back as the fourth or fifth centuries, have wording that must have been translated from *orgistheis*. The Diatessaron, the harmony of the Gospels by a late second-century Christian named Tatian, likewise has this reading, according to Ephrem's fourth-century commentary on it. But that is about it. Normally, no matter how easy it is to envision a scribe changing a difficult reading to a simpler one, if there is this little external evidence for the more difficult reading, textual critics do not support it.[6]

Ehrman does prefer it, however, and his logic makes good sense. What scribe would ever turn the perfectly sensible and common depiction of Jesus having compassion for a person in need of healing into a statement of him being upset, indignant, or even outraged? But it makes all the sense in the world that a scribe (or numerous scribes) seeing the word for "outraged" might imagine that the text they were copying had an error at this point, so that they changed it to "having had compassion." Forms of the same verb (*splanchnizō*) recur in Mark 6:34, 8:2, and 9:22, with one of those recurrences in the identical form (9:22). The verb appears five times in Matthew and three times in Luke, though not in their parallels to this specific account of Jesus's curing the leper. The verbal root *orgizō*, on the other hand, appears only in Matthew (three times), Luke-Acts (twice), Ephesians (once), and Revelation (twice). We can readily explain Jesus's anger as directed not toward the man with leprosy, nor to his request, but to the unknown spiritual forces that were afflicting him.[7] Gordon Fee, a brilliant Pentecostal scholar with a long and distinguished career in New Testament textual criticism, was responsible for convincing the Committee on Bible Translation for the 2011 edition of the New International Version of the Bible that there was just no way to envision scribes replacing "having compassion" with "being indignant." The reverse substitution, however, makes very good sense. Fee agreed that Jesus need not have been upset about the leper's presence or about his request but could easily have been incensed about the damage the disease caused to the man, both physically and socially.[8]

More recently, nevertheless, two studies have independently argued that we should return to *splanchnistheis* and view it as a word Mark knew he was going to use later, so that "showing compassion" should be our first and primary choice for the original Greek expression. Peter Williams argues that letters being misread, inverted, and omitted could have combined with the already existing similarity of the last six Greek letters to create an accidental change,[9] while Peter Lorenz points out that the Latin textual witnesses are most probably dependent on the Greek, thus shrinking the independent support for *orgistheis* all the more.[10] So it is clear that discussion will continue. The point here is not to decide definitively which is the original reading but rather to illustrate Ehrman's approach. When we assess the internal evidence, we realize that either word could have been transformed into the other. Each has its last six Greek letters in common (ΣΠΛΑΝΧΝΙΣΘΕΙΣ and ΟΡΓΙΣΘΕΙΣ). The point is that neither reading is inconsistent with Christian orthodoxy, even if many people are a little more surprised to read about Jesus's indignation than about his compassion. The so-called "orthodox corruption" of Scripture raised some eyebrows but hardly caused any big fuss.

It was not until 2005, therefore, when Ehrman published his very misleadingly entitled book, *Misquoting Jesus: The Story behind Who Changed the Bible and Why*, that he took the world by storm and popularized his views by making them accessible to a lay audience. Even here, most of what Ehrman wrote was accurate, reflecting what textual critics had long known. There are two twelve-verse textual variants in the New Testament, the longer ending of Mark (Mark 16:9–20) and the woman caught in adultery (John 7:53–8:11), which were almost certainly not part of what Mark and John originally wrote.

There are another dozen individual verses (or portions of a couple of verses) that were added in by later scribes, several of them to harmonize Gospel parallels. There are about the same number that were later left out, either accidentally or for theological reasons. There are hundreds of thousands of very tiny changes scattered about the roughly five thoussand or so Greek manuscripts and well over ten thousand manuscripts of early translations of the New Testament into other languages (if Ehrman's numbers are correct) before the invention of the printing press.

It was the spin that the book put on these observations that proved deceptive. Or perhaps better phrased, it was what the book never addressed that fueled doubts. Once one finished reading it, one was left wondering how many more twelve-verse passages might be discovered to have been added to the original text. Or one began to mull over how many shorter one- or two-verse segments of text might be discovered that should be added in (or shown to be spurious so that they would need to be removed). The nature of all the minor variations was scarcely spelled out.[11] In scholarly settings, Ehrman has acknowledged how comparatively insignificant the full range of textual variants is, but in popular contexts he sounds far more skeptical.[12] It is very difficult to know what he actually believes.

Elijah Hixson and Peter Gurry have edited an important, very recent book on the "myths and mistakes" that New Testament textual critics have often made, including evangelicals (and including me!).[13] Because manuscripts vary so dramatically in size, from portions of a few verses to entire New Testaments, it is better to use statistics based on word counts. In his own essay in the anthology, Gurry estimates only one *unique* variant every 434 words in the manuscripts.[14] It is also important to acknowledge that with each successive century we have a greater quantity of handwritten manuscripts, exactly what we should expect given the nature of the preservation of materials from antiquity. So the majority of our manuscripts appear later rather than earlier. But we still have at least seventy-two manuscripts that date from the second or third century.[15] There are no other works from antiquity for which we possess anywhere close to that number from the first two centuries after the composition of the original book. In numerous instances, the oldest known copy of a work is separated by four hundred years or more from when it was first penned.[16]

Perhaps the most remarkable phenomena in recent New Testament textual criticism are how skeptical a few of its practitioners have become,[17] how much press those few have received, how little the general public is aware of the confidence that remains among a sizable majority of textual critics, and, above all, how there has been no new evidence to emerge in the discovery of ancient biblical manuscripts that warrants the changes in attitudes that we have seen.[18] All it takes is an atheist, agnostic, or very liberal Christian (especially if they are formerly evangelical) with an ax to grind who presents enough genuine information to sound credible but spins it in deceptive ways, and those who wish not to believe in Jesus investigate matters no further. Worse still, the faith of some Christians seems to be shaken, because they still have not learned to sift fact from fantasy either on the web or on the printed page. Churches, either ill-equipped to teach on the topic or fearful of the ire of the ultraconservatives in their midst who are unwilling to face the facts and accept even that the text changed as much as it did in its transmission, fail to prepare their congregants to have either informed conversations with others or well-founded beliefs for themselves.[19]

As a result, many "what if" questions proliferate. What if we found a portion of a New Testament text demonstrably earlier than anything we have discovered thus far, perhaps even datable to the late first century? What if it contained differences at various points from every other known manuscript in existence? The answer is actually quite simple. It would almost certainly represent an anomalous distortion of the text, whether intentionally or unintentionally. Textual critics have already found all kinds of minor differences in later manuscripts that set one or a very small number of manuscripts off from all the others.[20] Unless someone could devise a compelling explanation for how all traces of such distinctive readings disappeared from all of the thousands of later manuscripts, then the only rational conclusion is that some eccentric scribe was responsible for the anomalous text and others recognized that it should not be copied.[21]

A second unwarranted objection is refuted by the very process of preserving later manuscripts. Ehrman, like many people, imagines a papyrus or parchment being worn out like a popular modern paperback, discarded in perhaps a decade or two from its original publication, so that even the very oldest manuscripts we have are copies of copies of copies of copies of copies of—well, we get the idea.[22] But that is sheer assumption based on modern analogies and our culture of waste. It is certainly possible that some people treated manuscripts too casually so that they wore out unusually quickly and had to be replaced or that in making copies for dissemination originals were not always kept, but most everything we actually know about the preservation of sacred Scriptures or even highly valued documents in the ancient world, and certainly in the Judaism that birthed Christianity, tells us that the more revered the text, the more careful its preservation.[23] It is true that fledgling Islam, after the death of Muhammad, destroyed all versions of the Qur'an but one, and Islam since has worked very hard to preserve it intact, though without the perfectly flawless success rate that some claim.[24] Christianity by nature was more concerned about circulating the texts, translating them, getting them into the hands of as many people as could read, having them read aloud to groups of others who could not read, and, in short, disseminating the gospel message in an understandable and compelling fashion. Islam, historically, has been more concerned that its adherents memorize large portions of the original Arabic whether they can understand what they memorize or not. For Muslims, there is an almost magical quality to the original text that Christians have rarely ever ascribed to such a degree to their originals, even should any be discovered.[25]

What has only recently become crystal clear, however, is that ancient libraries and other depositories of valued scrolls and codices typically kept them in circulation for a minimum of 100–150 years and often considerably longer.[26] Libraries were primarily not lending libraries but places for the safe preservation of books and for people to come to use them. When a document was particularly highly valued, like the fourth-century Codex Vaticanus of the entire New Testament, it would be reinked. In the case of Vaticanus this occurred after five hundred years of use when it was not sitting in a library and had all the more reason to be worn and discarded![27] So the "copies of copies of copies of copies . . ." model is the exact opposite of what would have occurred with New Testament books. I regularly teach modular classes in Dublin at the Irish Bible Institute, a short bus ride from the Chester Beatty Library on the grounds of the Dublin Castle. In it are a variety of ancient manuscripts on display, including portions of both the Chester Beatty and (apparently) the Bodmer Papyri collections, which contain a number of manuscripts that date to the third century. I tell my students that it is theoretically possible that one or more of these manuscripts was copied directly from the original autographs, though given the distance the documents traveled in order to wind up in Ireland and the nature of their variants, they were more likely at least copies of copies. But one really need not postulate more than two rounds of scribal activity between these prized treasures and the New Testament originals, though of course it is very possible that their histories are more complex. The point is simply that all the imaginary gaps in time when all kinds of errors or distortions could have crept in undetected simply don't exist. It is certainly true that somewhat abberant manuscripts like Codex Bezae, in the fifth century, could add a lot of small, unique distinctives, especially with the book of Acts. But this "Western text" of the New Testament, to name it according to its text-type, hardly crept in undetected. Everyone recognized that it was different and, in some cases, may have even preserved historically accurate information that just wasn't in the earlier copies.[28]

Dan Wallace is not far from the mark, therefore, when he quips that we virtually do have the original texts of the New Testament books. When we look at the UBS or Nestle-Aland Greek New Testaments, for all intents and purposes we have the originals. We just don't always know whether the original readings appear in the text itself or in the textual apparatus that forms the footnotes.[29] Of course, to say this is to speak somewhat tongue-in-cheek. There are all kinds of very minor variants that are not represented even in the footnotes. But the rhetorical effect of such a quip is certainly less misleading than when Ehrman and others make it sound like we have little idea what the originals looked like at all. A massive project of international textual criticism to produce editions of the New Testament books that collate all the nontrivial variants in all available manuscripts of the first millennium of transmission, known as the Editio Critica Maior, will be an amazing boon for scholars. Yet even the small amounts that have thus far appeared are revealing no earth-shattering discoveries at all.[30]

An excellent example of a smaller project, already completed, that is showing how close to the originals the UBS/Nestle-Aland texts almost certainly are resulted in the Tyndale House Greek New Testament.[31] This was a painstaking effort of numerous scholars and student assistants at Tyndale House in Cambridge to create a fresh Greek New Testament not based on all the identical principles that textual critics typically use. With respect to external evidence, usually no reconstruction of any disputed text was used unless it could be shown to actually have existed in at least two manuscripts, one of them from the fifth century or earlier. Too often, eclectic textual criticism has picked and chosen from a variety of different manuscripts to create the wording of a particular verse or linguistic unit of thought that is not represented in any actual manuscript. The Tyndale House principles prevented this from occurring as frequently. With respect to internal evidence, when a change could plausibly be explained as due to an accidental scribal change, that view was preferred to one that had to be an intentional change. And when an intentional change for nontheological reasons could plausibly account for a variant, it was preferred to a theological rationale.[32] Still, the overall goal was the same as before: to postulate the earliest reading that best explained the origin of all the existing variants.

Contributors to the project expected that there would be quite a few places where different variants from what the editors of the standard text of the UBS/Nestle-Aland chose would wind up as the most likely original, but this only rarely happened and hardly ever with anything that made a significant difference to the meaning of the text. The results were surprisingly close to the existing text of the UBS/Nestle-Aland.[33] The same could be said of the only slightly older SBL Greek New Testament, which was also originally touted as a significant alternative to the two standard editions.[34] All that is really consistently interesting to anyone but the advanced specialist about these two newer Greek New Testaments is their differing textual apparatuses. The Tyndale House edition also adopts a different order of books, based on certain early arrangements of the New Testament, frequently makes different paragraph breaks, and does not make the spelling of words uniform when the manuscripts followed do not.[35] However, our knowledge of over 99 percent of the original New Testament text is more secure than ever.[36]

New Testament Perspectives

This is the one chapter in the book that has ventured well into the discussion of its topic without yet appealing to what the New Testament itself claims about it. But that is because nothing in the New Testament describes the process of its copying. How could it, since what it contains by definition is our best reconstruction of what was written before it was ever copied? Of course, it is theoretically possible that one of the later books of the New Testament could have written about the process of copying an earlier book, had that been relevant to its purposes, which it never was. But there are some passages that indirectly may hint at how the authors of the New Testament books might have addressed our question had they chosen to do so.

To begin with, we observe that the New Testament authors already had a Bible—the Hebrew Scriptures. By the time we have enough manuscripts to provide evidence for the copying processes of Old Testament books, as Christians now refer to them, we see a meticulous care, with checking, double-checking, and cross-checking that allows for noticeably fewer variations than even in New Testament textual criticism. This was the work of the Masoretic tradition of Hebrew scribes, which spanned from about AD 135 to 1000, though the oldest existing Hebrew Scriptures from this tradition date to about AD 900.[37] Comparing the portions of biblical books preserved in the Dead Sea Scrolls yields a greater breadth of practices. Still, the extraordinary similarities between the great Isaiah Scroll and its descendant one thousand years later is remarkable.[38] Other biblical books show that the copyists were not always that accurate, but overall the picture is certainly one of painstaking care.[39]

The first generation of Christian writers, therefore, already inherited a tradition of very careful copying of what was deemed to be sacred Scripture. As the convictions grew throughout the second century that the books that would become the New Testament were similarly sacred, scribes would have wanted to carefully preserve them as well, even if the results showed their efforts were not quite as painstaking. Jesus himself appealed to the partial pen strokes of various Hebrew letters when he declared, "For verily I say unto you, Till heaven and earth pass, one jot or one tittle shall in no wise pass from the law, till all be fulfilled" (Matt. 5:18 KJV). Modern translations admirably try to make "jot" and "tittle" more understandable for contemporary audiences but lose something of the text's original force. Of course, Jesus is not talking about the process of copying the text at all, but he is saying that every tiniest portion of the law will remain in force until its purposes have been fulfilled. But by appealing to even the smallest stroke of a pen, he may well be alluding to scribal habits of carefully copying every letter of every word. Likewise, even the smallest portion of the Scriptures will remain until entirely fulfilled.[40]

In Paul's original context, 2 Timothy 3:16 would likewise have referred solely to the Old Testament. It is "God-breathed and is useful for teaching, rebuking, correcting and training in righteousness." But as the Christian canon of the New Testament developed, one of the things that believers meant when they called an apostolic document part of Scripture was that it was equally truthful and useful.[41] Both of these convictions would have given believers a strong desire to ensure great care in the reproduction of these new-covenant documents, at least somewhat akin to the care with which they transmitted the old-covenant ones.

Luke 1:1–4 is usually cited to show the processes involved in the *composition* of this Gospel, and rightly so. Luke testifies that he has relied on eyewitness sources as well as those who were authorized transmitters of reliable Christian tradition, centered on the life and ministry of Jesus of Nazareth. He is aware of and has utilized previous written sources as well, but he takes all the material he has collected and puts his own distinctive arrangement and theological emphases on it so that his listeners may have great confidence in its accuracy. None of this includes a single word about how Luke hoped his two-volume work (Luke-Acts) would be *copied*, but it is difficult to imagine any scenario in which Luke's concern for accuracy would have made him tolerate anything but the greatest of care in the publication of his two volumes.

Paul, in 1 Thessalonians 2:13, authors a remarkable verse, explaining that "we also thank God continually because, when you received the word of God, which you heard from us, you accepted it not as a human word, but as it actually is, the word of God, which is indeed at work in you who believe." Even the faithfully *preached* message of the gospel can be called the very word of God. Paul was not just a good Jew, convinced of the carefulness with which his (Old Testament) Scriptures had been preserved; he also recognized the importance of fidelity in the oral proclamation of God's word.[42] How much more must he have insisted that written copies of his books were likewise God's word, worthy of great care in handling![43]

One New Testament text rises above all of these in its potential significance for this chapter. It is a passage, often misused, that may speak somewhat more directly to our topic than is usually recognized. Just before the last two verses of the book of Revelation, John writes, "I warn everyone who hears the words of the prophecy of this scroll: If anyone adds anything to them, God will add to that person the plagues described in this scroll. And if anyone takes words away from this scroll of prophecy, God will take away from that person any share in the tree of life and in the Holy City, which are described in this scroll" (Rev. 22:18–19). These verses are often used to support the notion of a closed canon of Scripture,[44] when in fact there is no way to demonstrate that John had any inkling he was writing the last book of the Bible when he wrote his Apocalypse.

It is not even the case that John necessarily had any other Scripture in mind when he wrote Revelation 22:18–19. John is talking about the book he has just written, pure and simple, nothing more and nothing less. His words warn particularly against any doctrinal distortion of his Apocalypse.[45] And while it is clear that he knows he has received extraordinary revelation about dramatic present and future events in the visions God gave him while he was "in the Spirit" (Rev. 1:10), we cannot even know whether he had any special sense of inspiration when he recorded these descriptions of his visions. It is true that there are a variety of allusions to Genesis in Revelation, and "a new heaven and a new earth" (21:1) allude in various ways to the pristine glories of the garden of Eden. It is obvious that the book provides a very fitting end both to the New Testament and to the combination of Old and New Testaments together. Very indirectly, once the process of canonization began and once Revelation was placed at the end of a collection of books deemed to be inspired and authoritative, these closing words would have functioned in the eyes of some as a warning against adding or deleting books from the canon. Still, nothing suggests that John had any idea he was writing the last book of the Bible.[46]

On the other hand, the moment Revelation began to be read even as a book on its own, anyone tasked with *copying* it would have found its closing warnings very sobering indeed. Scribes would most likely have worked as carefully as they possibly could to avoid even the slightest chance of falling under the curses enunciated over those who would add to or delete from the book. Then, as the canon began to take shape and the New Testament began to be viewed as a book itself with twenty-seven parts to it (rather than a collection of twenty-seven unrelated books), many scribes copying other parts of the New

Testament would have seen at least an implicit warning to them to do their work with meticulous care as well. Again, this does not mean the results were as flawless as might have been desired, but it would certainly seem to preclude any cavalier attitudes in approaching their task. As copies of the Septuagint (the Greek translation of the Hebrew Old Testament) were combined with the copies of the New Testament books, and the resulting collection was then recopied as one whole (or at least as a unified set of volumes), the same care would have been extended to the entire Bible.[47]

How does this square with the kinds of variations we know exist? We may assume that God forgives accidental mistakes. We may assume that scribes for the vast majority of the time when they intentionally made changes did so because they thought that they were restoring the original meaning, and that the exemplars they were copying were defective at the points where they were making their changes. What at times was "the orthodox corruption of Scripture" was probably thought to be the orthodox restoration of Scripture. We may assume that God looked on this heart motive in all these instances as well, even when the scribes' assumptions turned out to be wrong. None of this suggests that out of the thousands of instances of copying parts or all of the New Testament there were no "rogue" scribes who intentionally made changes they did not believe were simply restoring the original meaning. Any such rogues would also have then realized that they were not instantly struck dead or necessarily punished with bad life circumstances (as Rev. 22:18–19 might have been taken to imply). Most scribes, however, would have realized that Revelation's warning applies to people who would consciously rewrite John's visions to make them teach something that they were never intended to. Still, for Christian scribes with any kind of a conscience, John's words would have given them much pause before they arbitrarily added or deleted anything.[48] And the ensuing history of the transmission of the text still remains sufficiently unique to mesh with the conviction that God worked remarkably well even with flawed human beings for his glorious and sovereign purposes.

Translations of the New Testament

It only makes sense to assume that translators of the New Testament books, from antiquity onward, were regularly motivated by the same sense of the sacredness of the text and the dangers of tampering with it in any way. I have elsewhere given a variety of samples of the different kinds of modern English translations that are the most popular, and how they translate various verses. The results make it virtually always clear that the same Greek or Hebrew must lie behind all the diverse renderings of a given passage. Every once in a while a word or expression is so rare that translations may vary considerably, but these are the very infrequent exceptions. In an era of computer programs that enable a display of a dozen or more translations at a time of any portion of Scripture one cares to scrutinize, readers with any doubts should try the experiment for themselves. Randomly choose a verse, as many times as you need to do so in order to convince yourself, look at the English renderings in as many of the established versions as you want to, and see the comparatively minor nature of the differences.[49]

Why, then, are there so many translations, especially in English? The cynic's answer would be that Bibles make money for their publishers, usually much more so than the other books or products that they sell. While this no doubt is true, many publishers also give away huge numbers of their Bibles. And the people who do the translation work, given the immense amount of time and energy they need, are almost always more nobly motivated. If there is any way to get Bibles in the hands of a cross-section of the public that might not otherwise have them, or to get people to read Bibles who may have other translations that they don't read, then the very value Christians ascribe to reading, understanding, and applying the text for oneself more than justifies the cost and effort of a new translation.[50]

At the risk of considerable oversimplification, I suggest that there are three major translation philosophies utilized today. *Formally equivalent* translations prioritize the form, structure, and accuracy of the translation over clarity and intelligibility. The King James Version was such a Bible in its day (1611), and the New American Standard Bible, the New Revised Standard Version, and the English Standard Version fall into that category today. *Dynamically equivalent* translations prioritize the readability, clarity, and intelligibility of the text over form and meaning. The New Living Translation is the best-known example of a Bible using this translation philosophy today. Other examples include the Contemporary English Version, the Good News Bible, and the New International Reader's Version. *Optimally equivalent* translations prioritize neither clarity over accuracy nor accuracy over clarity but try to achieve as much of both as possible in every text, realizing that overall they will then not have quite as much accuracy as formally equivalent translations or quite as much clarity as dynamically equivalent translations. But they will have considerably more clarity than formally equivalent translations and considerably more accuracy than dynamically equivalent ones. The New International Version, the world's best-selling translation by far, is the prototype in this category. Others include the Christian Standard Bible, the Common English Bible, and the New English Translation or NET Bible.[51]

Whichever kind of Bible translation one uses, nevertheless, one will get a more than adequate grasp of Scripture's teaching on salvation and sanctification—how to get right with God and grow in following him. No significant teaching of Christianity depends solely on a verse or passage that is textually or translationally uncertain. Using claims that the original books of Scripture were not carefully enough transmitted or accurately enough copied as a reason for not accepting Christianity or its God boils down to a smokescreen of massive proportions. The evidence of their accuracy is far greater than it is for many ordinary things we rely on (by faith!) every day—whether it is the belief that our cars will run, that we won't fall as we walk, or that the food we purchase will not make us sick!

Conclusion

Just as the best way for the average English reader of the Bible to determine how significant New Testament textual variants are is to skim through an English New Testament and pay attention to the footnotes, so also the best way to determine how different all the various translations are is to skim through a cross-section of them. Simpler still, get a computerized program like Logos or Accordance and toggle among any random cross-section of English translations of a single verse. Then do that several times from various parts of Scripture. For those who don't own such programs, Bible Gateway allows you to select a verse and an English version, with several dozen to choose from.[52] You can then look at its renderings one by one. On rare occasions, a word or phrase is so obscure that there will be enough differences in translation to make you wonder if they were all reading the same original. Or, if the footnotes refer to what "some manuscripts read," then you know they are translating a different textual variant. But these phenomena occur in only a very tiny fraction of the texts of Scripture. In other words, don't believe someone who tells you the textual history of the Bible is hopelessly corrupt, just as you shouldn't believe someone who says it has been preserved perfectly. Check it out for yourself, and decide who is closer to the truth.

Nevertheless, what if something did come in and distort the text in one of the few chronologically longer gaps in the manuscript evidence? We would have to deal with that when it was discovered, but we have no reason to suspect that will happen. What if there were a conspiracy to materially change things at some point, despite the fact that Christianity had no platform for doing so for its first three hundred years? We would have to offer an answer, but we have no actual evidence to make that scenario likely. What if an original reading that would have significantly changed our understanding of Christian origins were entirely lost sight of because the error or change came so early in the process of copying that everyone else followed it? We would have to address the question when it arose, but there is no actual evidence to make that scenario any likelier. As long as one crafts "what ifs" for which we have no actual evidence, we can doubt the undeniable facts of our own lives. But if we focus on everything for which we have actual evidence, we have no reason whatsoever to believe that we cannot reconstruct with remarkable accuracy the original texts of the New Testament.

The Alleged Undesirability
of the Christian Life

From time to time, someone will be honest with me and say up front that they don't believe in the Christian God because they are unwilling to live like they know the Bible teaches that Christians should. More often, my atheist acquaintances suggest one of the other issues I have discussed in one of the last nine chapters as their first or primary reason for not believing in God. Still, the more we talk, the more it becomes clear that these are subordinate issues, and the big issue is that they want to run their own life without any interference from anyone, not even God himself. I have a friend who teaches apologetics at a well-known evangelical seminary on the American West Coast who insists that this is the bottom-line issue for *all* atheists. I disagree. I have met several who are genuinely perplexed by one or more of the issues I have already discussed in this volume, or by others. But I have little doubt that a significant number of those who do not believe in the God and Father of Jesus Christ simply don't want the accountability that comes with making a profession of faith in Jesus.

Of course, as we have seen already, believing or not believing in God has no logical connection to whether he exists. If he does exist, whether or not I believe in him will not affect his existence. If there is a judgment day to come when all human beings who have ever lived will stand before God, accountable for what they have done with their lives, the fact that not everyone in the world believes in such a God will not prevent him from being their Judge.

Conversely, if such a God does not exist, no amount of belief in him will bring him into existence. Ironically, then, this last objection is a non sequitur. Whether or not I want to believe what Christians believe or live as Christians are supposed to live has no bearing whatsoever on God's existence. Yet, the rhetoric of many people makes it seem they think it does. "Oh, I could never believe in a God who . . ." say many individuals, not realizing that if such a God exists, then their choice to remain estranged from him throughout their whole lives by continually rejecting his gracious offer of salvation will give them what they desire, keeping them estranged from him throughout eternity, through no one's fault but their own.

Oftentimes, nevertheless, when someone rejects Christianity, they are rejecting something that they have been told is an essential Christian belief or behavior when in fact it is not. Throughout church history, plenty of people have added requirements to the Christian life that do not appear in Scripture at all or do not appear as issues related to anyone's salvation. Perhaps they have to do with a set of beliefs that in fact only one wing or certain wings of Christianity actually believe. As we have seen in earlier chapters, people may think that a Christian must have a certain kind of view about hell or about the fate of the unevangelized, about predestination, about gender roles, about war and peace, or about various other debated issues. Other topics on which Bible-believing Christians have multiple, potentially valid positions include, but are not limited to, details about the end times, the organization of the church, the interplay between divine and human roles in a person's salvation, the nature of biblical inspiration, spiritual gifts, baptism, the age of the earth and how God created the universe, the extent of sin and human depravity, and so on.[1] It is tragic when a person rejects Christianity because they think being a believer requires them to hold a view they find untenable on something, when in fact there is considerable legitimate diversity within Christian circles on that particular topic.

Many times, however, when people reject Christianity because they hold different views on important topics, they are thinking about ethical or behavioral issues. Here, again, there can be mistaken notions about breadth of perspectives. People may associate Christian ethics or social justice with just one or two topics. One group of Christians may look to opposing abortion and homosexual behavior or supporting a fairly free-market economy as the most important issues to address, whereas another may look to the alleviation of poverty, the need for health care, and gun control as more pressing concerns. Both groups are in fact correct in finding their concerns supported by Scripture—if not in specific passages, then at least in the Bible's overall concern for human flourishing—but wrong in thinking the other concerns are unbiblical.[2] And both groups can misidentify what Scripture actually prioritizes. Still, the focus of this chapter lies elsewhere, specifically, on the belief that Christian faith enslaves rather than liberates and that the Christian life is thus just too undesirable to countenance.

The objection to belief in God that stems from a desire to run one's own life rather than submitting to any external authority, even an all-powerful and all-loving one, is typically an objection that recognizes that biblical Christianity does contain certain nonnegotiables (notwithstanding some Christians' attempts to negotiate them!).[3] But these nonnegotiables simply prove too objectionable for the person in question to accept the Christian God. For example, there are individuals who recognize that not committing adultery is one of the ten most central commandments in the Old Testament and a moral absolute enshrined as equally important in the New Testament. Yet they want to feel free to cheat on their spouse or perhaps go further and live an intentionally polyamorous lifestyle. At least they have the integrity to recognize that one cannot legitimate such behavior within a Christian framework (or almost every other theistic framework) and so they refuse to believe in God, or they reject him even if they once claimed to follow him.[4] Again, whether or not a person agrees with Christian ethics has no logical bearing on the truth or falsity of those ethics. Even on the purely human level, I may resent and choose not to obey certain laws of my country or city, believing them to be unfair, misguided, or even evil. Yet my attitudes will have no bearing on the legal system's ability to hold me accountable to them. The burden of this chapter, however, is to highlight certain *New Testament* texts that make the claims that Christian ethics actually involve behaviors and commitments that serve the best interests of all people, even while permitting a fair amount of freedom of lifestyle.[5] I will begin by making a caveat about what I am not claiming, proceed by looking at certain texts on freedom from the law and freedom to serve, and finally, turn to a slightly more detailed focus on two key passages that somewhat balance freedom and concern for others in morally gray areas. Still, freedom trumps legalism every time.

A Caveat: The Dangers of Belief in God

A generation ago, a popular Christian song contained the following refrain: "But if heaven never [were] promised to me, . . . it's been worth just having the Lord in my life."[6] Even at that time, as a young believer, I realized that this was horrible theology. Imagine the apostle Paul with all of the sufferings and persecution he experienced for his faith (summarized in 2 Cor. 11:23b–28) penning such lyrics![7] Rather, Paul's views are encapsulated in 1 Corinthians 15:13–19:

> If there is no resurrection of the dead, then not even Christ has been raised. And if Christ has not been raised, our preaching is useless and so is your faith. More than that, we are then found to be false witnesses about God, for we have testified about God that he raised Christ from the dead. But he did not raise him if in fact the dead are not raised. For if the dead are not raised, then Christ has not been raised either. And if Christ has not been raised, your faith is futile; you are still in your sins. Then those also who have fallen asleep in Christ are lost. If only for this life we have hope in Christ, we are of all people most to be pitied.

This is a far cry from saying that it's worth having God in our lives just for what we gain in this world. After all, the God we would be relating to, if he existed at all, would be a liar and untrustworthy, since he promised us eternal life.[8]

What Paul wrote was true for his fellow apostles in the first century. It has been true at times and places of great persecution against the church, as it is in certain parts of the world today. Paul also recognized that all faithful believers will at times experience hardship because of their commitments—he told Timothy that "everyone who wants to live a godly life in Christ Jesus will be persecuted" (2 Tim. 3:12).[9] Serving Christ *can* nevertheless yield enormous benefit even just in this life, long before the arrival of the eternal state of humanity. John 10:10 quotes Jesus promising his followers life in abundance (NIV, "life . . . to the full"). While this has nothing to do with the so-called health and wealth gospel, it does mean that we can enjoy life in the here and now as much as anyone, as we know that what we do pleases God and as we use the gifts he has given us for others as much as we can.[10]

Church history discloses many periods and parts of the world when overt hostility toward believers has not characterized the majority of people's lives. Individuals have accepted Jesus because they have recognized that Christian principles of living make for better relationships, families, and societies. Those who have begun their lives without God have discovered greater "love, joy, peace, patience, kindness, goodness, faithfulness, gentleness, self-control" (Gal. 5:22–23a ESV). Loving God and neighbor (Matt. 22:37–40) has relieved stress and conflict.[11] Belief in an orderly creation by a benevolent God has provided the foundations of modern scientific inquiry and the principles for various societies' laws. Compassion for the needy led to the establishment of public education, the development of new medical procedures and medicines, humanitarian aid, and relief. Belief that all people are equally created in God's image fueled emancipation and civil rights movements.[12]

A number of years ago I was invited to speak at a men's retreat for one of the flagship Messianic Jewish congregations in Colorado.[13] Exactly thirty men attended, of whom only three were ethnically Jewish. I knew the number of Gentiles participating in this congregation was high, but I was surprised to learn that it was this high. I asked them to each in a sentence or two tell me why they had joined a Messianic congregation as non-Jewish people. The vast majority gave the same answer: they had seen the lawless behavior of too many people in the typical Christian church, and as a result they delighted in submitting themselves to a large number of the Old Testament laws and believed that God would be pleased with them also. They apparently had not experienced a church with a healthy balance between freedom from rules and regulations and internally guided, Spirit-filled Christian living that didn't allow that freedom to become a license for sin. By way of contrast, almost every church I have been a part of during my adult life, wherever I have lived, has had a good balance, so I know it is possible to achieve such balance—not perfectly, but to a significant degree.

One of my wife's relatives who has been a part of the Church of Jesus Christ of Latter-day Saints for more than thirty-five years now, though she was raised in a largely irreligious family, not too long ago admitted, "I guess what attracted me to Mormonism were the clear rules. Just tell me what I need to do, and I'll do it. I like living that way." She is hardly alone, and the Latter-day Saints are hardly the only religious group that is often enamored with rules and regulations. In a constantly changing world with information overload, conflicting perspectives on just about any topic of importance, and too little time to reflect deeply on any such topic, a surprising number of people in "the land of the free and the home of the brave" want to be neither free nor brave.[14] Instead, they just want to be told what to think or how to live by authority figures they can trust. Freedom is always harder and requires more bravery!

Freedom from the Law

It is surprising how often the New Testament writers speak of the freedom that Christianity offers. In his programmatic sermon in the Nazareth synagogue, Jesus (as summarized by Luke) proclaims freedom for the prisoners and promises to set the oppressed free, along with proclaiming the year of the Lord's favor (Luke 4:18–19, quoting a prophecy in Isa. 61:1–2)—the Jubilee, in which slaves were to receive their freedom and debts were to be forgiven (Lev. 25).[15] As so often in his teaching, Jesus combines the material and the spiritual, so that we dare not jettison either one. God forgives a person's sins when they follow Jesus, but he also wants them to live in material and political freedom. In John 8:31–32, Jesus explains to a group of his new followers, "If you hold to my teaching, you are really my disciples. Then you will know the truth, and the truth will set you free." Today, the last statement in this quotation is emblazoned over the doorways of various university buildings around the world and interpreted as applying to intellectual truth, but Jesus was speaking of divine revelation and freedom from sin and death.[16] Christian truth was never designed primarily to restrict human behavior or in any way to enslave people, but it was designed to free them to become what their deepest longings desire and that for which God in fact created them.[17]

Not surprisingly, James twice describes the law of Moses, as it is interpreted by and fulfilled in Christ and his new-covenant teachings, as the perfect or royal "law that gives freedom" (James 1:25; 2:12).[18] Peter commands his churches, "Live as free people, but do not use your freedom as a cover-up for evil; live as God's slaves" (1 Pet. 2:16).[19] The sexually immoral teachers Peter has to counter in verse 19 are claiming to be free to live however they like, but in fact they have become enslaved to their uncontrolled desires. They promise other people freedom, "while they themselves are slaves of depravity—for 'people are slaves to whatever has mastered them.'"[20] Internet trolls who do nothing but mock Christianity, just like supposed Christians who consistently bad-mouth their fellow believers (or others), seem to be enslaved to these patterns of behavior and unable to quit. Little freedom appears present in their lives.

The author to the Hebrews puts his finger on a frequent characteristic of pagan religion in the ancient Mediterranean world: their fear in the face of death as the great unknown. We read that "since [Jesus's followers] have flesh and blood, [Jesus] too shared in their humanity so that by his death he might break the power of him who holds the power of death—that is, the devil—and free those who all their lives were held in slavery by their fear of death" (Heb. 2:14–15).[21] Modern beliefs and superstitions show that sinful humanity has not progressed much from the days of Greco-Roman antiquity. Hardened secular people turn remarkably sentimental, contradicting their avowed beliefs, when well-liked people die. "Rest in peace," they say, or "They're in a better place." Yet if persons have no souls that exist beyond the grave, a rotting corpse is hardly resting in peace or in a better place or condition for anyone.

Freedom to Serve

Paul, in Galatians, the book that many from the days of Martin Luther onward have dubbed the Magna Carta of Christian liberty, takes a quite different tack.[22] After spending two-thirds of his letter defending justification by faith rather than by the works of the law, Paul declares, "It is for freedom that Christ has set us free. Stand firm, then, and do not let yourselves be burdened again by a yoke of slavery" (Gal. 5:1).[23] Christianity was never intended to be a long list of dos and don'ts; it is a living, loving relationship between human beings and God and among humans themselves. Still, before Paul unfolds the new thought with which Galatians 5 begins, he feels compelled to once again stress that it is faith and not the works of the law, not even so central a law as the Jewish initiation rite of circumcision, that produces righteousness and salvation (vv. 2–12). Only then he is ready to unpack his claim, "You, my brothers and sisters, were called to be free. But do not use your freedom to indulge the flesh; rather, serve one another humbly in love" (v. 13).[24]

What Paul is stressing is that freedom in Christ through the Spirit is freedom to serve, not freedom to live life in any way one imagines might be desirable. Romans 6–7 contains some remarkable teaching on this topic. Romans 6:1–10 establishes as decisively as any New Testament passage does that sin is done away with in the Christian's life. Verse 6 insists that "we know that our old self was crucified with him so that the body ruled by sin might be done away with, that we should no longer be slaves to sin." Paul does not envision the life apart from Christ as one of great individual freedom to live in any way that he likes. He sees it as a kind of slavery—slavery to sin and all its consequences, many of them in this life already and the rest in the life to come. The person looking for the greatest amount of freedom, paradoxically, finds it only in serving Jesus the Messiah (vv. 6b–10).[25]

Verse 11 turns from the indicative to the imperative, from stating what circumstances actually are to commanding believers not to do what it seemed Paul just said they couldn't do anyway! They must "count" themselves "dead to sin but alive to God in Christ Jesus." They must "not let sin reign in [their] mortal body so that [they] obey its evil desires" (v. 12). They must "not offer any part of [themselves] to sin as an instrument of wickedness, but rather offer [themselves] to God as those who have been brought from death to life; and offer every part of [themselves] to him as an instrument of righteousness" (v. 13). The rationale for all this appears in the concluding verse of the little paragraph begun at verse 11: "For sin shall no longer be your master, because you are not under the law, but under grace" (v. 14). In the midst of all the other commands from verse 11 onward, it seems likely that this is an imperatival rather than a predictive future—that is, "sin must not be your master" rather than "sin can never again be your master" (cf. NAB, NLT).[26]

Paul's next paragraph makes the telling point that all people are always slaves to something. The verb *douleuō*, of course, can be translated both "to be enslaved to" and "to serve." Precisely because of Western society's proper objection to slavery, older translations tended to render this verb in contexts like this one as "serve" (KJV, ASV), but its power is thereby considerably diminished. Precisely when we use forms of "slave" in our translations do we feel its force: "Don't you know that when you offer yourselves to someone as obedient slaves, you are slaves of the one you obey—whether you are slaves to sin, which leads to death, or to obedience, which leads to righteousness?" (v. 16). People who reject God often think they are free as a result, whereas the New Testament maintains that they are slaves to sin, including the sinful identity or patterns of behavior that they have chosen for themselves. Conversely, Christians should never imagine that freedom in Christ means freedom to live any way they want. Acknowledging Jesus as Lord means becoming his slave or indentured servant. But since no one can escape being a slave, Paul longs for people to choose well whom or what they will serve. He is convinced righteous living is far more desirable, so he wants as many as possible to serve "obedience" (to God), "which leads to righteousness" (v. 16). This obedience also frees people from enslavement to sin (v. 18).[27]

Verse 21 raises a powerful rhetorical question that can be answered only in the negative: "What benefit did you reap at that time from the things you are now ashamed of?" Paul can reply merely by exclaiming, "Those things result in death!" The fleeting but sinful pleasures of life bring very temporary satisfaction—if even that, compared with the longer-term personal suffering they create. God forbade drunkenness, gluttony, malice, bitterness, sexual immorality, theft, murder, and idolatry not to make human existence less enjoyable but to make it more so. Overextending bodily appetites sooner or later damages ourselves or others or both. Unloving treatment of other people may allow us to gain something at their expense in the short run, but it ruins relationships in the long run. Wholesome, self-giving relationships with others, which put their well-being above our own (Phil. 2:4),[28] may require sacrifice, but they allow our consciences to accuse us less and less. And even if one's conscience is already so seared that one has nothing to fear from it, living a life of self-giving means that other people are more likely to treat one better.

Many Shades of Gray

Countless issues in Christian living, nevertheless, do not remain clear-cut. Romans 14:1–15:13 and 1 Corinthians 8:1–11:1 both deal at some length with these *adiaphora* (issues on which believers may legitimately differ). In the first-century Greco-Roman world, the issues that fledgling Christianity often had to deal with involved food sacrificed to idols, dietary laws, circumcision, hairstyles and head coverings, special holidays, and the like. In both passages, Paul insists that believers are fundamentally free to do as they please. They may agree to participate in the activity in question. But if there is a "weaker brother or sister" present, then they should refrain from the activity.[29] It is important, however, to note the implied definitions of the weaker brother or sister. These are fellow believers whose consciences do not permit them to participate in the debated actions. The weaker spiritual sibling is also someone who would be tempted actually to imitate their fellow Christian without a clear conscience and/or move beyond the potentially permissible activity to something that is clearly sinful.[30] Examples include the freedom to drink alcohol in moderation tempting a recovering alcoholic to fall off the wagon, or the freedom to play violent video games tempting a disturbed "loner" to become an active shooter of real human beings in some public place.

Unfortunately, some Christians have applied the principles of these chapters in Romans and 1 Corinthians inappropriately, labeling every believer who is ever offended by some morally neutral practice a weaker brother or sister. However, if someone is offended by a practice, they are not likely to imitate the person they are criticizing, much less be led into a real sin. I am not saying that Christians should unnecessarily offend one another. Still, if the unavoidable choice were between removing an *unnecessary* obstacle to someone coming to Christ and hurting the feelings of a fellow believer, Scripture would remove the unnecessary obstacle every time.[31] Paul explicitly says, "I have become all things to all people so that by all possible means I might save some" (1 Cor. 9:22). The "foolishness" of the cross (1:18) is the necessary obstacle that we cannot remove.[32]

Romans 14:1–15:13

The structure of Romans 14:1–15:13 reinforces the conviction that the scales tip in favor of freedom over unneeded restraint. The passage falls into three main sections: 14:1–12; 14:13–15:6; 15:7–13. While Paul does speak about freedom and restraint in each section, the main point of the first and third sections is freedom. The first section (14:1–12) stresses mutual acceptance.[33] Verses 1–4 teach that the person who wants to refrain from the morally neutral issue (in this case what foods to eat) should be allowed to, and the person who wants to practice it should be allowed to, because God will judge us all individually. We are not to judge one another on such issues. Verses 5–9 repeat the same point, only with respect to holy days, and then return to the issue of food. Verses 10–12 expand on the concept of each person individually giving an account before God of their behavior.

The second section (14:13–15:6) begins by reiterating the point that we should "stop passing judgment on one another" (v. 13a) but then moves on to the balancing point about not causing a Christian brother or sister to stumble or fall (vv. 13b, 20, 21).[34] Verse 15 contains two verbs that at first blush prove ambiguous. It speaks of a brother or sister who is "distressed" because of another's behavior and warns us not to "destroy someone for whom Christ died." But with verses 20–21 coming after verse 15, it is obvious that they clarify the earlier statement. And verse 23 speaks of those who have doubts being condemned if they practice the disputed activity, because "everything that does not come from faith is sin." So there is nothing here about someone who is simply upset that another Christian likes something that they don't. Such a person by definition is not going to imitate the other in their practice, going against their conscience and thus sinning. Even in this central section on restraint, Paul still inserts the warning to "not let what you know is good be spoken of as evil" (v. 16).[35] This middle section is rounded out by 15:1–6, which introduces the language of the "strong" and the "weak" for the first time in the context of the strong trying to minimize the damage they do to the weak.

Verse 7, nevertheless, starts off the third section by repeating the point of the first: "Accept one another, then, just as Christ accepted you" (v. 7a). Then comes the explicit application to Jews and Gentiles in the mixed congregation of the church in Rome: Paul wants God's promises of salvation for both groups to be fulfilled, so evangelism trumps in-house preferences.[36] Then follow a barrage of Old Testament quotations about God's desires for the Gentiles to be incorporated into the family of God, desires that are in part thwarted by people already in the family squabbling over what others can and cannot do.

1 Corinthians 8:1–11:1

First Corinthians 8:1–11:1 leads us to the same conclusion. Paul introduces the weaker brother or sister earlier in his discussion, in 8:7–13, but with the same definition. It is someone who is emboldened to do what their conscience doesn't permit them to do (vv. 10–12) or to do what is actually sinful (v. 13).[37] Interestingly, 9:1–18 seems to have moved on to a new topic—the freedom to receive money for ministry—but it turns out to be a second application of the similar principle: inherent freedom is tempered by voluntary restraint, but only when there is real likelihood of serious damage to Paul's freedom in the faith. Here the danger is that the patron-client relationships in Corinth might lead benefactors to try to "control the purse strings" as a way to limit what

Paul teaches.[38] So Paul's voluntary restraint in accepting money in Corinth is actually in service of maximizing his freedom to preach exactly as he believes Christ is leading him. Verses 19–23 then explicitly articulate Paul's "all things to all people" philosophy, while verses 24–27 liken the self-discipline needed for this strategy to that of an athlete in training.[39]

In 10:1–22 Paul then reminds the Corinthians that these principles for morally neutral matters cannot be extended to inherently immoral issues. Freedom to drink does not mean freedom for drunkenness. Freedom to be paid for ministry does not mean freedom for covetousness or to insist on money for ministry. Freedom to eat food sacrificed to idols does not mean freedom to worship false gods while eating food sacrificed to them.[40] Still, just as in Romans, Paul ends by stressing freedom. He then begins 10:23–11:1 by qualifying the Corinthian slogan that they have the freedom to do absolutely anything (vv. 23–24). But verses 25–27 restate the principle of freedom with respect to food sacrificed to idols: "Eat anything sold in the meat market without raising questions of conscience, for, 'The earth is the Lord's, and everything in it.' If an unbeliever invites you to a meal and you want to go, eat whatever is put before you without raising questions of conscience." The fundamental principle is freedom.[41]

Only if someone else points out that the meat had been sacrificed to idols— presumably meaning that they do not feel free to eat it—should the believer with the more robust conscience refrain. The RSV and NLT helpfully put parentheses around verses 28–29a.[42] Verses 29b–30 make little sense as the continuation of the thought of verse 29a but follow up nicely on where Paul left off at the end of verse 27 before his parenthetical remarks. Paul's freedom should *not* be limited by what other people think. That is the general principle. The one exceptional circumstance where Paul qualifies his general principle should not be treated as his emphasis, thereby blurring his main point. Verses 31–33 round out the discussion by reiterating three key points of chapters 8–10: (1) do all to God's glory (v. 31); (2) don't use your freedom in ways that lead others to commit sin (v. 32); (3) think of what will best aid in other people's salvation (v. 33). In today's world, countless unbelievers need to see that Christians are not "uptight" about morally neutral matters. Not a few are freed thereby to begin to look at belief in Jesus differently and eventually come to faith themselves.[43]

Conclusion

Many of the reasons that unbelievers have viewed the Christian life as undesirable involve a caricature of that life rather than the real thing. Unfortunately, enough believers pursue and promote that caricature that it is understandable why the stereotypes have endured. Christianity is not fundamentally about removing fun from one's life! It offers purpose, fulfillment, and a destiny that is unmatched by any other worldview. It gives hope for eternal life, even if temporal life is cut short, whether by disease, injury, or actual martyrdom for one's faith. Suffering of some kind is promised, but so is God's comfort and empowerment to endure. And countless Christians have testified that the latter far outweighs the former. Nor is suffering unrelenting for most; it is merely interspersed between far more amenable circumstances. Freedom to serve is far more rewarding than slavery to sin, even if at first slavery to sin may feel like freedom without any restraints. The genuine freedom that Christians have is far more widespread and sweeping than the legalists in our midst ever let on, and it needs to be advertised much more widely as well.

CONCLUSION

T he New Testament makes significant contributions to the ten questions or clusters of questions that I have addressed. In many instances these contributions point us in directions that are not as well known as those indicated by theologians, historians, ethicists, philosophers, and even Old Testament scholars. Even if one does not presuppose the complete reliability of the New Testament, these commonsense answers afford great wisdom to aid in making the questions not as perplexing as they might have been. None of the questions is so difficult that it has to prove a barrier to belief in God.

I will not attempt to summarize each chapter at this juncture; chapter conclusions have done that. I will highlight, however, what may be the one most significant contribution of the New Testament to each area of inquiry.

1. With respect to the problem of suffering and evil, 2 Peter 3:8–9 points us in a key direction. God isn't slow to deal with wickedness and its consequences, as it seems from a human perspective, because his sense of timing is measured by the eternal. Whatever seeming delay emerges is wholly to give more people a chance to repent and turn to him.

2. With the issue of the unevangelized, the New Testament does *not* teach that no one is saved unless they have heard of Jesus and consciously trusted in him, but it does teach that whoever is saved finds forgiveness only through Jesus's atoning cross-work (John 14:6; Acts 4:12). Whatever else hell may be, it is eternal, conscious separation from God (2 Thess. 1:9), but it is never foisted on someone against their will. Just as there are degrees of wickedness in this life, there will be degrees of punishment in the life to come (Luke 12:47–48).

3. Debates about slavery, gender roles, and same-sex relations in today's world tend to be all about human rights. The New Testament's perspectives are all about the responsibilities of believers to give up their rights for others

and to find true freedom in that. Nevertheless, 1 Corinthians 7:21 and the Letter to Philemon both support slaves gaining their freedom whenever they can. On the matter of gender roles, both a "soft complementarian" and a "soft egalitarian" perspective are defensible from the Scriptures, and we need to allow one another freedom to disagree within those parameters. Still, no woman or man should ever be stifled in the full use of their *spiritual gifts*, whatever one decides about certain controversial offices. Homosexual *practice*, however, is never condoned, but that restriction must be kept separate from anything that would discriminate against a person simply for their sexual orientation. Sexual release and interpersonal intimacy likewise need to be distinguished. The experience of countless straight and gay women and men throughout history who have trusted that biblical teaching, rightly interpreted, actually does have their best interests in view needs to be trusted much more than counterclaims that have been tested only for a generation or less in our modern world and with mixed results even then.

4. What distinguished the New Testament miracles from all other accounts or collections of accounts of supernatural activity in antiquity is their role in demonstrating the arrival of the kingdom of God (esp. Matt. 12:28). If the kingdom is present, then the king of that kingdom must be present as well. Unless one from the outset rules out both God and the supernatural more generally, the nature of the New Testament miracles supports the existence of the God who is said to have produced them.

5. The superficial similarities between the historical narratives of the New Testament and Greco-Roman myths and legends turn out to be not nearly as significant as the fact that the New Testament, including its most extraordinary narratives, is deeply embedded in the Jewish world of its day and consistently draws on the Jewish Scriptures (the Christian Old Testament). The God of Israel is thus also the God of Jesus Christ, who discloses the eminently credible nature of the Being who is depicted as the true and living God of the universe.

6. Divine violence and warfare are transmuted from their physical plane in the Old Testament to a spiritual plane in the New (see esp. Eph. 6:10–20). This does not automatically mean that pacifism is to be preferred to just-war theory. Yet it *does* mean that the problem of a God who sanctions physical violence is more acute for the Orthodox Jew than it is for the Christian who discerns progress in God's revelation between the two ages. Final judgment nevertheless remains, for without judgment there can ultimately be no justice.

7. People who pray need not think they are changing God's mind (and thus worshiping a God not worthy of their allegiance), for God has promised to give us certain good things contingent on our asking for them (James 4:2).

Predestination is "single," not "double," and therefore merely confirms what we can know experientially as well: we can never take ultimate credit for being saved, but we have only ourselves to blame for being lost (Rom. 9:22–23).

8. The three accounts of Saul's conversion, the three narratives of Peter with Cornelius, and the three rehearsals of the apostolic decree, all in the book of Acts, show the amount of diversity one biographer and historian in New Testament times deemed acceptable in compiling his narratives (cf. Luke 1:1–4). Similar differences among the Gospel parallels, therefore, should cause no surprise or skepticism about their reliability. Those who would reject the God of Scripture because they perceive too many contradictions in Scripture, with Gospel parallels as their signature example, must look elsewhere if they want to support that kind of thinking.

9. A careful analysis of the textual variants in the New Testament shows that the texts have been copied extraordinarily well, while a similar study of the footnotes of modern English translations shows we have nothing to fear from textual criticism. A thoughtful comparison of the numerous standard and common English translations of the New Testament likewise yields valuable insights. All are more than accurate enough to teach us God's plan of salvation and the ways in which we should grow in our Christian faith. We scarcely need to abandon our faith commitments on the grounds that we cannot really know what God's word says, due either to copyists' mistakes or to translators' confusion.

10. Finally, resisting belief in God because of a desire to rule one's own life misconstrues the benevolent ways Jesus wishes to empower us when he comes to live inside us, and it ignores the scriptural teaching that God's rule in our lives is for our goodness and benefit. We do not have to fear that obedience to his commandments will reduce true pleasure or fulfillment in life. Christ offers freedom from anxiety and purposelessness, even though we do translate our allegiance from enslavement to sin to whole-life service of God when we become believers. We may have to suffer or even be martyred, but the eternal glory that will then be ours will far more than compensate for such suffering (Rom. 8:18; 2 Cor. 4:17).

As I said in the introduction, these are not the only significant obstacles to belief in God. Even at the time when they were being compiled for this book, others vied for inclusion. Still, these seemed to reappear as often as any did. Sometimes, an individual's rhetoric masks the fact that they aren't actually giving *reasons* for disbelief; they are simply restating their presuppositions. A good example is, "I am an atheist because there is no actual evidence for God." Of course, there are at least four major classic arguments for God's existence throughout the history of philosophy—the cosmological, teleological, moral, and ontological arguments.[1] Yet instead of discussing and trying to refute each of these, the speaker or writer simply continues to their next point. Or, if they do try to support their assertion, they may explain that what would count as evidence has to be empirical, subject to scientific laws of cause and effect, repeatable under laboratory conditions, or the like.

There are at least three problems here. First, this restriction to the empirical cannot itself be demonstrated empirically, by scientific principles and experimentation. Second, the classic arguments for God's existence do include empirical evidence in places.[2] But third, and perhaps most importantly, the entire line of reasoning boils down to a non sequitur: A person doesn't believe in God, who by definition transcends nature. Why? Because that person finds no natural evidence for him. Shouldn't we allow supernatural options to determine whether or not God exists? No, because that's not scientific method. Fine. All that has been proven is that science can't adjudicate on the existence of God.[3] It's no more convincing than saying that a given farmer isn't growing any wheat this year after looking only in his cornfield and not checking to see if he has any other fields!

Nevertheless, this is not the kind of conversation that appears in the New Testament. Atheism was almost nonexistent in the ancient Mediterranean world. This *is* the kind of conversation, moreover, that philosophers have had many times, so that it need not be repeated here. Can we still believe in God? Of course, anyone is able to do so if they choose to. The question is really shorthand for, Can we still believe in God as a logical or rational thing to do, especially in light of a number of the most common reasons people have given for not doing so? The answer to that question is also a resounding yes. The New Testament itself provides some of the best reasons for that affirmation, whether or not one begins from a perspective of confidence in its overall testimony.

NOTES

Chapter 1 If There Is a God, Why Does He Allow So Much Suffering and Evil?

1. As of April 2019. That figure, however, was nearly two billion in 1990, so encouraging strides have been taken in less than thirty years. Much work nevertheless remains. See "Poverty: Overview," The World Bank, updated April 3, 2019, https://www.worldbank.org/en/topic/pov erty/overview. For some of what needs to be done, see Craig L. Blomberg, *Christians in an Age of Wealth: A Biblical Theology of Stewardship* (Grand Rapids: Zondervan, 2013).

2. "About Chronic Diseases," National Health Council, revised July 29, 2014, https://www .nationalhealthcouncil.org/sites/default/files/AboutChronicDisease.pdf.

3. Michael L. Peterson, "The Problem of Evil," in *The Oxford Handbook of Atheism*, ed. Stephen Bullivant and Michael Ruse (Oxford: Oxford University Press, 2013), 71. Cf. Carl Stecher's contributions to Carl Stecher and Craig Blomberg, *Resurrection: Faith or Fact?*, with contributions by Richard Carrier and Peter S. Williams (Durham, NC: Pitchstone, 2019).

4. See, e.g., Clay Jones, *Why Does God Allow Evil?* (Eugene, OR: Harvest House, 2017). For a representative spectrum of theistic positions, see Chad Meister and James K. Dew Jr., *God and the Problem of Evil: Five Views* (Downers Grove, IL: IVP Academic, 2017).

5. Compare, respectively, J. P. Moreland and William Lane Craig, *Philosophical Foundations for a Christian Worldview*, 2nd ed. (Downers Grove, IL: IVP Academic, 2017), 536–53, with Terrance Tiessen, *Providence and Prayer: How Does God Work in the World?* (Downers Grove, IL: InterVarsity, 2000), 184–93.

6. Part of the "moral argument" for God's existence. Cf., e.g., Douglas L. Groothuis, *Christian Apologetics: A Comprehensive Case for Biblical Faith* (Downers Grove, IL: IVP Academic, 2011), 330–63.

7. Millard J. Erickson, *Christian Theology*, 3rd ed. (Grand Rapids: Baker Academic, 2013), 513–83; Gordon R. Lewis and Bruce A. Demarest, *Integrative Theology* (Grand Rapids: Zondervan, 1990), 2:183–245.

8. For a variety of options, see John H. Walton, *The Lost World of Adam and Eve: Genesis 2–3 and the Human Origins Debate* (Downers Grove, IL: IVP Academic, 2015); Richard S. Hess and David Toshio Tsumura, eds., *I Studied Inscriptions from before the Flood: Ancient Near Eastern, Literary, and Linguistic Approaches to Genesis 1–11*, Sources for Biblical and Theological Study 4 (Winona Lake, IN: Eisenbrauns, 1994); Conrad Hyers, *The Meaning of Creation: Genesis and Modern Science* (Atlanta: John Knox, 1984).

9. See esp. D. A. Carson, *Divine Sovereignty and Human Responsibility: Biblical Perspectives in Tension* (1994; repr., Eugene, OR: Wipf & Stock, 2002).

10. "Classically" articulated by Gustaf Aulén, *Christus Victor: An Historical Study of the Three Main Types of the Idea of the Atonement* (1931; repr., London: SPCK, 2010). More briefly, see Gregory A. Boyd and Paul R. Eddy, *Across the Spectrum: Understanding Issues in Evangelical Theology*, 2nd ed. (Grand Rapids: Baker Academic, 2009), 124–44.

11. See throughout Craig L. Blomberg, *A New Testament Theology* (Waco: Baylor University Press, 2018).

12. Craig L. Blomberg, "The Posttribulationism of the New Testament: Leaving *Left Behind* Behind," in *A Case for Historic Premillennialism: An Alternative to "Left Behind" Eschatology*, ed. Craig L. Blomberg and Sung Wook Chung (Grand Rapids: Baker Academic, 2009), 82.

13. For a thorough study, see Martin Hengel, *Crucifixion in the Ancient World and the Folly of the Message of the Cross* (Philadelphia: Fortress, 1977). See also David Tombs, "Crucifixion, State Terror, and Sexual Abuse," *Union Seminary Quarterly Review* 53 (1999): 89–109. For a modern scientific analysis, see W. D. Edwards, W. J. Gabel, and F. E. Hosmer, "On the Physical Death of Jesus Christ," *Journal of the American Medical Association* 255 (1986): 1455–63.

14. In other words, they do not hold to a young-earth theory of creation but accept the standard scientific hypotheses about the date of the emergence of human beings. For the compatibility of an old earth and early date for the creation of humanity with a high view of Scripture, see David Snoke, *A Biblical Case for an Old Earth* (Grand Rapids: Baker Books, 2006).

15. Intriguingly, this psalm was the most-often-quoted biblical explanation for the delay of God's final judgment within pre-Christian Judaism. See Richard Bauckham, "The Delay of the Parousia," *Tyndale Bulletin* 31 (1980): 3–36.

16. One has to think only of Josef Stalin, Mao Zedong, or Pol Pot, in the twentieth century alone, whose pogroms were directly the product of their particular forms of atheism. Countless others in the history of the world exploited religion to their political ends but could scarcely have believed in a judgment day when they would have to account for their horrific misdeeds before an almighty God.

17. For a more balanced perspective, see Rodney Stark, *God's Battalions: The Case for the Crusades* (New York: HarperOne, 2009).

18. See esp. Jonathan Hill, *What Has Christianity Ever Done for Us? How It Shaped the Modern World* (Downers Grove, IL: InterVarsity, 2005); David Bentley Hart, *Atheist Delusions: The Christian Revolution and Its Fashionable Enemies* (New Haven: Yale University Press, 2009).

19. For massive documentation of this phenomenon, see Craig S. Keener, *Miracles: The Credibility of the New Testament Accounts* (Grand Rapids: Baker Academic, 2011), 1:209–599.

20. Cf. esp. Siu Fung Wu, *Suffering in Romans* (Eugene, OR: Pickwick, 2015), 57–60.

21. For the probable historical setting of Hebrews and 1 Peter, see Craig L. Blomberg, *From Pentecost to Patmos: Acts to Revelation—An Introduction and Survey* (Nottingham: Apollos, 2006), 409–13, 441–46.

22. Joy here "may be defined as a settled contentment in every situation or 'an unnatural reaction of deep, steady and unadulterated thankful trust in God.'" Craig L. Blomberg and Mariam J. Kamell, *James*, ZECNT (Grand Rapids: Zondervan, 2008), quoting Derek Tidball, *Wisdom from Heaven: The Message of the Letter of James for Today* (Fearn, Scotland: Christian Focus, 2003), 22.

23. C. S. Lewis, *The Problem of Pain* (New York: Harper & Row, 1940), 91. In the same vein and equally helpful is Paul Brand and Philip Yancey, *Pain: The Gift Nobody Wants* (New York: HarperCollins, 1993).

24. On the imagery in these verses, see esp. Jack T. Fitzgerald, *Cracks in an Earthen Vessel: An Examination of the Catalogues of Hardships in the Corinthian Correspondence* (Atlanta: Scholars Press, 1988). For powerful illustrations of these principles, see George H. Guthrie, *2 Corinthians*, BECNT (Grand Rapids: Baker Academic, 2015), 266–67.

25. For a profound exploration of this theme throughout the epistle, see Timothy B. Savage, *Power through Weakness: Paul's Understanding of the Christian Ministry in 2 Corinthians* (New

York: Cambridge University Press, 1997). On the principles of these verses (here and elsewhere in Paul's writings), more specifically, see Petrus J. Gräbe, *The Power of God in Paul's Letters* (Tübingen: Mohr Siebeck, 2000).

26. The depth of a good pastor's daily concern for his or her "flock" is a hardship that few people appreciate if they are not in such a position. Cf. Frank J. Matera, *II Corinthians: A Commentary*, NTL (Louisville: Westminster John Knox, 2003), 220.

27. Anthony C. Thiselton (*The First Epistle to the Corinthians*, NIGTC [Grand Rapids: Eerdmans, 2000], 365) refers to it as "the lowest, strongest, most earthy language."

28. For an excellent introduction to the prosperity gospel, along with its debunking, see David W. Jones and Russell S. Woodbridge, *Health, Wealth and Happiness: How the Prosperity Gospel Overshadows the Gospel of Christ* (Grand Rapids: Kregel, 2011).

29. On the strings that patrons could pull, see John K. Chow, *Patronage and Power: A Study of Social Networks in Corinth* (Sheffield: JSOT Press, 1992).

30. Alicia S. Duprée, "Paul and the Filling of Afflictions: A Messianic-Missional Conversation about Colossians 1:24 and 2 Corinthians 1:3–7" (paper presented at the Annual Meeting of the Rocky Mountain/Great Plains Region of the SBL/AAR, Provo, UT, March 2018).

31. L. Ann Jervis (*At the Heart of the Gospel: Suffering in the Earliest Christian Message* [Grand Rapids: Eerdmans, 2007], 61) argues that Paul goes beyond urging his readers to suffer for or like Christ and actually commands that they take on suffering by sharing Christ's mindset. Cf. Barry D. Smith, *Paul's Seven Explanations of the Suffering of the Righteous* (New York: Peter Lang, 2002), 174–200.

32. It is important to follow the NIV in the translation here because it is most likely that *panta* is an adverbial accusative. God does *not* work all things together for good; he works together *in* all things for the good. See esp. Carroll D. Osburn, "The Interpretation of Romans 8:28," *Westminster Theological Journal* 44 (1982): 99–109.

33. Cf. esp. A. E. Harvey, *Renewal through Suffering: A Study of 2 Corinthians* (Edinburgh: T&T Clark, 1996). Harvey notes how unparalleled this perspective is in the history of religion. On Rom. 8:18, see esp. Andrzej Gieniusz, *Romans 8:18–30: "Suffering Does Not Thwart the Future Glory"* (Atlanta: Scholars Press, 1999).

34. "None of the evils and threats of the old world can hinder the saints from fully enjoying the consummate presence of God" (G. K. Beale, *The Book of Revelation*, NIGTC [Grand Rapids: Eerdmans, 1999], 1049). David Mathewson (*A New Heaven and a New Earth: The Meaning and Function of the Old Testament in Revelation 21.1–22.5* [New York: Sheffield Academic, 2003], 58–60) shows how this verse flows directly from Isa. 25:8 and 65:19.

35. Groothuis, *Christian Apologetics*, 641–44.

36. Craig L. Blomberg, *Matthew*, NAC (Nashville: Broadman, 1992), 101.

37. Nicholas Perrin, *Jesus the Temple* (Grand Rapids: Baker Academic, 2010), 152–54.

38. "Death is a dreadful reversal, but not the most extreme one possible. Fear of God is to displace fear of death-dealing persecutors. The stakes are higher with God." John Nolland, *The Gospel of Matthew*, NIGTC (Grand Rapids: Eerdmans, 2005), 436.

39. Whether or not the messianic woes are in view in Col. 1:24 (see above, in the discussion of God's present action), they almost certainly are here. See D. A. Carson, *The Gospel according to John*, PNTC (Grand Rapids: Eerdmans, 1991), 544.

40. See esp. John Christopher Thomas, "'Stop Sinning Lest Something Worse Come upon You,'" *Journal for the Study of the New Testament* 59 (1995): 3–20. See also A. T. Lincoln, *The Gospel according to Saint John*, BNTC (New York: Continuum, 2005), 195.

41. See esp. D. A. Carson, *How Long, O Lord? Reflections on Suffering and Evil*, 2nd ed. (Grand Rapids: Baker Academic, 2006), 60–62. Note also I. Howard Marshall, *The Gospel of Luke*, NIGTC (Grand Rapids: Eerdmans, 1978), 554: "The point is then that natural calamities afford no proof that those who suffer in them are any worse sinners than anybody else; far more important is the fact that all sinners face the judgment of God unless they repent."

42. Though they require a response, on which, see esp. John M. G. Barclay, *Paul and the Gift* (Grand Rapids: Eerdmans, 2015).

43. See Blomberg, *From Pentecost to Patmos*, 32–33. For a helpful book-length treatment of this passage, see David R. McCabe, *How to Kill Things with Words: Ananias and Sapphira under the Prophetic Speech-Act of Divine Judgment* (New York: T&T Clark, 2011).

44. Though it may also be the case that Paul is saying the Corinthian church has experienced an unusual number of illnesses and deaths because of the overall abuse of the Lord's Supper by the community. Some of those sick may have been the most egregious sinners but not necessarily all of them. See Roy E. Ciampa and Brian S. Rosner, *The First Letter to the Corinthians*, PNTC (Grand Rapids: Eerdmans, 2010), 556.

45. More specifically, God does not promise to take temptation to sin away, but believers do not have to give in to it, "because God is faithful and powerful. Such an escape, however, depends on people understanding their sin and depending on the faithful God for the help they need." Paul Gardner, *1 Corinthians*, ZECNT (Grand Rapids: Zondervan, 2018), 442.

46. After all, "the Sinless One knows the force of temptation in a way that we who sin do not. We give in before the temptation has fully spent itself; only he who does not yield knows its full force." Leon Morris, "Hebrews," in *The Expositor's Bible Commentary*, ed. Frank E. Gaebelein (Grand Rapids: Zondervan, 1981), 12:46.

47. Cf. Paul Little and Marie E. Little, *Know Why You Believe*, 4th ed. (Downers Grove, IL: InterVarsity, 2000), 169; Jones, *Why Does God Allow Evil?*, 140–43.

48. Jones, *Why Does God Allow Evil?*, 145–57.

49. "It is God's desire or wish that none perish, however, this does not stop people from rejecting God's truth for falsehood and bringing divine judgment upon themselves." Andrew M. Mbuvi, *Jude and 2 Peter*, NCCS (Eugene, OR: Cascade, 2015), 145. Thomas R. Schreiner (*1, 2 Peter, Jude*, NAC [Nashville: Broadman & Holman, 2003], 381) helpfully appeals to the classic theological distinction between the decretive and the desired wills of God.

50. Moreover, "the hearers have the advantage of living after the ministry of the 'perfecter of faith,' and having his example as the crowning paradigm of trust in action. Those who now respond in trust respond to the 'something better' that brings all the people of faith to the eternal inheritance." David A. deSilva, *Perseverance in Gratitude: A Socio-Rhetorical Commentary on the Epistle "to the Hebrews"* (Grand Rapids: Eerdmans, 2000), 424.

51. For statistics about how rampant such sins are, see Ronald J. Sider, *The Scandal of the Evangelical Conscience: Why Are Christians Living Just Like the Rest of the World?* (Grand Rapids: Baker Books, 2005).

Chapter 2 Must All the Unevangelized Go to Hell (and What Is Hell)?

1. See the full taxonomy of options in John Sanders, *No Other Name: An Investigation into the Destiny of the Unevangelized* (Grand Rapids: Eerdmans, 1992).

2. E.g., Ronald H. Nash, "Restrictivism," in *What about Those Who Have Never Heard? Three Views on the Destiny of the Unevangelized*, ed. John Sanders (Downers Grove, IL: InterVarsity, 1995), 107–39.

3. R. Bryan Widbin, "Salvation for People outside Israel's Covenant?," in *Through No Fault of Their Own? The Fate of Those Who Have Never Heard*, ed. William V. Crockett and James G. Sigountos (Grand Rapids: Baker, 1991), 73–83. Cf. Don Richardson, *Eternity in Their Hearts*, 3rd ed. (Grand Rapids: Bethany House, 2014).

4. See a number of the accounts in Helena Smrcek, *Kingdom beyond Borders: Finding Hope along the Refugee Highway* (Bloomington, IN: WestBow, 2011).

5. Ronald H. Nash, *When a Baby Dies: Answers to Comfort Grieving Parents* (Grand Rapids: Zondervan, 1999), 59–100. A danger of this approach is that it could turn into an argument for abortion or even infanticide, though Nash certainly does not intend it to do so. Another

serious problem is the sheer lack of exegetical support in Scripture, however logical it might sound to someone with Nash's presuppositions.

6. Cf. Dale Moody, *The Word of Truth: A Summary of Christian Doctrine Based on Biblical Revelation* (Grand Rapids: Eerdmans, 1981), 341–48, though with some modifications.

7. For an excellent introduction to middle knowledge, see William L. Craig, *The Only Wise God: The Compatibility of Divine Knowledge and Human Freedom* (1987; repr., Eugene, OR: Wipf & Stock, 1999), 127–52. A slightly less encouraging form of this view appears in J. P. Moreland and William L. Craig, *Philosophical Foundations for a Christian Worldview* (Downers Grove, IL: InterVarsity, 2003), 623–24, in which God ensures that the gospel does make it to all whom he knew would respond positively to it. It is less encouraging because it does not hold out the same hope for those who died without having heard the gospel.

8. E.g., Gabriel J. Fackre, "Divine Perseverance," in Sanders, *What about Those Who Have Never Heard?*, 71–95.

9. Most notably the Church of Jesus Christ of Latter-day Saints, or Mormons. See Robert L. Millet, "Salvation for the Dead," in *LDS Beliefs: A Doctrinal Reference*, by Robert L. Millet et al. (Salt Lake City: Deseret, 2011), 557–59.

10. David A. deSilva (*Perseverance in Gratitude: A Socio-Rhetorical Commentary on the Epistle "to the Hebrews"* [Grand Rapids: Eerdmans, 2000], 315) explains, "The maxim about death followed by judgment reinforces the author's strategic warning that leaving the group does not mean escaping danger, specifically in the form of being held accountable by the God whose Son they spurned." Were there a second chance after death, this logic would prove specious. Cf. Thomas R. Schreiner, *Commentary on Hebrews*, BTCP (Nashville: B&H, 2015), 286.

11. Sometimes also called (or slightly distinguished from) *conditional immortality* (which can mean that all people are annihilated but only believers resurrected). The most famous potential exponent of this position in recent decades has been John R. W. Stott (see David L. Edwards, with a response from John Stott, *Evangelical Essentials: A Liberal-Evangelical Dialogue* [Downers Grove, IL: InterVarsity, 1988], 315–29), who stops just short of saying he actually affirms it but "tentatively" (320) argues that it seemed to be a legitimate "possibility" (315).

12. E.g., John Sanders, "Inclusivism," in Sanders, *What about Those Who Have Never Heard?*, 21–55.

13. A view held almost exclusively outside evangelicalism. But see Gregory Macdonald, *The Evangelical Universalist*, 2nd ed. (Eugene, OR: Cascade, 2012). The author's published name is a pseudonym. In between the book's two editions, the author disclosed that he was in fact Robin A. Parry.

14. See, classically, John Hick, *An Interpretation of Religion*, 2nd ed. (New Haven: Yale University Press, 1989), 233–96.

15. Sir Norman Anderson, ed., *The World's Religions*, rev. ed. (London: Inter-Varsity, 1975; Grand Rapids: Eerdmans, 1976), 234.

16. Anderson, *World's Religions*, 235–36. Cf. Sanders, *No Other Name*, 241–49.

17. As a matter of fact, it has never happened in recorded history, but it has come close enough that it very much could happen. See Tom Skilling, "Ask Tom: Has Lake Michigan Ever Completely Frozen Over?," *Chicago Tribune*, December 19, 2017, https://www.chicagotribune.com/weather/ct-wea-asktom-1220-20171219-column.html.

18. William V. Crockett, "The Metaphorical View," in *Four Views on Hell*, ed. William Crockett (Grand Rapids: Zondervan, 1996), 43–76.

19. A view popularized in recent years particularly by Rob Bell, *Love Wins: A Book about Heaven, Hell, and the Fate of Every Person Who Ever Lived* (New York: HarperOne, 2011), 63–93. After this finite period of time, the position resolves into either annihilationism or universalism.

20. Best known among Roman Catholics and Latter-day Saints, respectively. For purgatory, see, e.g., Jerry L. Walls, "Purgatory and Hell," in *Four Views on Hell*, 2nd ed., ed. Preston

Sprinkle (Grand Rapids: Zondervan, 2016), 145–73. For the Latter-day Saints and hell, see Robert L. Millet, "Hell," in Millet et al., *LDS Beliefs*, 302–3. I will express my preferences below.

21. See esp. Heikki Räisänen, *Paul and the Law*, 2nd ed. (Eugene, OR: Wipf & Stock, 2010).

22. Martin Luther, *Commentary on Romans* (Grand Rapids: Zondervan, 1954), 57–61. For Calvin and other prominent supporters, see Douglas J. Moo, *The Epistle to the Romans*, NICNT (Grand Rapids: Eerdmans, 1996), 148n27.

23. C. K. Barrett (*The Epistle to the Romans*, 3rd ed., BNTC [Peabody, MA: Hendrickson, 1991], 35) explains, "Observation of created life is sufficient to show that creation does not provide the key to its own existence."

24. Grant R. Osborne (*Romans*, IVPNTC [Downers Grove, IL: InterVarsity, 2004], 58) remarks, "The main point is that every human being has been given by God a deep awareness of two things: (1) the existence and power of God and (2) each person's general guilt before God because of sin."

25. For a philosopher's introduction to each of these three arguments for God's existence, see Douglas L. Groothuis, *Christian Apologetics: A Comprehensive Case for Biblical Faith* (Downers Grove, IL: IVP Academic, 2011), 207–363. The foundational work for intelligent design is Michael Behe, *Darwin's Black Box: The Biochemical Challenge to Evolution* (New York: Simon & Schuster, 1996). But see now his *Darwin Devolves: The New Science about DNA that Challenges Evolution* (New York: HarperOne, 2019).

26. Cf. Moo, *Epistle to the Romans*, 142, though he prefers not to use the term "hypothetical" for the view.

27. Thus leading some to the view that these are *Christian* Gentiles. See esp. C. E. B. Cranfield, *A Critical and Exegetical Commentary on the Epistle to the Romans*, ICC (Edinburgh: T&T Clark, 1975), 1:162.

28. Luther, *Commentary on Romans*, 63.

29. Moo, *Epistle to the Romans*, 149n28.

30. Cranfield, *Epistle to the Romans*, 1:151–53.

31. Cf. Richard N. Longenecker, *The Epistle to the Romans*, NIGTC (Grand Rapids: Eerdmans, 2016), 277. Longenecker hints that he is moving in the direction of the third view I present, but he concludes, "Such teaching as appears in this passage is not given so that we might speculate further about how God deals with people other than ourselves. Rather, it is given so that those of us who know God by means of his 'special revelation,' however that revelation has been given, might be shamed into doing God's will when compared to those who have been given and know far less and yet do far more" (286).

32. Klyne R. Snodgrass, "Justification by Grace—to the Doers: An Analysis of the Place of Romans 2 in the Theology of Paul," *New Testament Studies* 32 (1986): 81.

33. E.g., John Wesley, as quoted in Sanders, *No Other Name*, 250. Another key Reformer holding this view was Ulrich Zwingli. Among modern commentators, see esp. James D. G. Dunn, *Romans 1–8*, WBC (Dallas: Word, 1988), 107. See also Moo, *Epistle to the Romans*, 150n34.

34. Further supporters of this position, in varying ways, include Glenn N. Davies, *Faith and Obedience in Romans: A Study in Romans 1–4* (Sheffield: JSOT Press, 1990), 53–71; Snodgrass, "Justification by Grace."

35. For an excellent survey of the various arguments utilized by "inclusivists" and their proponents (some of whom are quite theologically conservative and hold open the door just a crack for this kind of perspective), see Sanders, *No Other Name*, 215–80.

36. For a thorough discussion of the pros and cons of this kind of a position, see David K. Clark, "Is Special Revelation Necessary for Salvation?," in Crockett and Sigountos, *Through No Fault of Their Own?*, 35–45. Clark calls this the "implicit faith" view.

37. Cf. Craig L. Blomberg, "From Dialogue to Contextualization," in *Perspectives on Post-Christendom Spiritualities: Reflections on New Religious Movements and Western Spiritualities*, ed. Michael T. Cooper (Sydney: Morling, 2010), 100.

38. See, classically, Acts 1:8, which functions as a miniature outline of the entire book of Acts.

39. Alternately, he may be referring to what his own ministry and its offshoots have spawned thus far. Leon Morris (*The Epistle to the Romans*, PNTC [Grand Rapids: Eerdmans, 1988], 393) comments, "Does Paul really mean that every person in all the earth had heard the gospel? Or even every Jew? The answer in either case can scarcely be 'Yes.' In this very letter Paul is envisaging a missionary trip to Spain which implies that there were people there who had not heard the gospel. His meaning is rather what Bruce calls 'representative universalism'; the gospel had been widely enough preached for it to be said that representatives of Judaism throughout the known world had heard it (for this way of speaking cf. Col. 1:5–6, 23)."

40. "Any hint at universalism, syncretistic patterns of salvation, or reaching the Father through any other means than Jesus is here completely eliminated." Gerald L. Borchert, *John 12–21*, NAC (Nashville: Broadman & Holman, 2002), 110.

41. John 8:56 suggests simply that Abram looked forward to the day that God's promises (esp. in Gen. 12:1–4) would be fulfilled, not that the details of the life of Jesus of Nazareth were disclosed to him. Compare how Gal. 3:8 states that Abraham had the gospel preached in advance to him, by which Paul goes on to explain that he is referring to the promise of Gen. 15:6 that all nations would be blessed through Abraham.

42. Rodney A. Whitacre (*John*, IVPNTC [Downers Grove, IL: InterVarsity, 1999], 352) puts it this way: "This verse does not address the ways in which Jesus brings people to the Father, but what it does say is that no one who ends up sharing God's life will do so apart from Jesus, the unique Son of God who *is*, not just who conveys, truth and life." Of course, the degree to which one resonates with differences between the ages of salvation history depends in part on where one falls on the spectrum between classic dispensationalism and classic covenant theology.

43. Moisés Silva, ed., *New International Dictionary of New Testament Theology and Exegesis*, 2nd ed. (Grand Rapids: Zondervan, 2014), s.v. "ὄνομα," 3:514–22.

44. Clark H. Pinnock, "Acts 4:12—No Other Name under Heaven," in Crockett and Sigountos, *Through No Fault of Their Own?*, 107–15.

45. E.g., R. E. O. White, "'No One Comes to the Father but by Me,'" *Expository Times* 113 (2002): 116–17.

46. See further Peter Stuhlmacher, *Paul's Letter to the Romans: A Commentary*, trans. Scott J. Hafemann (Louisville: Westminster John Knox, 1994), 87–88.

47. Anthony C. Thiselton, *The First Epistle to the Corinthians*, NIGTC (Grand Rapids: Eerdmans, 2000), 1227.

48. Ben Witherington III, *Paul's Letter to the Philippians: A Socio-Rhetorical Commentary* (Grand Rapids: Eerdmans, 2011), 153–54.

49. But those who are not saved will nevertheless find themselves "submitting against their wills to a power which they cannot resist" (F. F. Bruce and E. K. Simpson, *Commentary on the Epistles to the Ephesians and the Colossians*, NICNT [Grand Rapids: Eerdmans, 1957], 210). Cf. Peter T. O'Brien, *Colossians, Philemon*, WBC (Waco: Word, 1982), 56, 129.

50. George E. Ladd, *A Theology of the New Testament*, rev. ed., ed. Donald A. Hagner (Grand Rapids: Eerdmans, 1993), 196.

51. This verse does not dispute the omnipresence of God; it merely indicates that his comfort remains unavailable to people in hell. See Charles L. Quarles, "The *'Apo* of 2 Thessalonians 1:9 and the Nature of Eternal Punishment," *Westminster Theological Journal* 59 (1997): 201–11.

52. Cf. Craig S. Keener, *The Gospel of Matthew: A Socio-Rhetorical Commentary*, 2nd ed. (Grand Rapids: Eerdmans, 2009), 269.

53. See throughout Craig L. Blomberg, *Interpreting the Parables*, 2nd ed. (Downers Grove, IL: IVP Academic, 2012).

54. Gregory K. Beale, *1–2 Thessalonians*, IVPNTC (Downers Grove, IL: InterVarsity, 2003), 188, with special reference to 4 Macc. 10:15. It is also worth asking if a soul can even be destroyed; even if it can, what then takes its place? Destruction of material things leads to other products resulting from the dissolution; why should it be any different with immaterial things?

55. Cf. Robert H. Gundry, *Mark: A Commentary on His Apology for the Cross* (Grand Rapids: Eerdmans, 1993), 839: "Taken strictly, the implied judgment might be less frightful than eternal damnation but more frightful than never having come into existence. One wonders what besides eternal damnation would be more frightful, however."

56. Leon Morris, *The Gospel according to Matthew*, PNTC (Grand Rapids: Eerdmans, 1992), 641.

57. The parallelism with the resurrection of the righteous is all the more significant because John never spells out in any detail what eternal condemnation looks like. See also 3:17–18; 5:24; 12:48; and Colin G. Kruse, *The Gospel according to John*, TNTC (Grand Rapids: Eerdmans, 2003), 154–55.

58. "The brief outbreak of evil at the end of the thousand years is John's way of saying that Satan's activity is not limited to the immediate threat to Christians from the Roman Empire in his own time. It can happen at any time and under a variety of circumstances. But the outcome is always the same. Satan is always defeated, whether thrown down from heaven (12:9), bound in the abyss (20:1–3) or thrown into the lake of fire (v. 10)." J. Ramsey Michaels, *Revelation*, IVPNTC (Downers Grove, IL: InterVarsity, 1997), 226–27. Apparently the same cycles would repeat throughout eternity if they were allowed to.

59. C. S. Lewis, *The Problem of Pain* (London: Geoffrey Bles, 1940), 115.

60. C. S. Lewis, *The Great Divorce* (London: Geoffrey Bles, 1948), 66–67.

61. See further Craig L. Blomberg, "Degrees of Reward in the Kingdom of Heaven?," *Journal of the Evangelical Theological Society* 35 (1992): 159–72.

62. Norval Geldenhuys, *Commentary on the Gospel of Luke*, NICNT (Grand Rapids: Eerdmans, 1951), 365. See further Craig L. Blomberg, "Eschatology and the Church: Some New Testament Perspectives," *Themelios* 23, no. 3 (1998): 3–26.

63. A favorite comment of international celebrity atheist apologist Richard Dawkins in his public appearances.

64. The seminal work in this area, which also contains a history of interpretation, is William J. Dalton, *Christ's Proclamation to the Spirits: A Study of 1 Peter 3:18–4:6*, rev. ed. (Rome: Pontificio Istituto Biblico, 1989).

65. See esp. John H. Elliott, *1 Peter: A New Translation with Introduction and Commentary*, AB (New York: Doubleday, 2000), 731–40. I have alluded to C. S. Lewis's views above, and he is sometimes charged with teaching postmortem evangelization. But he explicitly disavows it in *Problem of Pain*, 126.

66. The pioneering work in this area was Raymond A. Moody, *Life after Life*, now in a 3rd ed. (New York: HarperOne, 2015). See also esp. Eben Alexander, *Proof of Heaven: A Neurosurgeon's Journey into the Afterlife* (New York: Simon & Schuster, 2012); Todd Burpo with Lynn Vincent, *Heaven Is For Real: A Little Boy's Astounding Story of His Trip to Heaven and Back* (Nashville: Nelson, 2010).

67. That a few such claims have been fabricated and later discredited scarcely disproves the experience altogether.

68. "James's assertion can sound universalist if taken out of context, as if one day all would be saved. Here, however, he is discussing how mercy triumphs over judgment for the Christian. Those who never show any mercy cannot have internalized and accepted God's mercy." Craig L. Blomberg and Mariam J. Kamell, *James*, ZECNT (Grand Rapids: Zondervan, 2008), 120.

69. For the exact quote, see Vernon C. Grounds, "Heaven's Surprises," *Our Daily Bread*, March 21, 1996, https://odb.org/1996/03/21/heavens-surprises/.

Chapter 3 Slavery, Gender Roles, and Same-Sex Sexual Relations

1. See esp. D. A. Carson, *The Intolerance of Tolerance* (Grand Rapids: Eerdmans, 2012).

2. This debate deals with the question of whether it is possible to submit to others in practice (functionally) while still retaining equal intrinsic (ontological) worth as a person with others.

Contrast, e.g., Rebecca Merrill Groothuis, *Good News for Women: A Biblical Picture of Gender Equality* (Grand Rapids: Baker, 1997), 41–64, with Raymond C. Ortlund Jr., "Male-Female Equality and Male Headship," in *Recovering Biblical Manhood and Womanhood*, ed. John Piper and Wayne Grudem, rev. ed. (Wheaton: Crossway, 2006), 95–112.

3. E.g., Peter J. Paris, ed., with Julius Crump, *African-American Theological Ethics* (Louisville: Westminster John Knox, 2015).

4. See esp. William Webb, *Slaves, Women and Homosexuals: Exploring the Hermeneutics of Cultural Analysis* (Downers Grove, IL: InterVarsity, 2001).

5. E.g., Gregory C. Chirichigno, *Debt-Slavery in Israel and the Ancient Near East* (Sheffield: JSOT Press, 1993).

6. E.g., Hector Avalos, *Slavery, Abolitionism, and the Ethics of Biblical Scholarship* (Sheffield: Sheffield Phoenix, 2013).

7. See esp. Thomas Schirrmacher, ed., *The Humanisation of Slavery in the Old Testament* (Eugene, OR: Wipf & Stock, 2018). The most famous example is that of *limiting* revenge to an eye for an eye or a tooth for a tooth.

8. See esp. Christopher J. H. Wright, *Old Testament Ethics for the People of God* (Downers Grove, IL: InterVarsity, 2004).

9. For a good overview, see K. R. Bradley, *Slavery and Society at Rome* (Cambridge: Cambridge University Press, 1994).

10. Cf., e.g., James D. G. Dunn, *The Theology of Paul the Apostle* (Grand Rapids: Eerdmans, 1998), 698–701.

11. "To see those of different social classes . . . as equals, as brothers and sisters in Christ, is to establish an entirely new order, and such an order will witness against the Roman Empire's exploitative systemic injustices and more 'benign' world of status and honor. The power differential of slave and master is diminished dramatically in these two words: 'right and fair.'" Scot McKnight, *The Letter to the Colossians*, NICNT (Grand Rapids: Eerdmans, 2018), 367.

12. "The really remarkable thing is . . . that household life was so transformed 'in the Lord' that each person was precious to God, and that husbands and masters recognized that they had duties no less than rights" (C. F. D. Moule, *The Epistles of Paul the Apostle to the Colossians and to Philemon*, CGTC [Cambridge: Cambridge University Press, 1957], 128). Robert McL. Wilson (*A Critical and Exegetical Commentary on Colossians and Philemon*, ICC [New York: T&T Clark, 2005], 277n14) points out, "No small part of the problems of modern society is quite simply due to emphasis on rights to the neglect of responsibilities."

13. The main point of Richard W. Hove, *Equality in Christ? Galatians 3:28 and the Gender Dispute* (Wheaton: Crossway, 1999).

14. On which, see esp. Ben Witherington III, "Rite and Rights for Women—Galatians 3.28," *New Testament Studies* 27 (1981): 593–604.

15. Cf. Gordon D. Fee, *The First Epistle to the Corinthians*, rev. ed., NICNT (Grand Rapids: Eerdmans, 2014), 352–54.

16. For a fuller discussion of proslavery arguments from the Bible, see Willard Swartley, *Slavery, Sabbath, War, and Women: Case Studies in Biblical Interpretation* (Scottdale, PA: Herald, 1983), 31–37.

17. Scott Bartchy, *ΜΑΛΛΟΝ ΧΡΗΣΑΙ: First-Century Slavery and 1 Corinthians 7:21* (Missoula, MT: Scholars Press, 1973).

18. Alternately, he may have been sent to find Paul and ask him to function as an *amicus domini* (a "friend of the master") in mediating some dispute between Philemon and him. See esp. Chris Frilingos, "'For My Child, Onesimus': Paul and Domestic Power in Philemon," *Journal of Biblical Literature* 119 (2000): 91–104. See also Brian M. Rapske, "The Prisoner Paul in the Eyes of Onesimus," *New Testament Studies* 37 (1991): 187–203.

19. By modern standards, Paul sometimes seems to be manipulative, but by ancient standards his rhetoric is considerably toned down from what would have been expected. On which, see

esp. Andrew Wilson, "The Pragmatics of Politeness and Pauline Epistolography: A Case Study of the Letter to Philemon," *Journal for the Study of the New Testament* 48 (1992): 107–19. Carl R. Holladay (*A Critical Introduction to the New Testament: Interpreting the Message and Meaning of Jesus Christ* [Nashville: Abingdon, 2003], 383) terms it "a diplomatic masterpiece because of its sensitive handling of a delicate situation."

20. Ben Witherington III, *The Letters to Philemon, the Colossians, and the Ephesians: A Socio-Rhetorical Commentary on the Captivity Epistles* (Grand Rapids: Eerdmans, 2007), 75–76. Bernardo Cho ("Subverting Slavery: Philemon, Onesimus, and Paul's Gospel of Reconciliation," *Evangelical Quarterly* 86 [2014]: 99–115) shows how radical even the request to welcome Onesimus back as a beloved brother was.

21. E.g., David W. Pao, *Colossians and Philemon*, ZECNT (Grand Rapids: Zondervan, 2012), 395–96; Scot McKnight, *The Letter to Philemon*, NICNT (Grand Rapids: Eerdmans, 2017), 97–98.

22. Joseph A. Fitzmyer, *The Letter to Philemon: A New Translation with Introduction and Commentary*, AB (Garden City, NY: Doubleday, 2000), 24; Murray J. Harris, *Colossians and Philemon*, rev. ed., EGGNT (Nashville: B&H Academic, 2010), 278–79; Douglas J. Moo, *The Letters to the Colossians and to Philemon*, PNTC (Grand Rapids: Eerdmans, 2008), 436. Many commentators stop just short of affirming this because Paul never says so in so many words, but they nevertheless agree that Paul *hoped* for it.

23. For more on the formation of the Christian "canon" of Scripture, see Craig L. Blomberg, *Can We Still Believe the Bible? An Evangelical Engagement with Contemporary Questions* (Grand Rapids: Brazos, 2014), 43–84, and the literature cited there.

24. Jeremiah J. Johnston, *Unimaginable: What Our World Would Be Like without Christianity* (Grand Rapids: Bethany House, 2017), 180–86.

25. See esp. throughout Ruth A. Tucker and Walter Liefeld, *Daughters of the Church: Women and Ministry from New Testament Times to the Present* (Grand Rapids: Zondervan, 1987).

26. Including the Evangelical Free Church of America and Moody Bible Institute. See Janette Hassey, *Evangelical Women in Public Ministry around the Turn of the Century* (1986; repr., Minneapolis: Christians for Biblical Equality, 2008).

27. Key works of complementarians and egalitarians, respectively, were John Piper and Wayne Grudem, eds., *Recovering Biblical Manhood and Womanhood*, rev. ed. (Wheaton: Crossway, 2006); Ronald W. Pierce and Rebecca Merrill Groothuis, eds., *Discovering Biblical Equality: Complementarity without Hierarchy*, 2nd ed. (Downers Grove, IL: InterVarsity, 2005).

28. Craig L. Blomberg, "Women in Ministry: A Complementarian Perspective," in *Two Views on Women in Ministry*, ed. James R. Beck (Grand Rapids: Zondervan, 2005), 121–84. I have elsewhere argued that this position is really a third option; see Craig L. Blomberg, "Neither Hierarchicalist nor Egalitarian: Gender Roles in Paul," in *Paul and His Theology*, ed. Stanley E. Porter (Boston: Brill, 2006), 283–326.

29. See esp. Blomberg, "Women in Ministry," 169–72.

30. See esp. David Hill, *New Testament Prophecy* (Atlanta: John Knox, 1979), esp. 193–213.

31. On which, see Craig L. Blomberg, *1 Corinthians*, NIVAC (Grand Rapids: Zondervan, 1994), 211, and the literature cited there.

32. Wayne Grudem, *The Gift of Prophecy in 1 Corinthians* (1982; repr., Eugene, OR: Wipf & Stock, 1999), 239–55.

33. Philip B. Payne, "1 Tim 2.12 and the Use of *Oude* to Combine Two Elements to Express a Single Idea," *New Testament Studies* 54 (2008): 235–53.

34. Ben Witherington III (*The Letters to Philemon, the Colossians, and the Ephesians*, 328) explains that "the husband is to 'go ahead' or take the lead or initiative in active loving and self-sacrificial service as Christ has done in relationship to the church. 'Head' then means head servant, and refers to a sort of servant leadership (cf. Luke 22.25ff). If Christ, the one who lovingly offered himself as a sacrifice, is the model of headship, then general patriarchy and the assumptions of a patriarchal culture are not providing the model or the way it is to be enacted."

35. See further Steven Tracy, "Domestic Violence in the Church and Redemptive Suffering in 1 Peter," *Calvin Theological Journal* 41 (2006): 294.

36. There are several mediating perspectives that bring complementarian and egalitarian models very close together, and they deserve a continued hearing. See esp. Sarah Sumner, *Men and Women in the Church: Building Consensus on Christian Leadership* (Downers Grove, IL: InterVarsity, 2003); Michelle Lee-Barnewall, *Neither Complementarian nor Egalitarian: A Kingdom Corrective to the Evangelical Gender Debate* (Grand Rapids: Baker Academic, 2016).

37. For a full study, see Joan C. Campbell, *Phoebe: Patron and Emissary* (Collegeville, MN: Liturgical Press, 2009).

38. On whom, see esp. Eldon J. Epp, *Junia: The First Woman Apostle* (Minneapolis: Fortress, 2005).

39. Craig S. Keener, *Acts: An Exegetical Commentary* (Grand Rapids: Baker Academic, 2014), 3:2809–11. Cf. John B. Polhill, *Acts*, NAC (Nashville: Broadman, 1992), 382.

40. E.g., Wayne Grudem, *The Gift of Prophecy in the New Testament and Today*, rev. ed. (Wheaton: Crossway, 2000), 183–92.

41. Xenophon of Ephesus, *Anthia and Habrocomes*, in *Longus, Daphnis and Chloe, and Xenophon of Ephesus, Anthia and Habrocomes*, ed. and trans. Jeffrey Henderson, Loeb Classical Library 69 (Cambridge: Harvard University Press, 2009).

42. Gary G. Hoag, *Wealth in Ancient Ephesus and the First Letter to Timothy: Fresh Insights from Ephesiaca by Xenophon of Ephesus* (Winona Lake, IN: Eisenbrauns, 2015), 61–99.

43. The standard Greek lexica agree that "fear," "reverence," and "respect" are the three main meanings of the Greek verb (*phobeomai*) used here, and the major translations are in remarkable agreement that "respect" is the appropriate choice in this context. The KJV used "reverence" and the ASV "fear," but CEB, CJB, CSB, ESV, NAB, NASB, NET, NIV, NJB, NKJV, NLT, NRSV, and RSV all use "respect."

44. The most accurate translation of Phil. 2:4 is "not looking to your own interests (things) but each of you to the interests (things) of the others" (cf. CEB, KJV, NAB, NIV, NJB, NRSV), rather than the weakened form "not looking *merely* to your own interests (things) but each of you (also) to the interests (things) of the others" (cf. CSB, ESV, NASB, NET, NLT). There is no word in the Greek text corresponding to "merely."

45. As in the title of Webb's book, *Slaves, Women and Homosexuals*.

46. It is often alleged as well that the ancients knew nothing of sexual *orientation*, but this is simply not true. See esp. Branson Parler, "Worlds Apart: James Brownson and the Sexual Diversity of the Greco-Roman World," *Trinity Journal* 38 (2017): 183–200; see also James B. de Young, *Homosexuality* (Grand Rapids: Kregel, 2000), 152–53, 205–13.

47. See esp. Linda L. Belleville, *Sex, Lies, and the Truth: Developing a Christian Ethic in a Post-Christian Society* (Eugene, OR: Wipf & Stock, 2010), 51–105. To a lesser extent, the same or similar campaigns convinced countless Americans that all sex among consenting adults should be considered acceptable, with the possible exception of adultery. See the rest of Belleville's volume.

48. This is the main point of Webb, *Slaves, Women and Homosexuals*. The most thorough and accurate treatment of all the passages on this third topic is Robert A. J. Gagnon, *The Bible and Homosexual Practice: Texts and Hermeneutics* (Nashville: Abingdon, 2002). Unfortunately, the tone is not always as charitable as it might have been.

49. David E. Malick, "The Condemnation of Homosexuality in 1 Corinthians 6:9," *Bibliotheca Sacra* 150 (1993): 479–92.

50. David F. Wright, "Translating ΑΡΣΕΝΟΚΟΙΤΑΙ (1 Cor. 6:9; 1 Tim. 1:10)," *Vigilae Christianae* 41 (1987): 396–98.

51. Anthony C. Thiselton (*The First Epistle to the Corinthians*, NIGTC [Grand Rapids: Eerdmans, 2000], 439) puts it superbly: "*[Paul] is not describing the qualifications required for an entrance examination; he is comparing habituated actions, which by definition can find*

no place in God's reign for the welfare of all, with those qualities in accordance with which Christian believers need to be transformed if they belong authentically to God's new creation in Christ. Everything which persistently opposes what it is to be Christlike *must undergo change if those who practice such things wish to call themselves Christians and to look forward to resurrection with Christ"* (italics original).

52. Cf. Walter C. Kaiser Jr., "The Weightier and Lighter Matters of the Law: Moses, Jesus and Paul," in *Current Issues in Biblical and Patristic Interpretation*, ed. Gerald F. Hawthorne (Grand Rapids: Eerdmans, 1975), 176–92.

53. Most Jewish teachers recognized distinctions among the various laws of torah, distinguishing between more and less important ones. See Craig S. Keener, *The Gospel of Matthew: A Socio-Rhetorical Commentary*, 2nd ed. (Grand Rapids: Eerdmans, 2009), 551.

54. In fact, D. A. Carson ("Matthew," in *The Expositor's Bible Commentary*, ed. Tremper Longman III and David Garland, rev. ed. [Grand Rapids: Zondervan, 2010], 9:184), following a study by Klaus Haacker, argues that the Greek of Matt. 5:28 should be translated as "so as to get her to lust after him" rather than "so as to lust after her." It is the actual involvement of the second person that makes it comparable to (but not as wicked as) adultery.

55. *Porneia* (KJV "fornication"; NIV "sexual immorality"), an item commonly found in New Testament vice lists, in fact refers to all sexual relations with a person other than one's monogamous, heterosexually married spouse. See Joseph F. Jensen, "Does *Porneia* Mean Fornication? A Critique of Bruce Malina," *Novum Testamentum* 20 (1978): 161–84.

56. As noted above, the ancients did have a sense of sexual *orientation*. See esp. Parler, "Worlds Apart"; de Young, *Homosexuality*, 152–53, 205–13.

57. For elaboration of a number of these revisionist arguments against traditional exegesis here, see esp. James V. Brownson, *Bible, Gender, Sexuality: Reframing the Church's Debate on Same-Sex Relationships* (Grand Rapids: Eerdmans, 2013).

58. Convincingly rebutting Brownson is Preston M. Sprinkle, "Romans 1 and Homosexuality: A Critical Review of James Brownson's *Bible, Gender, Sexuality*," *Bulletin for Biblical Research* 24 (2014): 515–28. See also Sprinkle, "Paul and Homosexual Behavior: A Critical Evaluation of the Excessive-Lust Interpretation of Romans 1:26–27," *Bulletin for Biblical Research* 25 (2015): 497–517.

59. See esp. Stanton L. Jones and Mark A. Yarhouse, *Ex-Gays? A Longitudinal Study of Religiously Mediated Change in Sexual Orientation* (Downers Grove, IL: IVP Academic, 2007). For a fascinating history of the last century, see Tom Waidzunas, *The Straight Line: How the Fringe Science of Ex-Gay Therapy Reoriented Sexuality* (Minneapolis: University of Minnesota Press, 2015). He highlights the role of social constructivism in people's identification of their sexual orientation rather than the existence of any essentialist nature.

60. See esp. Wesley Hill, *Washed and Waiting: Reflections on Christian Faithfulness and Homosexuality*, rev. ed. (Grand Rapids: Zondervan, 2016).

61. For a thorough and wide-ranging treatment, see Elizabeth Abbott, *A History of Celibacy* (New York: Scribner, 2000).

62. St. Augustine, in his classic *Confessions* (10.31), describes how when he finally decided to stop having almost daily sex with his mistress, he realized he had to tackle his problem of gluttony. All of us struggle with self-restraint in some area or another!

63. See esp. Jenell Williams Paris, *The End of Sexual Identity: Why Sex Is Too Important to Define Who We Are* (Downers Grove, IL: InterVarsity, 2011).

64. For further debate, see esp. Preston M. Sprinkle, ed., *Two Views on Homosexuality, the Bible, and the Church* (Grand Rapids: Zondervan, 2016). See also Dan O. Via and Robert A. J. Gagnon, *Homosexuality and the Bible: Two Views* (Minneapolis: Fortress, 2003); Jeffrey S. Siker, ed., *Homosexuality in the Church: Both Sides of the Debate* (Nashville: Abingdon, 1994). For a robust defense of the historic Christian position and a demonstration that it is the very uniform view throughout church history (unlike views on slavery and gender roles, which have varied

considerably over the ages), see S. Donald Forston and Rollin G. Grams, *Unchanging Witness: The Consistent Teaching on Homosexuality in Scripture and Tradition* (Nashville: B&H, 2016).

Chapter 4 The Meaning of the Miracles

1. Thomas Jefferson, *The Jefferson Bible: The Life and Morals of Jesus of Nazareth, Extracted Textually from the Gospels in Greek, Latin, French & English* (Washington, DC: Smithsonian Books, 2011).

2. Robert W. Funk and the Jesus Seminar, *The Five Gospels: The Search for the Authentic Words of Jesus* (New York: Macmillan, 1993), 2–3.

3. For Funk's own perspective, even more radical than the Jesus Seminar's overall, see his *Honest to Jesus: Jesus for a New Millennium* (San Francisco: HarperSanFrancisco, 1996).

4. See, e.g., David Basinger, *Miracles* (Cambridge: Cambridge University Press, 2018); David Corner, *The Philosophy of Miracles* (New York: Continuum, 2007). A classic modern study is Richard Swinburne, *The Concept of Miracle* (New York: Macmillan, 1970).

5. The standard work here remains Peter Medawar, *The Limits of Science* (Oxford: Oxford University Press, 1984). See also Stephen M. Barr, *Modern Physics and Ancient Faith* (Notre Dame, IN: Notre Dame University Press, 2003); Francis S. Collins, *The Language of God: A Scientist Presents Evidence for Belief* (New York: Free Press, 2006).

6. For a recent example, see M. David Litwa, *Iesus Deus: The Early Christian Depiction of Jesus as a Mediterranean God* (Minneapolis: Fortress, 2014).

7. For the debate, see Craig L. Blomberg, *Can We Still Believe the Bible? An Evangelical Engagement with Contemporary Questions* (Grand Rapids: Brazos, 2014), 179–212, and the literature cited there.

8. See esp. Leah Bronner, *The Stories of Elijah and Elisha as Polemics against Baal Worship* (Leiden: Brill, 1968).

9. See esp. David Seccombe, *The King of God's Kingdom: A Solution to the Puzzle of Jesus* (Waynesboro, GA: Paternoster, 2000), 277–318.

10. For these and other arguments for the authenticity of the cores of the sizable majority of the Synoptic miracles, see John P. Meier, *A Marginal Jew: Rethinking the Historical Jesus*, vol. 2, *Mentor, Message, and Miracles* (New York: Doubleday, 1991), 509–1038.

11. For how this pairing plays itself out in determining a plausible outline for the entire Gospel, see Craig L. Blomberg, *Matthew*, NAC (Nashville: Broadman, 1992), 22–25.

12. Demonstrating his power for resurrection, Jesus shows his ability to give life in all its fullness both now and for eternity, roughly equivalent in Johannine idiom to what the Synoptics teach about the present and future kingdom. On the authenticity of this narrative, see esp. René Latourelle, *The Miracles of Jesus and the Theology of Miracles* (New York: Paulist Press, 1988), 229–38.

13. Craig L. Blomberg, *The Historical Reliability of John's Gospel* (Downers Grove, IL: InterVarsity, 2001).

14. Favoring the link are, e.g., Robert H. Stein, *Mark*, BECNT (Grand Rapids: Baker Academic, 2008), 410–11; Craig A. Evans, *Mark 8:27–16:20*, WBC (Nashville: Nelson, 2001), 29.

15. See further R. T. France, *The Gospel of Mark*, NIGTC (Grand Rapids: Eerdmans, 2002), 344–46.

16. See further Daniel Johansson, "'Who Can Forgive Sins but God Alone?' Human and Angelic Agents, and Divine Forgiveness in Early Judaism," *Journal for the Study of the New Testament* 33 (2011): 351–94.

17. For something similar, though not quite reasoning from the perceived fulfillment of the Isaianic prophecies to the arrival of the new age, see among the Dead Sea Scrolls 4Q521 II, 5–13.

18. See throughout Graham H. Twelftree, *Jesus the Exorcist: A Contribution to the Study of the Historical Jesus* (Peabody, MA: Hendrickson, 1993); Twelftree, *Jesus, the Miracle Worker: A Historical and Theological Study* (Downers Grove, IL: InterVarsity, 1999).

19. See further Graham H. Twelftree, " 'ΕΙ ΔΕ . . . ΕΓΩ ΕΚΒΑΛΛΩ ΤΑ ΔΑΙΜΟΝΙΑ'. . . ," in *Gospel Perspectives*, vol. 6, *The Miracles of Jesus*, ed. David Wenham and Craig Blomberg (1986; repr., Eugene, OR: Wipf & Stock, 2003), 361–400.

20. Cf. Amanda Witmer, *Jesus, the Galilean Exorcist: The Exorcisms in Social and Political Context* (New York: T&T Clark, 2012); Gerd Theissen and Annette Merz, *The Historical Jesus: A Comprehensive Guide* (Minneapolis: Fortress, 1996), 281–325; John Dominic Crossan, *The Historical Jesus: The Life of a Mediterranean Jewish Peasant* (San Francisco: HarperSanFrancisco, 1991), 303–53; Howard C. Kee, *Miracle in the Early Christian World* (New Haven: Yale University Press, 1983). The Jesus Seminar's skepticism in this arena was actually an anomaly.

21. Cf., e.g., Pieter F. Craffert, *The Life of a Galilean Shaman: Jesus of Nazareth in Anthropological-Historical Perspective* (Eugene, OR: Cascade, 2008).

22. See esp. Heinz Noetzel, *Christus und Dionysos: Bemerkungen zum religionsgeschichtlichen Hintergrund von Johannes 2,1–11* (Stuttgart: Calwer, 1960). There is no English-language equivalent to this work.

23. D. A. Carson, *The Gospel according to John*, PNTC (Grand Rapids: Eerdmans, 1991), 173.

24. See further Craig L. Blomberg, "The Miracles as Parables," in Wenham and Blomberg, *Gospel Perspectives*, 6:333–37.

25. E.g., Robert H. Gundry, *Mark: A Commentary on His Apology for the Cross* (Grand Rapids: Eerdmans, 1993), 636.

26. Steven M. Bryan, *Jesus and Israel's Traditions of Judgement and Restoration* (Cambridge: Cambridge University Press, 2002), 48.

27. James R. Edwards, "Markan Sandwiches: The Significance of Interpolations in Markan Narratives," *Novum Testamentum* 31 (1989): 193–216.

28. Joel R. Marcus, *Mark 1–8: A New Translation with Introduction and Commentary*, AB (New York: Doubleday, 2000), 404–21.

29. Cf. Stein, *Mark*, 326, 598; Ethelbert Stauffer, *Jesus and His Story*, trans. Richard and Clara Winston (New York: Knopf, 1960), 124–26.

30. Cf. James R. Edwards, *The Gospel according to Mark*, PNTC (Grand Rapids: Eerdmans, 2002), 198–99; William L. Lane, *The Gospel according to Mark*, NICNT (Grand Rapids: Eerdmans, 1974), 236.

31. Lane, *The Gospel according to Mark*, 266.

32. Murray J. Harris, "'The Dead Are Restored to Life': Miracles of Revivification in the Gospels," in Wenham and Blomberg, *Gospel Perspectives*, 6:298–99.

33. Indeed, a full slate of Elijah-Elisha comparisons with Jesus can be discerned in Luke. See John S. Kloppenborg and Joseph Verheyden, eds., *The Elijah-Elisha Narrative in the Composition of Luke* (London: Bloomsbury T&T Clark, 2014).

34. At the very least, "we perhaps glimpse the concept of a messianic community which in some sense shares the Messiah's special relationship to God." R. T. France, *The Gospel of Matthew*, NICNT (Grand Rapids: Eerdmans, 2007), 670.

35. F. F. Bruce, *The New Testament Documents: Are They Reliable?*, 5th ed. (Downers Grove, IL: InterVarsity, 1960), 73.

36. Gerd Theissen, *The Miracle Stories of the Early Christian Tradition*, trans. Francis McDonagh (Philadelphia: Fortress, 1983), 65–72.

37. Michael J. Wilkins, *Matthew*, NIVAC (Grand Rapids: Zondervan, 2004), 600.

38. Cf. Richard Bauckham, "The Coin in the Fish's Mouth," in Wenham and Blomberg, *Gospel Perspectives*, 6:219–52.

39. Hendrik van der Loos, *The Miracles of Jesus*, trans. T. S. Preston (Leiden: Brill, 1965), 686–87.

40. Of course, interpreters have to do this all the time, but it is not a little ironic if some who do this accuse those who stick solely with what the text does or doesn't say of having a lower view of Scripture's accuracy or authority than they do. It's not a case of the pot calling the kettle black; it's a case of the grass calling the elephant green! No fewer than six times in *Vital Issues in the Inerrancy Debate* (ed. F. David Farnell and Norman L. Geisler [Eugene, OR: Wipf & Stock, 2016], 187, 242, 269, 376, 390, 411) am I accused of denying the historicity of the catch of the fish with the coin in its mouth, when not once in any published writing have I ever suggested that we can know one way or the other. Readers of *Vital Issues* should assiduously check any quotations or summaries of others' views for accuracy, because many individuals have been falsely vilified here. The same is true of Norman L. Geisler and William C. Roach, *Defending Inerrancy: Affirming the Accuracy of Scripture for a New Generation* (Grand Rapids: Baker Books, 2011); Norman L. Geisler and F. David Farnell, *The Jesus Quest: The Danger from Within* (Camarillo, CA: Xulon, 2014).

41. See further Craig L. Blomberg, "New Testament Miracles and Higher Criticism: Climbing Up the Slippery Slope," *Journal of the Evangelical Theological Society* 27 (1984): 425–38.

42. The Greek word for "compassion" comes from a root that the KJV often translated as "bowels" (e.g., Phil. 1:8; Col. 3:12; 1 John 3:17), because the internal abdominal organs were often thought to be the seat of emotions. Edwards (*The Gospel according to Mark*, 230) attempts a modern equivalent when he speaks of "Jesus' gut-wrenching emotion on behalf of the crowd" here in 8:2.

43. Craig S. Keener (*Matthew: A Socio-Rhetorical Commentary* [Grand Rapids: Eerdmans, 2009], 434) thinks that "Jesus' compassion was the ultimate motivation for his acting," but using the adjective "ultimate" goes beyond what the text actually says and does not explain all the sick and disabled people Jesus encountered without healing them (e.g., at the pool of Bethesda in John 5:1–15).

44. The issue continues to be debated, however. Compare Bart D. Ehrman, "Did Jesus Get Angry or Agonize? A Text Critic Pursues the Original Jesus Story," *Bible Review* 21 (2005): 17–26, with Peter J. Williams, "An Examination of Ehrman's Case for ὀργισθείς in Mark 1:41," *Novum Testamentum* 54 (2012): 1–12. Darrell L. Bock (*Mark*, NCBC [Cambridge: Cambridge University Press, 2015], 137n68) notes that he has changed his mind from believing "compassion" to be original to now accepting "indignant" as original.

45. See further Craig L. Blomberg, "'Your Faith Has Made You Whole': The Evangelical Liberation Theology of Jesus," in *Jesus of Nazareth, Lord and Christ: Essays on the Historical Jesus and New Testament Christology*, ed. Joel B. Green and Max Turner (Grand Rapids: Eerdmans, 1994), 75–93.

46. The man must have had some extraordinary confidence in Jesus to come to him in the first place, as other synagogue authorities were already demonstrating hostility toward him. So Ronald J. Kernaghan (*Mark*, IVPNTC [Downers Grove, IL: InterVarsity, 2007], 111) may be correct in suggesting that the present imperative verb in v. 36 should be translated as "keep on believing."

47. Note how often Mark begins a sentence or clause with *kai* when the subsequent syntax shows a connection other than additive. See E. J. Pryke, *Redactional Style in the Marcan Gospel: A Study of Syntax and Vocabulary as Guides to Redaction in Mark* (Cambridge: Cambridge University Press, 1978), 32–135.

48. Ben Witherington III (*The Gospel of Mark: A Socio-Rhetorical Commentary* [Grand Rapids: Eerdmans, 2001], 200) observes, "The problem with hometown folks is that they know both too much and too little about a person. What they know has to do with their memories of what a person was like while growing up and becoming an adult. Once one has left town

and gone elsewhere, they know little about what is or is not true about the person over that period of time."

49. Most famously in Günther Bornkamm, Gerhard Barth, and Heinz Joachim Held, *Tradition and Interpretation in Matthew*, trans. Percy Scott (Philadelphia: Westminster, 1963), 52–57.

50. Paul F. Feiler, "The Stilling of the Storm in Matthew: A Response to Günther Bornkamm," *Journal of the Evangelical Theological Society* 26 (1983): 399–406.

51. For this somewhat ironic interpretation, see Robert Kysar, *John, the Maverick Gospel*, rev. ed. (Louisville: Westminster John Knox, 2007), 98–99. Kysar charts a middle ground between purely negative and positive interpretations.

52. Jack Deere, *Surprised by the Power of the Spirit: Discovering How God Speaks and Heals Today* (Grand Rapids: Zondervan, 1993), 117–43.

53. See esp. Michael H. Burer, *Divine Sabbath Work* (Winona Lake, IN: Eisenbrauns, 2012), 103–35.

54. The focus is thrown back on the authority of the one who challenges the law so directly. See further Sven-Olav Back, "Jesus and the Sabbath," in *Handbook for the Study of the Historical Jesus*, ed. Tom Holmén and Stanley E. Porter (Leiden: Brill, 2011), 3:2597–633.

55. Speaking about the centurion, Grant R. Osborne (*Matthew*, ZECNT [Grand Rapids: Zondervan, 2010], 292) notes, "That one of the very people most mistrusted by the Jewish people would be the one who showed them what faith really was is astounding."

56. The nobleman and his son in John 4:46–54 are most likely Gentiles; Malchus in Luke 22:49–51 was the slave of a wealthy person, not that rich person himself. Moreover, Malchus's injury was caused by Peter, Jesus's disciple, which sets it apart from all the other people Jesus heals. Jesus is restoring what Peter wrongly took from Malchus—his ear!

57. See Peter G. Bolt, "Life, Death, and the Afterlife in the Greco-Roman World," in *Life in the Face of Death: The Resurrection Message of the New Testament*, ed. Richard N. Longenecker (Grand Rapids: Eerdmans, 1998), 56–57.

58. Cf. Craig L. Blomberg, *Contagious Holiness: Jesus' Meals with Sinners* (Downers Grove, IL: InterVarsity, 2005).

59. Cf. Kelly R. Iverson, *Gentiles in the Gospel of Mark: "Even the Dogs under the Table Eat the Children's Crumbs"* (New York: T&T Clark, 2007), 183.

60. John Christopher Thomas, "'Stop Sinning Lest Something Worse Come upon You': The Man at the Pool in John 5," *Journal for the Study of the New Testament* 18 (1996): 3–20.

61. Most interpreters take v. 3b (literally, "in order that the works of God might be displayed in him") to explain why the man was born blind (vv. 1–3a). But this clause could also modify the next one, giving the reason for why Jesus must do the work of the one who sent him (v. 4). See Gary M. Burge, *John*, NIVAC (Grand Rapids: Zondervan, 2000), 272–73. In this case the text simply would not supply the reason for the man's congenital condition.

62. Hans-Josef Klauck (*Apocryphal Gospels: An Introduction*, trans. Brian McNeil [New York: T&T Clark, 2003], 223) approvingly cites Walter Bauer's summary of the relevant motives: "a pious yearning to know more, a naïve curiosity, delight in colourful pictures and folktales." It is possible that some of these emerged from the felt need to have Jesus "outdo" the pagan miracle workers of the day with respect to their kind of portents. Cf. Ulrike Riemer, "Miracle Stories and Their Narrative Intent in the Context of the Ruler Cult of Classical Antiquity," in *Wonders Never Cease: The Purpose of Narrating Miracle Stories in the New Testament and Its Religious Environment*, ed. Michael Labahn and Bert Jan Lietaert Peerbolte (New York: T&T Clark, 2006), 32–47.

63. See Craig L. Blomberg, *The Historical Reliability of the Gospels*, rev. ed. (Downers Grove, IL: IVP Academic, 2007), 115–19, and the literature cited there. Cf. also Tryggve N. D. Mettinger, *The Riddle of Resurrection: "Dying and Rising Gods" in the Ancient Near East* (Stockholm: Almqvist & Wiksell, 2001).

64. See Blomberg, *Can We Still Believe the Bible?*, 190–200, and the literature cited there.

65. Paul Fullmer (*Resurrection in Mark's Literary-Historical Perspective* [New York: T&T Clark, 2007]) surveys in detail the ancient literature on this one form of miracle, showing that in the Greco-Roman world the most common model is death and revival—to continued existence in this life—with the subject moving from confusion to enlightenment. In most cases the focus is not on a miracle worker; indeed, the gods must be the agents, but we do not learn more about them as a result.

66. See esp. Graham H. Twelftree, *In the Name of Jesus: Exorcism among Early Christians* (Grand Rapids: Baker Academic, 2007); see also Twelftree, *Paul and the Miraculous: A Historical Reconstruction* (Grand Rapids: Baker Academic, 2013).

Chapter 5 Weren't the Stories of Jesus Made Up from Greco-Roman Myths?

1. For a concise introduction, see Wayne A. Meeks, "The History of Religions School," in *The New Cambridge History of the Bible* (Cambridge: Cambridge University Press, 2015), 4:127–38. Put simply, 100–150 years ago, many biblical scholars thought that much of the Bible could be derived from pagan parallels in its world. The last century has turned predominantly to Jewish parallels as closer ones and biblical distinctives as preventing significant pagan derivation. More likely, the biblical authors were contrasting their views with pagan counterparts.

2. Wilhelm Bousset, *Kyrios Christos: A History of the Belief in Christ from the Beginnings of Christianity to Irenaeus*, rev. ed., trans. John E. Steely (Waco: Baylor University Press, 2013), originally published in German in 1913.

3. E.g., Reginald H. Fuller, *The Foundations of New Testament Christology* (New York: Scribner's Sons, 1965).

4. Nicely summarized in Andrew Ter Ern Loke, *The Origin of Divine Christology* (Cambridge: Cambridge University Press, 2017). Cf. esp. Chris Tilling, *Paul's Divine Christology* (Grand Rapids: Eerdmans, 2015); David B. Capes, *Old Testament Yahweh Texts in Paul's Christology* (Waco: Baylor University Press, 2017).

5. Larry W. Hurtado, "The Gospel of Mark: Evolutionary or Revolutionary Document?," *Journal for the Study of the New Testament* 40 (1990): 15–32.

6. See esp. Larry W. Hurtado, *Lord Jesus Christ: Devotion to Jesus in Earliest Christianity* (Grand Rapids: Eerdmans, 2003).

7. Loke, *Origin of Divine Christology*, 26–32; Larry W. Hurtado, *Honoring the Son: Jesus in Earliest Christian Devotional Practice* (Bellingham, WA: Lexham, 2018), 44–45.

8. Cf. N. T. Wright, *What Saint Paul Really Said: Was Paul of Tarsus the Real Founder of Christianity?* (Grand Rapids: Eerdmans, 1997), 65–67.

9. For a very scholarly anthology, see Thomas R. Blanton IV, Robert Matthew Calhoun, and Clare K. Rothschild, eds., *The History of Religions School Today: Essays on the New Testament and Related Ancient Mediterranean Texts* (Tübingen: Mohr Siebeck, 2014). The historical conclusions are not always as skeptical as a century ago, but sometimes they are.

10. A classic example is James G. Frazer, *The Golden Bough: A Study in Magic and Religion* (New York: Macmillan, 1922). Although this was a foundational work in its time, Frazer is now widely acknowledged to have too readily grouped together too many religious phenomena without always making the finer distinctions that were needed.

11. One of the more egregious combinations of genuine information, half-truths, and flat-out lies is Kersey Graves, *The World's Sixteen Crucified Saviors; Or, Christianity before Christ* (New York: Scriptura, 2015), originally published in 1875. For an online example, see the Listverse website, whose staff took over much of this and even more mythical works and reproduced selected contents uncritically in a post called "10 Christ-like Figures Who Pre-date Jesus," Listverse, April 3, 2009, https://listverse.com/2009/04/13/10-christ-like-figures-who-pre-date-jesus/. For a trenchant debunking of these approaches, see esp. Maurice Casey, *Jesus: Evidence and Argument or Mythicist Myths?* (New York: Bloomsbury T&T Clark, 2014).

12. In a work that has never been refuted but has been widely ignored, J. Gresham Machen (*The Virgin Birth of Christ* [New York: Harper, 1930]) presented the contents of these alleged parallels in detail and showed just how different they actually are.

13. E.g., the god Adonis is born from a myrrh tree; Dionysus comes from Zeus's sex with his daughter Persephone; Osiris and Horus are born from relations between gods and goddesses. Not one of these figures was ever even believed to be a human being, and none of the "mothers" are human beings, much less virgins! See also Mary Jo Sharp, "Is the Story of Jesus Borrowed from Pagan Myths?," in *In Defense of the Bible: A Comprehensive Apologetic for the Authority of Scripture*, ed. Steven B. Cowan and Terry L. Wilder (Nashville: B&H, 2013), 193–94.

14. Raymond E. Brown, *The Birth of the Messiah: A Commentary on the Infancy Narratives in the Gospels of Matthew and Luke* (New York: Doubleday, 1993), 523.

15. Plutarch, *Life of Alexander*, in *Lives*, vol. 7, *Demosthenes and Cicero. Alexander and Caesar.*, trans. Bernadotte Perrin, Loeb Classical Library 99 (New York: G. P. Putnam's Sons, 1919), 227.

16. Suetonius, *Life of Augustus*, in *Lives of the Caesars*, vol. 1, *Julius. Augustus. Tiberius. Gaius. Caligula.*, trans. J. C. Rolfe, Loeb Classical Library 31 (Cambridge, MA: Harvard University Press, 1914), 265, 267.

17. Cf. W. D. Davies and Dale C. Allison Jr., *A Critical and Exegetical Commentary on the Gospel according to Saint Matthew*, ICC (Edinburgh: T&T Clark, 1988), 1:214–16.

18. Isaiah 7:14, of course, is the prophecy of this very event, so it is not an exception to my statement. If an event occurred in Isaiah's day as a foreshadowing of the virginal conception, it was the special children of Isaiah and his wife (7:1; 8:1, 3), but they were offspring by normal sexual relations.

19. The unusually Semitic style of Luke 1–2 and its distinctive focus on Mary's and Elizabeth's perspectives have often been noted, and can plausibly be attributed to Luke's interviewing Mary during his two years in Israel (AD 57–59) while Paul languished in detention in Caesarea (Acts 23:12–24:27). For those who don't find the tradition of Lukan authorship of these two works compelling, the 80s remain the most commonly suggested date for their composition.

20. See, e.g., Otto Rank, Lord Raglan, and Alan Dundes, *In Quest of the Hero* (Princeton: Princeton University Press, 1990).

21. This is a passage that, though unique to John's account of the feeding of the five thousand, is nevertheless widely held to be authentic. See, e.g., C. H. Dodd, *Historical Tradition in the Fourth Gospel* (Cambridge: Cambridge University Press, 1963), 213–15.

22. In John's Gospel, for example, "eternal life" seems to function as something of an equivalent concept, inasmuch as such life begins now already in the present. But the "kingdom of God" theme is actually more pervasive in John than this. See Hannah F. Robinson, "The Fourth Gospel and the Mystery of the Kingdom of God" (PhD thesis, Middlesex University, 2015).

23. See esp. Bruce Chilton, *Pure Kingdom: Jesus' Vision of God* (Grand Rapids: Eerdmans, 1996); G. R. Beasley-Murray, *Jesus and the Kingdom of God* (Grand Rapids: Eerdmans, 1986).

24. Mary Ann Beavis ("Parable and Fable," *Catholic Bibilical Quarterly* 52 [1990]: 473–98) compares and contrasts Jesus's parables with Greek fables, especially those of Aesop, pointing out that the differences are not always as great as they have sometimes been alleged and that they create an expectation that such narratives were to be interpreted morally.

25. For this as the heart of Jesus's parables, see Craig L. Blomberg, *Interpreting the Parables*, rev. ed. (Downers Grove, IL: IVP Academic, 2012).

26. Cf. throughout Robert M. Johnston and Harvey K. McArthur, *They Also Taught in Parables: Rabbinic Parables from the First Centuries of the Christian Era* (Grand Rapids: Zondervan, 1990).

27. Craig L. Blomberg, *The Historical Reliability of the Gospels*, 2nd ed. (Downers Grove, IL: IVP Academic, 2007), 116.

28. See throughout Glen W. Bowersock, *Fiction as History: Nero to Julian* (Berkeley: University of California Press, 1994).

29. For a plausible reconstruction of the historical Apollonius, see B. F. Harris, "Apollonius of Tyana: Fact and Fiction," *Journal of Religious History* 5 (1969): 189–99.

30. See further Murray J. Harris, "'The Dead Are Restored to Life': Miracles of Revivification in the Gospels," in *Gospel Perspectives*, vol. 6, *The Miracles of Jesus*, ed. David Wenham and Craig Blomberg (1986; repr., Eugene, OR: Wipf & Stock, 2003), 299–301.

31. "Asclepius: Greco-Roman God," *Encyclopaedia Britannica*, accessed December 3, 2018, https://www.britannica.com/topic/Asclepius.

32. Cf. Graham H. Twelftree, "ΕΙ ΔΕ . . . ΕΓΩ ΕΚΒΑΛΛΩ ΤΑ ΔΑΙΜΟΝΙΑ . . . ," in Wenham and Blomberg, *Gospel Perspectives*, 6:383.

33. A. E. Harvey, *Jesus and the Constraints of History* (Philadelphia: Westminster, 1982), 100–104.

34. See further Graham H. Twelftree, *Jesus the Exorcist: A Contribution to the Study of the Historical Jesus* (Peabody, MA: Hendrickson, 1993), 13–52.

35. See esp. Maurice Casey, *The Solution to the "Son of Man" Problem* (New York: T&T Clark, 2007).

36. See esp. Larry W. Hurtado and Paul L. Owen, eds., *"Who Is This Son of Man?": The Latest Scholarship on a Puzzling Expression of the Historical Jesus* (New York: T&T Clark, 2012).

37. Michael F. Bird, "Christ," in *Dictionary of Jesus and the Gospels*, 2nd ed., ed. Joel B. Green, Jeannine K. Brown, and Nicholas Perrin (Downers Grove, IL: IVP Academic, 2013), 115.

38. For a good introduction, see Michael F. Bird, *Are You the One Who Is to Come? The Historical Jesus and the Messianic Question* (Grand Rapids: Baker Academic, 2009), 36–72.

39. Joseph A. Fitzmyer, *To Advance the Gospel: New Testament Studies*, 2nd ed. (Grand Rapids: Eerdmans, 1968), 218–35.

40. See esp. Barry Blackburn, *Theios Anēr and the Markan Miracle Traditions: A Critique of the Theios Anēr Concept as an Interpretative Background of the Miracle Traditions Used by Mark* (Tübingen: Mohr, 1991).

41. See esp. M. David Litwa, *Iesus Deus: The Early Christian Depiction of Jesus as a Mediterranean God* (Minneapolis: Fortress, 2014). See also Michael Patella, *Lord of the Cosmos: Mithras, Paul, and the Gospel of Mark* (New York: T&T Clark, 2006).

42. Samuel Sandmel, "Parallelomania," *Journal of Biblical Literature* 81 (1962): 1–13.

43. Prudentius, *Peristephanon* 10.1011–50.

44. Tertullian, *On Baptism* 5. For a good introduction, see Manfred Clauss, *The Roman Cult of Mithras: The God and His Mysteries* (New York: Routledge, 2001), 108–13.

45. Known only from Justin Martyr, *First Apology* 66. One liturgy for Mithraic worship has come to light; for the debate surrounding it, see Hans Dieter Betz, *The "Mithras Liturgy": Text, Translation, and Commentary* (Tübingen: Mohr Siebeck, 2005).

46. Affirmed nevertheless by, e.g., Acharya S/D. M. Murdock, "Mithra: The Pagan Christ," Truth Be Known, accessed June 1, 2016, http://www.truthbeknown.com/mithra.htm, who is widely cited by others online.

47. See esp. Everett Ferguson, *Baptism in the Early Church: History, Theology, and Liturgy in the First Five Centuries* (Grand Rapids: Eerdmans, 2009), 60–96.

48. See esp. Brant Pitre, *Jesus and the Jewish Roots of the Eucharist: Unlocking the Secrets of the Last Supper* (New York: Penguin, 2011).

49. See, e.g., Mary Douglas, ed., *Food in the Social Order: Studies of Food and Festivities in Three American Communities* (New York: Routledge, 1973).

50. Dennis E. Smith, *From Symposium to Eucharist: The Banquet in the Early Christian World* (Minneapolis: Fortress, 2003), 13–46.

51. Craig L. Blomberg, *Contagious Holiness: Jesus' Meals with Sinners* (Downers Grove, IL: InterVarsity, 2005), 86–93; Gerd Theissen, *The Social Setting of Pauline Christianity: Essays on Corinth*, trans. and ed. John H. Schütz (Philadelphia: Fortress, 1982), 145–74.

52. Cf. David W. Chapman, *Ancient Jewish and Christian Perceptions of Crucifixion* (Tübingen: Mohr Siebeck, 2008; Grand Rapids: Baker Academic, 2010), 43–96.

53. See throughout Chapman, *Ancient Jewish and Christian Perceptions of Crucifixion*, and for the primary sources, see David W. Chapman and Eckhard Schnabel, *The Trial and Crucifixion of Jesus: Texts and Commentary* (Tübingen: Mohr Siebeck, 2015).

54. For the historical narratives, see Richard A. Horsley with John S. Hanson, *Bandits, Prophets, Messiahs: Popular Movements at the Time of Jesus*, rev. ed. (Valley Forge, PA: Trinity Press International, 1999).

55. See, e.g., Richard Carrier, *On the Historicity of Jesus: Why We Might Have Reason for Doubt* (Sheffield: Sheffield Phoenix, 2014), 62. Carrier defines "resurrection" as "any restoration of life to the dead." He purports not to include "the survival or ascension of an already-immortal soul," but apparently the emphasis is on "already" because most of the so-called parallels in Greco-Roman mythology did involve the immortality of a soul and a new status conferred on it after death, sometimes temporarily visible in ethereal form.

56. On the immortality of the soul and the resurrection of the body, see N. T. Wright, *The Resurrection of the Son of God*, Christian Origins and the Question of God 3 (Minneapolis: Fortress, 2003), 32–84 and 129–206, respectively. For the exceptions, see Stanley E. Porter, "Resurrection, the Greeks and the New Testament," in *Resurrection*, ed. Stanley E. Porter, Michael A. Hayes, and David Tombs (Sheffield: Sheffield Academic, 1999), 52–81.

57. Murray J. Harris, *From Grave to Glory: Resurrection in the New Testament* (Grand Rapids: Zondervan, 1990), 31–36.

58. For a detailed treatment, see Tryggve N. D. Mettinger, *The Riddle of Resurrection: "Dying and Rising Gods" in the Ancient Near East* (Stockholm: Almqvist & Wiksell, 2001).

59. See, e.g., Wright, *What Saint Paul Really Said*, 34.

60. See, e.g., Pinchas Lapide, *The Resurrection of Jesus: A Jewish Perspective* (Philadelphia: Fortress, 1982).

61. His main work on the last of these is Carrier, *On the Historicity of Jesus*.

62. Carrier, *On the Historicity of Jesus*, 53.

63. As demonstrated by Casey, *Jesus*; Bart D. Ehrman, *Did Jesus Exist? The Historical Argument for Jesus of Nazareth* (New York: HarperCollins, 2012).

64. Carrier, *On the Historicity of Jesus*, 227. See Richard C. Miller, "Mark's Empty Tomb and Other Translation Fables in Classical Antiquity," *Journal of Biblical Literature* 129 (2010): 759–76.

65. For the fullest recent study, explicitly focusing on Plutarch, see Michael Licona, *Why Are There Differences in the Gospels? What We Can Learn from Ancient Biography* (Oxford: Oxford University Press, 2010).

66. Miller, "Mark's Empty Tomb," 772–73.

67. Bayes's theorem. See esp. Carrier, *On the Historicity of Jesus*, 596–601.

68. Carrier, *On the Historicity of Jesus*, 226.

69. Carrier (*On the Historicity of Jesus*, 62) intentionally erases this distinction by referring to "translation"-to-heaven accounts as resurrections if the person is ever said to be visible (apparently his definition of a "body") at any point after death, whether or not an actual ascension is ever narrated (227). Carrier also takes Miller's twenty categories, all of which I have quoted verbatim, and embellishes them just enough to make the parallels appear even more striking. Calling Mars Romulus's father becomes for Miller "son of god" and for Carrier "the son of God." Miller's "frightened subjects" becomes for Carrier "witnesses are frightened by his appearance and/or disappearance," neither of which is the case with Romulus. "Flight" becomes "some witnesses flee," even though none who fled the mayhem in the senate were said

to have witnessed anything with respect to Romulus. Miller's "great commission" is glossed as "instruction to future followers," though Romulus has no disciples who set out to spread his message. Some of this may be unintentional, but it is an important reminder always to research original stories that are being described rather than simply relying on later summaries (including mine!). For more of Carrier's and my views on resurrection, see Carl Stecher and Craig L. Blomberg, *Resurrection: Faith or Fact?*, with contributions by Richard Carrier and Peter S. Williams (Durham, NC: Pitchstone, 2019), 195–219 and 125–51, respectively.

70. See, respectively, Dennis R. MacDonald, *The Homeric Epics and the Gospel of Mark* (New Haven: Yale University Press, 2000); MacDonald, *Luke and Vergil: Imitations of Classical Greek Literature* (Lanham, MD: Rowman & Littlefield, 2015); MacDonald, *The Dionysian Gospel: The Fourth Gospel and Euripides* (Minneapolis: Fortress, 2017).

71. MacDonald, *Dionysian Gospel*, 23–123.

72. Dennis R. MacDonald, *Mythologizing Jesus: From Jewish Teacher to Epic Hero* (Lanham, MD: Rowman & Littlefield, 2015), 42–43.

73. MacDonald, *Mythologizing Jesus*, 43–44.

74. For one collection of very astute assessments of strengths and weaknesses, see Margaret M. Mitchell, "Review: Homer in the New Testament?," *Journal of Religion* 83 (2003): 244–60.

75. Craig S. Keener, *The Gospel of Matthew: A Socio-Historical Perspective* (Grand Rapids: Eerdmans, 2009); Keener, *The Gospel of John*, 2 vols. (Peabody, MA: Hendrickson, 2003).

76. For this concept and a response to it, with respect to the passion narratives, see Craig A. Evans, "The Passion of Jesus: History Remembered or Prophecy Historicized?," *Bulletin for Biblical Research* 6 (1996): 159–65.

77. It is widely agreed that what accounts for both the overlap and unique features of Matthew's infancy narrative (esp. versus Luke's) is that he is narrating the events required to make sense of the five fulfillment passages he cites in this material.

78. Cf. Steve Moyise, *Was the Birth of Jesus according to Scripture?* (Eugene, OR: Cascade, 2013).

79. The two most common and plausible explanations for this are both based on the fact that here, uniquely, Matthew speaks of the "prophets" in the plural as being fulfilled, suggesting that this summarizes a theme found in multiple places rather than quoting explicitly from a single passage. See further Craig L. Blomberg, *Matthew*, NAC (Nashville: Broadman, 1992), 69–70. The only point that is relevant here is that there is no Old Testament declaration that the Messiah was to be related to the town of Nazareth in any way, which could then have encouraged Matthew to make up a story associating him with that location.

80. See esp. Leonhard Goppelt, *Typos: The Typological Interpretation of the Old Testament in the New* (Grand Rapids: Eerdmans, 1982).

81. For detailed discussion of a classic example of this, in the Old Testament quotations in Matt. 1–2, see R. T. France, "Scripture, Tradition, and History in the Infancy Narratives of Matthew," in *Gospel Perspectives*, vol. 2, *Studies of History and Tradition in the Four Gospels*, ed. R. T. France and David Wenham (Sheffield: JSOT Press, 1982), 239–66.

82. See esp. the articles on each of the four Gospels in D. A. Carson and G. K. Beale, eds., *Commentary on the New Testament Use of the Old Testament* (Grand Rapids: Baker Academic, 2007).

83. A half century ago, classical scholar Moses Hadas and historian Morton Smith, both professors at Columbia University and neither a particular friend of Christianity, commented much more soberly than many of today's atheists do: "It is not unlikely that Jesus may have deliberately acted like a conventional (or conventionally unconventional) 'sage.' There is no doubt that the Greek ideal of the philosopher exercised a great influence in shaping the 'wise man' (the *hakam*) of rabbinic Judaism, and this influence was exercised and this figure shaped in Palestine during the century within which Jesus' lifetime fell. Jesus seems to have been in closer

touch with the Hellenizing elements of the Palestinian population than were the Pharisees; it would be surprising if he were less open to Hellenistic influences." *Heroes and Gods: Spiritual Biographies in Antiquity* (New York: Harper & Row, 1965), 162–63.

84. For both of these conclusions with key issues arising out of Paul, Hebrews, and John, see Ronald A. Nash, *The Gospel and the Greeks: Did the New Testament Borrow from Pagan Thought?*, 2nd ed. (Phillipsburg, NJ: P&R, 2003).

85. Samuel T. Lachs, *A Rabbinic Commentary on the New Testament: The Gospels of Matthew, Mark, and Luke* (New York: KTAV, 1987); John Lightfoot, *Commentary on the New Testament from the Talmud and Hebraica*, 4 vols. (Peabody, MA: Hendrickson, 1989).

Chapter 6 How Should We Respond to All the Violence in the Bible?

1. See esp. L. Daniel Hawk, *The Violence of the Biblical God: Canonical Narrative and Christian Faith* (Grand Rapids: Eerdmans, 2019); Heath A. Thomas, Jeremy Evans, and Paul Copan, *Holy War in the Bible: Christian Morality and an Old Testament Problem* (Downers Grove, IL: IVP Academic, 2013); C. S. Cowles et al., *Show Them No Mercy: Four Views on God and Canaanite Genocide* (Grand Rapids: Zondervan, 2003).

2. I owe most of the observations in this paragraph to my Old Testament colleague Richard S. Hess. Many of them can be found in his *Joshua*, TOTC (Downers Grove, IL: InterVarsity, 1996). For a very different though less convincing perspective that disputes many of these points, see John H. Walton and J. Harvey Walton, *The Lost World of the Israelite Conquest: Covenant, Retribution, and the Fate of the Canaanites* (Downers Grove, IL: IVP Academic, 2017).

3. See esp. Paul Copan and Matthew Flannagan, *Did God Really Command Genocide? Coming to Terms with the Justice of God* (Grand Rapids: Baker Books, 2014); Christian Hofreiter, *Making Sense of Old Testament Genocide: Christian Interpretations of* Herem *Passages* (Oxford: Oxford University Press, 2018); Paul Copan, *Is God a Moral Monster? Making Sense of the Old Testament God* (Grand Rapids: Baker Books, 2011).

4. See esp. throughout Craig L. Blomberg, *A New Testament Theology* (Waco: Baylor University Press, 2018).

5. E.g., André Trocmé, *Jesus and the Nonviolent Revolution*, rev. ed. (Walden, NY: Plough, 2003); Donald B. Kraybill, *The Upside-Down Kingdom*, 4th ed. (Scottdale, PA: Herald, 2011).

6. Glen H. Stassen, *Just Peacemaking: Transforming Initiatives for Justice and Peace* (Louisville: Westminster John Knox, 1992); Stassen, *Living the Sermon on the Mount: A Practical Hope for Grace and Deliverance* (San Francisco: Jossey-Bass, 2006); Stassen, ed., *Formation for Life: Just Peacemaking and Twenty-First Century Discipleship* (Eugene, OR: Wipf & Stock, 2013).

7. Cf. Craig S. Keener, *The Gospel of Matthew: A Socio-Rhetorical Commentary*, rev. ed. (Grand Rapids: Eerdmans, 2009), 197.

8. E.g., John R. W. Stott, *The Message of the Sermon on the Mount (Matthew 5–7): Christian Counter-Culture*, BST (originally published as *Christian Counter-Culture*; Downers Grove, IL: InterVarsity, 1978), 115.

9. See esp. Douglas J. Moo, "Jesus and the Authority of the Mosaic Law," *Journal for the Study of the New Testament* 20 (1984): 3–49.

10. John Nolland (*The Gospel of Matthew*, NIGTC [Grand Rapids: Eerdmans, 2005], 494) adds, "What is normally thought to be beyond valuing is preserved from its expected fate."

11. See further Craig L. Blomberg, *Interpreting the Parables*, rev. ed. (Downers Grove, IL: IVP Academic, 2012), 245–50.

12. Luke 22:35–38 is almost certainly a metaphorical command to be prepared for hostility. When Peter picks up two swords and Jesus replies, "That's enough!" he is showing that Peter has misunderstood him by interpreting him literally, not that two swords are sufficient for self-defense! Cf., e.g., I. Howard Marshall, *The Gospel of Luke*, NIGTC (Grand Rapids: Eerdmans, 1978), 827.

13. See further Marshall, *The Gospel of Luke*, 295–303.

14. The action was a dramatic prophetic object lesson, threatening the coming destruction of the temple if its leadership did not repent. See esp. E. P. Sanders, *Jesus and Judaism* (Philadelphia: Fortress, 1985), 61–71.

15. Not all translations are equally clear at this point. Compare the ESV ("And making a whip of cords, he drove them all out of the temple, with the sheep and oxen") with the NIV ("So he made a whip out of cords, and drove all from the temple courts, both sheep and cattle"). The Greek has nothing corresponding to either the "them" or the "with" of the ESV, while the *te . . . kai* construction regularly denotes "both . . . and," as in the NIV.

16. Since Paul was in Jerusalem when Stephen was stoned to death (Acts 7:59–8:1), he would almost certainly have heard about previous encounters between the first Christian leaders and the Sanhedrin there, no more than two or three years earlier. This may well have been the very period during which he was studying under Gamaliel, one of the Sanhedrin's most prominent members (5:34–40; 22:3).

17. These include (1) as a last resort; (2) sanctioned by a legitimate authority; (3) to redress a wrong suffered; (4) with a realistic chance of succeeding; (5) in order to reestablish peace and order; (6) proportionate to the wrong suffered; and (7) minimizing civilian casualties and collateral damage. For a good recent defense, see David Fisher, *Morality and War: Can War Be Just in the Twenty-First Century?* (Oxford: Oxford University Press, 2013).

18. But see Harold O. J. Brown, "The Crusade or Preventive War," in *War: Four Christian Views*, ed. Robert G. Clouse (Downers Grove, IL: InterVarsity, 1981), 151–88.

19. See the especially helpful comments of Grant R. Osborne, *Romans*, IVPNTC (Downers Grove, IL: InterVarsity, 2004), 343.

20. Cf. Stanley E. Porter, "Romans 13:1–7 as Pauline Political Rhetoric," *Filología Neotestamentaria* 3 (1990): 115–39.

21. "Nero had promised to abolish indirect taxes because of the abuses, but his advisors did not let him do so, which led to some general consternation." Ben Witherington III, *Paul's Letter to the Romans: A Socio-Rhetorical Commentary*, with Darlene Hyatt (Grand Rapids: Eerdmans, 2004), 313.

22. Michael B. Thompson, *Clothed with Christ: The Example and Teaching of Jesus in Romans 12.1–15.13* (1991; repr., Eugene, OR: Wipf & Stock, 2011), 90–110.

23. "Peter reminded his readers at the outset that rulers are merely creatures, created by God and existing under his lordship." Thomas R. Schreiner, *1, 2 Peter, Jude*, NAC (Nashville: Broadman & Holman, 2003), 128.

24. Johannes P. Louw and Eugene A. Nida (*Greek-English Lexicon of the New Testament Based on Semantic Domains*, 2nd ed. [New York: United Bible Societies, 1989], 1:474) place this use of the verb in the semantic domain of "Control, Restrain" and translate, "to the king who is the one who controls."

25. "In what is apparently mild irony Peter has put the emperor on the same level as 'all people.'" Wayne A. Grudem, *The First Epistle of Peter*, TNTC (Grand Rapids: Eerdmans, 1988), 123.

26. Bruce Winter (*Seek the Welfare of the City: Christians as Benefactors and Citizens* [Grand Rapids: Eerdmans, 1994], 25–40) demonstrates the prominent role of awarding civic honors to generous, private benefactors as part of the task of commending those who do right.

27. See esp. J. Nelson Kraybill, *Apocalypse and Allegiance: Worship, Politics, and Devotion in the Book of Revelation* (Grand Rapids: Brazos, 2010). See also Michael J. Gorman, *Reading Revelation Responsibly: Uncivil Worship and Witness; Following the Lamb into the New Creation* (Eugene, OR: Cascade, 2011).

28. Morna D. Hooker (*The Gospel according to Saint Mark*, BNTC [Peabody, MA: Hendrickson, 1991], 208) captures it succinctly: "The cost is comprehensive, but so is the reward."

29. On the utter shame of all this in Paul's cultures (Jewish, Greek, and Roman), see Jennifer A. Glancy, "Boasting of Beatings (2 Corinthians 11:23–25)," *Journal of Biblical Literature* 123 (2004): 99–135.

30. William R. Baker (*2 Corinthians*, CPNIVC [Joplin, MO: College Press, 1999], 433) rightly calls this verse the "signature motto" for the whole letter and for Paul's entire apostolic life. For a profound exploration of this theme throughout the epistle, see Timothy B. Savage, *Power through Weakness: Paul's Understanding of the Christian Ministry in 2 Corinthians* (Cambridge: Cambridge University Press, 1997).

31. Jean-Michel Hornus, *It Is Not Lawful for Me to Fight: Early Christian Attitudes toward War, Violence, and the State*, trans. Alan Kreider and Oliver Coburn (1980; repr., Eugene, OR: Wipf & Stock, 2009). For a full compilation of the primary sources, see George Kalantzis, *Caesar and the Lamb: Early Christian Attitudes toward War and Military Service* (Eugene, OR: Cascade, 2012).

32. It is also not thinking as a Christian when someone cites the American Constitution's Bill of Rights (or any other country's founding documents) as if they were somehow inspired or as if they justified holding to a view whether or not it squares with Scripture.

33. For a good anthology of studies, many of them reflecting this perspective, see Richard S. Hess and Elmer A. Martens, eds., *War in the Bible and Terrorism in the Twenty-First Century* (Winona Lake, IN: Eisenbrauns, 2008).

34. See esp. Tremper Longman III and Daniel G. Reid, *God Is a Warrior* (Grand Rapids: Zondervan, 1995), 91–192.

35. Some commentators speculate that Mark, in the way he narrates this event, is taking a swipe, as it were, against Rome, but it is harder to be sure about this. See, classically, Ched Myers, *Binding the Strong Man: A Political Reading of Mark's Story of Jesus*, rev. ed. (Maryknoll: Orbis, 2008), 190–94.

36. "Luke is trying to get across the idea that Christianity has nothing to do with magic, and that Jesus' name is no magical-incantation formula" (Joseph A. Fitzmyer, *The Acts of the Apostles: A New Translation with Introduction and Commentary*, AB [New York: Doubleday, 1998], 646). Clinton E. Arnold (*Ephesians: Power and Magic* [Cambridge: Cambridge University Press, 1989], 19) observes that "in religion one prays and requests from the gods; in magic one commands the gods and therefore expects guaranteed results."

37. Ernest Best, *A Critical and Exegetical Commentary on Ephesians*, ICC (Edinburgh: T&T Clark, 1998), 597.

38. It is certainly the case that God's word is central in fighting the devil's attacks through all of this world's false teaching. Cf. Rudolf Schnackenburg, *Ephesians: A Commentary*, trans. Helen Heron (Edinburgh: T&T Clark, 1991), 279–80.

39. "It is important to remember that spiritual warfare has nothing to do with literal, physical warfare against human enemies. It represents a struggle against the ultimate enemies—the spiritual forces that stand behind and incite acts of literal violence, aggression, strife, hatred, bitterness, and actual flesh and blood warfare. Spiritual warfare is the solution to human warfare." Clinton E. Arnold, *Ephesians*, ZECNT (Grand Rapids: Zondervan, 2010), 455.

40. Cf. Donald Guthrie, *The Relevance of John's Apocalypse* (Grand Rapids: Eerdmans, 1987), 46–51.

41. David E. Aune, *Revelation 6–16*, WBC (Nashville: Nelson, 1998), 527.

42. "John would no doubt have laughed at attempts to identify this horde with a group of human beings for he is talking about powers and principalities." Ben Witherington III, *Revelation*, NCBC (Cambridge: Cambridge University Press, 2003), 154.

43. Grant R. Osborne, *Revelation*, BECNT (Grand Rapids: Baker Academic, 2002), 595.

44. Alan F. Johnson, "Revelation," in *The Expositor's Bible Commentary*, ed. Frank E. Gaebelein (Grand Rapids: Zondervan, 1981), 12:552.

45. The army accompanying Christ "is never said to fight. In fact, they are wearing ceremonial garments, not armor or battle gear. Christ does whatever fighting is required, and that by his word" (Witherington, *Revelation*, 243).

46. Klyne R. Snodgrass, *Stories with Intent: A Comprehensive Guide to the Parables of Jesus*, 2nd ed. (Grand Rapids: Eerdmans, 2018).

47. See further R. T. France, *The Gospel of Matthew*, NICNT (Grand Rapids: Eerdmans, 2007), 536–37.

48. See esp. Glen H. Stassen and David P. Gushee, *Kingdom Ethics: Following Jesus in Contemporary Context* (Downers Grove, IL: InterVarsity, 2003), 194–214.

49. See Blomberg, *Interpreting the Parables*, 281–88.

50. Stopping just short of acknowledging this claim are Robertson McQuilkin and Paul Copan (*An Introduction to Biblical Ethics: Walking in the Way of Wisdom*, 3rd ed. [Downers Grove, IL: IVP Academic, 2014], 421), who nevertheless note the relative paucity of material.

51. Cf. Craig L. Blomberg and Mariam J. Kamell, *James*, ZECNT (Grand Rapids: Zondervan, 2008), 199–200.

52. Walter C. Kaiser Jr., *Toward Old Testament Ethics* (Grand Rapids: Zondervan, 1983), 175–77.

53. Moreover, "the law of reciprocity is not utterly repudiated but only taken out of human hands to be placed in divine hands" (W. D. Davies and Dale C. Allison Jr., *A Critical and Exegetical Commentary on the Gospel according to Saint Matthew*, ICC [Edinburgh: T&T Clark, 1988], 1:540). See also Rom. 12:19.

54. Ulrich Luz, *Matthew 21–28: A Commentary*, Hermeneia (Minneapolis: Fortress, 2005), 245.

55. Cf. Ben Witherington III, *Matthew*, SHBC (Macon, GA: Smyth & Helwys, 2006), 154: "It makes no sense whatsoever in light of the other discourses of Jesus in this Gospel, particularly the critiques of the Pharisees and other religious leaders, to see this as some sort of call never to criticize anyone or anything. . . . The issue here has to do with unfair critiques, uncharitable evaluations, and also, as the metaphorical illustration makes clear, judging others by a different standard than one uses to judge oneself."

56. Moisés Silva, ed., *New International Dictionary of New Testament Theology and Exegesis*, 2nd ed. (Grand Rapids: Zondervan, 2014), s.v. "κρίνω," 2:748.

57. If Christians would observe Paul's restrictions today, this would remove another key obstacle from belief in God: our negative attitudes to outsiders. See further Craig L. Blomberg, "The New Testament Definition of Heresy (or When Do Jesus and the Apostles Really Get Mad?)," *Journal of the Evangelical Theological Society* 45 (2002): 59–72.

58. Indeed, Paul does not forbid seeking justice for ourselves, merely that if it is in a dispute with fellow Christians, we do so via some intra-Christian conflict resolution mechanism, so as not to bring the gospel into still further disrepute before a watching world. See further Craig L. Blomberg, "Applying 1 Corinthians in the Early Twenty-First Century," *Southwestern Journal of Theology* 45 (2002): 19–38.

Chapter 7 The Problems of Prayer and Predestination

1. For a published version of this part of his story, see Carl Stecher, "Living without Gods," in *Resurrection: Faith or Fact?*, by Carl Stecher and Craig Blomberg with contributions by Richard Carrier and Peter S. Williams (Durham, NC: Pitchstone, 2019), 14.

2. Francis A. Schaeffer, *He Is There and He Is Not Silent* (Carol Stream, IL: Tyndale, 1972).

3. There are times, though, when even thoughtful scholars approach this language, as with Roger E. Olson's insistence to continue to speak of "Divine Determinism" as the strong Calvinist position (*Against Calvinism* [Grand Rapids: Zondervan, 2011], 70–101).

4. E.g., respectively, William L. Craig, *The Only Wise God: The Compatibility of Divine Foreknowledge and Human Freedom* (1987; repr., Eugene, OR: Wipf & Stock, 1999); Peter J.

Thuesen, *Predestination: The American Career of a Contentious Doctrine* (Oxford: Oxford University Press, 2009); Terrance Tiessen, *Providence and Prayer: How Does God Work in the World?* (Downers Grove, IL: InterVarsity, 2000).

5. Most recently, in Christopher Fisher, *God Is Open: Examining the Open Theism of the Biblical Authors* (Scotts Valley, CA: Create Space, 2017), 81–375.

6. For an excellent treatment of the teachings and the dangers, see David W. Jones and Russell S. Woodbridge, *Health, Wealth & Happiness: Has the Prosperity Gospel Overshadowed the Gospel of Christ?* (Grand Rapids: Kregel, 2011).

7. Cf. Craig S. Keener, *Matthew*, IVPNTC (Downers Grove, IL: InterVarsity, 1997), 160; David E. Garland, *Reading Matthew: A Literary and Theological Commentary on the First Gospel* (New York: Crossroad, 1993), 87.

8. See esp. William R. Telford, *The Barren Temple and the Withered Tree: A Redaction-Critical Analysis of the Cursing of the Fig-Tree Pericope in Mark's Gospel and Its Relation to the Cleansing of the Temple Tradition* (Sheffield: JSOT Press, 1980). See also Esther Miguel, "The Impatient Jesus and the Fig Tree: Marcan Disguised Discourse against the Temple," *Biblical Theology Bulletin* 45 (2015): 144–54.

9. Telford, *The Barren Temple and the Withered Tree*, 238–39.

10. David L. Turner, *Matthew*, BECNT (Grand Rapids: Baker Academic, 2008), 569; Leon Morris, *The Gospel according to Matthew*, PNTC (Grand Rapids: Eerdmans, 1992), 596.

11. Craig A. Evans, *Matthew*, NCBC (Cambridge: Cambridge University Press, 2012), 364; John Nolland, *The Gospel of Matthew*, NIGTC (Grand Rapids: Eerdmans, 2005), 865.

12. E.g., Joyce Meyer, quoted in Jones and Woodbridge, *Health, Wealth & Happiness*, 91.

13. Ronald Kernaghan, *Mark*, IVPNTC (Downers Grove, IL: InterVarsity, 2007), 220. Cf. Darrell L. Bock, *Mark*, NCBC (Cambridge: Cambridge University Press, 2015), 296: "It may be that the call is to trust that God will carry out the justice and accountability for the nation that Jesus has been dealing with in his most recent actions."

14. As often in the prosperity gospel or various parts of the charismatic movement.

15. Moisés Silva, ed., *New International Dictionary of New Testament Theology and Exegesis* (Grand Rapids: Zondervan, 2014), s.v. "ὄνομα," 3:514–22.

16. D. A. Carson, *The Gospel according to John*, PNTC (Grand Rapids: Eerdmans, 1991), 497. L. Scott Kellum (*The Unity of the Farewell Discourse: The Literary Integrity of John 13.31–16.33* [New York: T&T Clark, 2004], 158) adds that "the promise is not to benefit the believer alone; however, its purpose is to glorify the Father."

17. Cf. J. Carl Laney, "Abiding Is Believing: The Analogy of the Vine in John 15:1–6," *Bibliotheca Sacra* 146 (1989): 55–66. For an excellent study of the concept of abiding throughout John's Gospel, see Dean Wertz, "The Abide Project's Effect on Experiencing God in Daily Life" (DMin thesis, Denver Seminary, 2019), 28–91.

18. John C. Stube (*A Graeco-Roman Rhetorical Reading of the Farewell Discourse* [New York: T&T Clark, 2006], 144) notes that as believers abide in Jesus, "what they want will be what Jesus wants since he is in them and they in him. The content of their prayers, then, will be molded by the reciprocal relationship." Cf. Gerald L. Borchert, *John 12–21*, NAC (Nashville: Broadman & Holman, 2002), 145.

19. "Such suffering is part and parcel of the message of the Christian gospel. The gospel is not about an esoteric experience where adherents may be taken away from their troubles. It is about confronting problems head-on, without flinching." Kim Huat Tan, *Mark*, NCCS (Eugene, OR: Cascade, 2015), 219.

20. As alleged by, e.g., Kenneth E. Hagin, quoted in Bruce Barron, *The Health and Wealth Gospel: What's Going on Today in a Movement That Has Shaped the Faith of Millions?* (Downers Grove, IL: InterVarsity, 1987), 107–8.

21. And the rescue was complete at the exaltation. Cf. Harold W. Attridge, *The Epistle to the Hebrews: A Commentary*, Hermeneia (Philadelphia: Fortress, 1989), 150. God also heard

Christ in that he accepted his offering on the cross. Cf. Gareth L. Cockerill, *The Epistle to the Hebrews*, NICNT (Grand Rapids: Eerdmans, 2012), 246.

22. Three excellent treatments of prayer in Luke-Acts are David M. Crump, *Jesus the Intercessor: Prayer and Christology in Luke-Acts* (Tübingen: Mohr, 1992); Steven F. Plymale, *The Prayer Texts of Luke-Acts* (New York: Peter Lang, 1991); Geir Otto Holmås, *Prayer and Vindication in Luke-Acts: The Theme of Prayer within the Context of the Legitimating and Edifying Objective of the Lukan Narrative* (New York: T&T Clark, 2011).

23. See the excellent discussion of "the peace of God" here in Markus Bockmuehl, *The Epistle to the Philippians*, BNTC (Peabody, MA: Hendrickson, 1998), 247.

24. Cf. Ben Witherington III, *The Epistle to the Philippians: A Socio-Rhetorical Commentary* (Grand Rapids: Eerdmans, 2011), 276, who stresses how the verb "to do" has to be read into the verse; the CEB's "endure" is preferable in this context.

25. See further Craig L. Blomberg, *Christians in an Age of Wealth: A Biblical Theology of Stewardship* (Grand Rapids: Zondervan, 2013); Blomberg, *Neither Poverty nor Riches: A Biblical Theology of Possessions* (Downers Grove, IL: InterVarsity, 2001).

26. See the excellent and thorough survey of these three main categories of solutions, with similar results, in Murray J. Harris, *The Second Epistle to the Corinthians*, NIGTC (Grand Rapids: Eerdmans, 2005), 853–59. See also Margaret E. Thrall, *A Critical and Exegetical Commentary on the Second Epistle to the Corinthians*, ICC (Edinburgh: T&T Clark, 2000), 2:807–18.

27. We could easily imagine that one prayer guaranteed to reflect God's will would involve the salvation or sanctification of another person. But granting these requests also must not violate that other person's free will, and tragically people often choose to reject or to disobey Christ.

28. The church was Mission Hills Baptist Church, at that time located in Greenwood Village, Colorado.

29. See esp. the detailed documentation in Craig S. Keener, *Miracles: The Credibility of the New Testament Accounts*, 2 vols. (Grand Rapids: Baker Academic, 2011).

30. Cf. Luke Timothy Johnson, *The Letter of James: A New Translation with Introduction and Commentary*, AB (New York: Doubleday, 1995), 278; Scot McKnight, *The Letter of James*, NICNT (Grand Rapids: Eerdmans, 2011), 330.

31. Douglas J. Moo, *The Letter of James*, TNTC (Grand Rapids: Eerdmans, 1985), 182. Ben Witherington III (*Letters and Homilies for Jewish Christians: A Socio-Rhetorical Commentary on Hebrews, James and Jude* [Downers Grove, IL: IVP Academic, 2007], 544–45) adds that "this is probably not a prayer that believes something *specific* about what God will do, although that is not excluded, but a prayer that is offered out of a basic unconditional trust that God knows what is best and can handle the situation" (italics original).

32. In James alone, the commands to prayer are consistently in the present tense (a grammatical form used to indicate the unfolding nature of the action) and in the second-person plural, to James's entire communities. Cf. Chris A. Vlachos, *James*, EGGNT (Nashville: B&H, 2013), 25.

33. See esp. D. A. Carson, *Divine Sovereignty and Human Responsibility: Biblical Perspectives in Tension* (1994; repr., Eugene, OR: Wipf & Stock, 2002).

34. "God's work and the believer's efforts are coextensive, thereby excluding, as non-Pauline, any kind of synergism whereby some 'division of labor' might come into play between God and the Philippians." Joseph H. Hellerman, *Philippians*, EGGNT (Nashville: B&H, 2015), 132.

35. Even so, Paul's real point "is not to protect himself theologically, but to encourage the Philippians that God is on the side of his people, that he not only has their concern at heart, but actively works in their behalf for the sake of his own good pleasure." Gordon D. Fee, *Paul's Letter to the Philippians*, NICNT (Grand Rapids: Eerdmans, 1995), 237–38.

36. Cf. Carson, *Divine Sovereignty and Human Responsibility*, 9–10.

37. An excellent treatment of this concept appears in David P. Scaer, "The Doctrine of Election: A Lutheran Note," in *Perspectives in Contemporary Theology*, ed. Kenneth S. Kantzer and Stanley N. Gundry (Grand Rapids: Baker, 1979), 105–15.

38. The best treatment from this perspective is William W. Klein, *The New Chosen People: A Corporate View of Election*, 2nd ed. (Eugene, OR: Wipf & Stock, 2015).

39. This example comes from William W. Klein in oral communication. For an excellent treatment of the influence of preunderstandings and presuppositions in all of this, see his "Exegetical Rigor with Hermeneutical Humility: The Calvinist-Arminian Debate and the New Testament," in *New Testament Greek and Exegesis: Essays in Honor of Gerald F. Hawthorne*, ed. Amy M. Donaldson and Timothy B. Sailors (Grand Rapids: Eerdmans, 2003), 23–36.

40. See esp. Markus Barth, *Ephesians 1–3: A New Translation with Introduction and Commentary*, AB (Garden City, NY: Doubleday, 1974), 105–9.

41. Stanley K. Stowers, *The Diatribe and Paul's Letter to the Romans* (Chico, CA: Scholars Press, 1981), 113–14.

42. Thomas R. Schreiner, *Romans*, 2nd ed., BECNT (Grand Rapids: Baker Academic, 2018), 501–6.

43. Thoroughly argued in C. E. B. Cranfield, *A Critical and Exegetical Commentary on the Epistle to the Romans*, ICC (Edinburgh: T&T Clark, 1979), 2:492–97.

44. Gordon R. Lewis and Bruce A. Demarest, *Integrative Theology*, 3 vols. in 1 (Grand Rapids: Zondervan, 1996), 8.

45. Ben Witherington III, *Paul's Letter to the Romans: A Socio-Rhetorical Commentary*, with Darlene Hyatt (Grand Rapids: Eerdmans, 2004), 225, esp. n25. It is also important to distinguish between the verb used here, *proginōskein* ("to foreknow"), and the cognate noun *prognōsis* ("foreknowledge"). The latter, in its two uses in the Greek Bible, appears to have the sense of "election" (Acts 2:23; 1 Pet. 1:2). The former, in five of its seven uses outside of this passage in Romans, means simply to know ahead of time (Wis. 6:13; 8:8; 18:6; Acts 26:5; 2 Pet. 3:17).

46. See the excellent discussion in Grant R. Osborne, *Romans*, IVPNTC (Downers Grove, IL: InterVarsity, 2004), 221–22.

47. Intriguingly, middle knowledge has been defended from both a libertarian and a compatibilist approach to free will. This approach probably should be combined with the assumption that God also chose the scenario from which the maximum amount of good could issue, given the constraints necessitated by genuine human freedom. Note Richard N. Longenecker, *The Epistle to the Romans*, NIGTC (Grand Rapids: Eerdmans, 2016), 821: "If blame is to be assigned, it must be assigned solely to the person himself or herself who has exercised his or her own God-given freedom in rebellious and evil ways; but if mercy and grace are experienced in the life of a person, it is to be credited solely to God, who, it may be presumed, has selected the best of all the foreknown possibilities of a person's thoughts and actions and has sovereignly chosen the best of those potentialities and possibilities, with those divine choices being not only best for the person and situation in question but also best for God's overall plans and purposes."

48. As esp. in John Piper, *The Justification of God: An Exegetical and Theological Study of Romans 9:1–23*, 2nd ed. (Grand Rapids: Baker, 1993).

49. See esp. Gregory Boyd, *God of the Possible: A Biblical Introduction to the Open View of God* (Grand Rapids: Baker Books, 2000).

50. See esp. Carroll D. Osburn, "The Interpretation of Romans 8:28," *Westminster Theological Journal* 44 (1982): 99–109. Cf. Arland J. Hultgren, *Paul's Letter to the Romans: A Commentary* (Grand Rapids: Eerdmans, 2011), 326–27.

51. See further Alvin C. Plantinga, *God, Freedom, and Evil* (Grand Rapids: Eerdmans, 1974), 29–64.

Chapter 8   What about All the Apparent Contradictions in the Gospels?

1. See esp. John W. Loftus, *Why I Became an Atheist: A Former Preacher Rejects Christianity* (Amherst, NY: Prometheus, 2012), 255–448.

2. Robert L. Thomas and F. David Farnell, eds., *The Jesus Crisis: The Inroads of Historical Criticism into Jesus Scholarship* (Grand Rapids: Kregel, 1998), esp. the contributions by the two editors themselves.

3. Robert Funk, Roy W. Hoover, and the Jesus Seminar, *The Five Gospels: The Search for the Authentic Words of Jesus* (New York: Macmillan, 1993); Robert Funk and the Jesus Seminar, *The Acts of Jesus: The Search for the Authentic Deeds of Jesus* (New York: HarperCollins, 1998).

4. E.g., Paul Carlson, "New Testament Contradictions (1995)," The Secular Web, accessed April 23, 2019, https://infidels.org/library/modern/paul_carlson/nt_contradictions.html; Diogenes the Cynic, "Shredding the Gospels: Contradictions, Errors, Mistakes, Fictions," Evangelical Catholic Apologetics, March 2, 2005, http://www.biblicalcatholic.com/apologetics/ShreddingTheGospels.htm.

5. Jonathan T. Pennington, *The Sermon on the Mount and Human Flourishing: A Theological Commentary* (Grand Rapids: Baker Academic, 2017), 167, 211; Charles L. Quarles, *Sermon on the Mount: Restoring Christ's Message to the Modern Church*, NACSBT (Nashville: B&H Academic, 2011), 88, 173.

6. N. T. Wright, *The Resurrection of the Son of God*, Christian Origins and the Question of God 3 (Minneapolis: Fortress, 2003), 628, 648; John Wenham, *Easter Enigma: Are the Resurrection Accounts in Conflict?* (1992; repr., Eugene, OR: Wipf & Stock, 2005), 85–87.

7. Craig L. Blomberg, *The Historical Reliability of the Gospels*, 2nd ed. (Downers Grove, IL: IVP Academic, 2007), 152–240. Cf. Vern S. Poythress, *Inerrancy and the Gospels: A God-Centered Approach to Harmonization* (Wheaton: Crossway, 2012).

8. Craig L. Blomberg, *The Historical Reliability of the New Testament: Countering the Challenges to Evangelical Christian Beliefs* (Nashville: B&H Academic, 2016).

9. But see esp. Michael R. Licona, *Why Are There Differences in the Gospels? What We Can Learn from Ancient Biography* (Oxford: Oxford University Press, 2016). See also Craig L. Blomberg, *Can We Still Believe the Bible? An Evangelical Engagement with Contemporary Questions* (Grand Rapids: Brazos, 2014), 119–45.

10. The Greek word usually translated as "immediately" is used "to show connections and relations among sections of text" and indicates "a temporal or logical result." W. Pöhlmann, "εὐθύς, εὐθέως," in *Exegetical Dictionary of the New Testament*, ed. Horst Balz and Gerhard Schneider (Grand Rapids: Eerdmans, 1991), 2:77–78.

11. Craig S. Keener, "Ancient Biography and the Gospels: An Introduction," in *Biographies and Jesus: What Does It Mean for the Gospels to Be Biographies?*, ed. Craig S. Keener and Edward T. Wright (Lexington, KY: Emeth, 2016), 30.

12. Darrell L. Bock, "The Words of Jesus in the Gospels: Live, Jive, or Memorex?," in *Jesus under Fire: Modern Scholarship Reinvents the Historical Jesus*, ed. Michael J. Wilkins and J. P. Moreland (Grand Rapids: Zondervan, 1995), 73–100.

13. See esp. Gary Knoppers, "The Synoptic Problem: An Old Testament Perspective," *Bulletin for Biblical Research* 19 (2009): 11–34.

14. Licona, *Why Are There Differences in the Gospels?*, 112–84.

15. Licona, *Why Are There Differences in the Gospels?*, 20.

16. Craig L. Blomberg, "The Legitimacy and Limits of Harmonization," in *Hermeneutics, Authority, and Canon*, ed. D. A. Carson and John D. Woodbridge (1986; repr., Eugene, OR: Wipf & Stock, 2005), 135–74.

17. See esp. Loveday Alexander, *The Preface to Luke's Gospel: Literary Convention and Social Context in Luke 1.1–4 and Acts 1.1* (Cambridge: Cambridge University Press, 1993).

18. Keener, "Ancient Biography and the Gospels," 1–45. See also Youngju Kwon, "Charting the (Un)charted: Gospels as Biographies and Their (Un)explored Implications," in Keener and Wright, *Biographies and Jesus*, 59–75.

19. Darrell L. Bock, *Acts*, BECNT (Grand Rapids: Baker Academic, 2007), 315. David G. Peterson (*The Acts of the Apostles*, PNTC [Grand Rapids: Eerdmans, 2009], 268) thinks it implies that Saul "was already the acknowledged leader in the opposition to the early church."

20. Eckhard J. Schnabel, *Acts*, ZECNT (Grand Rapids: Zondervan, 2012), 392.

21. Classically articulated by A. T. Robertson, *A Grammar of the Greek New Testament in the Light of Historical Research* (Nashville: Broadman, 1934), 506.

22. John Polhill (*Acts*, NAC [Nashville: Broadman, 1992], 235n15) notes that the generalization does not hold up throughout Luke but adds, "The distinction is perhaps to be seen in the qualifying participial phrase of 22:9, hearing a 'voice' (φωνή) which was speaking, whereas 9:7 need mean no more than hearing a 'sound.'" For a full range of options, see Craig S. Keener, *Acts: An Exegetical Commentary* (Grand Rapids: Baker Academic, 2014), 3:3230–31.

23. See further Keener, *Acts*, 3:3195–204.

24. Peterson, *Acts of the Apostles*, 598, 602. For the rhetorical structure of Acts 22, itself also accounting for various differences from Acts 9 and 26, see Ben Witherington III, *The Acts of the Apostles: A Socio-Rhetorical Commentary* (Grand Rapids: Eerdmans, 1998), 665–68.

25. Cf. F. Scott Spencer, *Journeying through Acts: A Literary-Cultural Reading*, 2nd ed. (Grand Rapids: Baker Academic, 2004), 214.

26. Suppressing earlier narrated details also leaves "room for more details (vv. 16–18) about Paul's vocation." C. K. Barrett, *A Critical and Exegetical Commentary on the Acts of the Apostles*, ICC (Edinburgh: T&T Clark, 1998), 2:1151.

27. Those who distinguish between authentic and inauthentic parts of pronouncement stories thus find the climactic saying the most authentic part of a given narrative. See, classically, Rudolf Bultmann, *History of the Synoptic Tradition*, trans. John Marsh, rev. ed. (originally published in German in 1921; Peabody, MA: Hendrickson, 1994), 49.

28. Barrett, *Acts of the Apostles*, 2:1031. Barrett lists the invocation of the high priest and the council of elders to testify to Paul's Jewish zeal (Acts 22:5), Jesus as a Nazarene (v. 8), Ananias as a devout law-observer respected by all the local Jews (v. 12), speaking for "the God of our fathers" (v. 14), the temple as the place where Paul is instructed by God (v. 17), his Jewish credentials as a persecutor (vv. 19–20), and going to the Gentiles only when deliberately sent by God (vv. 21–22).

29. For a succinct overview with plausible theological interpretation, see Augustine Stock, "Is Matthew's Presentation of Peter Ironic?," *Biblical Theology Bulletin* 17 (1987): 64–69.

30. See, respectively, D. W. Geyer, *Fear, Anomaly, and Uncertainty in the Gospel of Mark* (Lanham, MD: Scarecrow, 2000); Jack D. Kingsbury, *Matthew: Structure, Christology, Kingdom* (Philadelphia: Fortress, 1975).

31. Craig S. Keener (*The Gospel of John: A Commentary* [Peabody, MA: Hendrickson, 2003], 1:673) believes that the disciples went from the northeast to the northwest shores of the Sea of Galilee.

32. Richard I. Pervo (*Acts: A Commentary*, Hermeneia [Minneapolis: Fortress, 2009], 559) sees Acts 22 as a Lukan composition, in part because of this piecemeal nature. But he also finds it "smoother and better integrated than Acts 9," while recognizing that in conflict with this observation is the fact that "chap. 22 would be difficult to understand apart from Acts 9" (561). Perhaps he has overestimated how smooth Acts 22 is, especially since he earlier identifies what he calls dissonances, particularly within chapters 22 and 26.

33. For the dynamics of the repetition, see Ronald D. Witherup, "Cornelius Over and Over and Over Again: Functional Redundancy in the Acts of the Apostles," in *Journal for the Study of the New Testament* 15 (1992): 67–85. For variations that correspond to who is narrating each account, see William S. Kurz, "Effects of Variant Narrators in Acts 10–11," *New Testament Studies* 43 (1997): 570–86.

34. It also "reinforces the divine initiative contained in the event." Craig S. Keener, *Acts: An Exegetical Commentary* (Grand Rapids: Baker Academic, 2013), 2:1816.

35. Compare how angels are described in Luke 1:11 and 24:4; and see Keener, *Acts*, 2:1793.

36. This renders the view that the man in Mark was the one from 14:52 rather than an angel very improbable. For a more detailed rebuttal, see R. T. France, *The Gospel of Mark*, NIGTC (Grand Rapids: Eerdmans, 2002), 679.

37. Licona, *Why Are There Differences in the Gospels?*, 13–14 and throughout.

38. Peterson, *Acts of the Apostles*, 424–25; Polhill, *Acts*, 326–27.

39. Luke Timothy Johnson, *The Acts of the Apostles*, SP (Collegeville, MN: Liturgical Press, 1992), 277.

40. Referring to an action that is in progress, developing, or unfolding as Paul is speaking. See David L. Mathewson and Elodie B. Emig, *Intermediate Greek Grammar: Syntax for Students of the New Testament* (Grand Rapids: Baker Academic, 2016), 113.

41. Whether he still does in every respect is another matter. For the major options, see Michael F. Bird, ed., *Four Views on the Apostle Paul* (Grand Rapids: Zondervan, 2012). For a classic balanced view of Paul, see Richard N. Longenecker, *Paul, Apostle of Liberty*, 2nd ed. (Grand Rapids: Eerdmans, 2015). For a quite new, fresh, and helpful perspective, see N. T. Wright, *Paul: A Biography* (New York: HarperOne, 2018).

42. The purpose of mentioning the decree again seems to be to assure Paul that the Jerusalem Christians are not going back on their earlier agreement. They do not intend to require more of Gentile believers in general, even if here they are asking more of Paul, as a Jewish believer, voluntarily. See Witherington, *Acts of the Apostles*, 650.

Chapter 9 Hasn't the Church Played Fast and Loose with Copying and Translating the New Testament?

1. In fact, Kenton L. Sparks (*God's Word in Human Words: An Evangelical Appropriation of Critical Biblical Scholarship* [Grand Rapids: Baker Academic, 2008], 168) chides evangelicals who did this, believing them to have been motivated by the desire not to have to confront the world of critical scholarship while still getting credentialed!

2. The Nestle-Aland version is now in its 28th edition (*Novum Testamentum Graece*, ed. Barbara Aland et al. [Stuttgart: Deutsche Bibelgesellschaft, 2012]), and the UBS in its 5th (*The Greek New Testament*, ed. Barbara Aland et al. [Stuttgart: Deutsche Bibelgesellschaft; American Bible Society; United Bible Societies, 2014]).

3. Rodney R. Reeves, "What Do We Do Now? Approaching the Crossroads of New Testament Textual Criticism," *Perspectives in Religious Studies* 23 (1996): 61–73.

4. Now available as Bart D. Ehrman, *The Orthodox Corruption of Scripture: The Effect of Early Christological Controversies on the Text of the New Testament*, rev. ed. (Oxford: Oxford University Press, 2011).

5. E.g., "without God" instead of "by the grace of God" in Heb. 2:9. See Ehrman, *Orthodox Corruption of Scripture*, 171–76.

6. The UBS 4th ed. chose *splanchnistheis* with a B-level of confidence, meaning that the editors believed their choice was almost certainly the correct reading, even though there was some slight reason for doubt. In his *Textual Commentary on the Greek New Testament* (2nd ed. [New York: American Bible Society, 1994], 65), Bruce M. Metzger explains that the paucity of external evidence, combined with the fact that Mark's use of *orgizō* twice elsewhere with Jesus did not yield such a variant, led the committee to accept it with this high degree of confidence.

7. Treated more fully in Bart D. Ehrman, *Misquoting Jesus: The Story behind Who Changed the Bible and Why* (New York: HarperCollins, 2005), 133–39; and in great detail in Ehrman, "A Leper in the Hands of an Angry Jesus," in *New Testament Greek and Exegesis: Essays in Honor of Gerald F. Hawthorne*, ed. Amy M. Donaldson and Timothy B. Sailors (Grand Rapids: Eerdmans, 2003), 77–98.

8. Gordon D. Fee, in the Committee on Bible Translation, when the TNIV was first produced and again just before the publication of the NIV 2011. The REB, CEB, and LEB have all

followed suit. The CEB translates "incensed"; the LEB, "becoming angry." See also Jean-Claude Haelewyck, "The Healing of a Leper (Mark 1,40–45): A Textual Commentary," *Ephemerides Theologicae Lovaniensum* 89 (2013): 15–36.

9. Peter J. Williams, "An Examination of Ehrman's Case for ὀργισθείς in Mark 1:41," *Novum Testamentum* 54 (2012): 1–12. For a theological reason for preferring *splanchnistheis* as the original reading, see Nicholas Perrin, "Managing Jesus' Anger: Revisiting a Text-Critical Conundrum (Mark 1:41)," *Criswell Theological Review* 13, no. 2 (2016): 3–16.

10. Peter E. Lorenz, "Counting Witnesses for the Angry Jesus in Mark 1:41: Interdependence and Insularity in the Latin Tradition," *Tyndale Bulletin* 67 (2016): 183–216. See also Nathan C. Johnson, "Anger Issues: Mark 1.41 in Ephrem the Syrian, the Old Latin Gospels and Codex Bezae," *New Testament Studies* 63, no. 2 (2017): 183–202.

11. For a thorough critique, see Timothy P. Jones, *Misquoting Truth: A Guide to the Fallacies of Bart Ehrman's* Misquoting Jesus (Downers Grove, IL: InterVarsity, 2007).

12. See the catena of conflicting quotations from Ehrman, cited in Daniel B. Wallace, ed., *Revisiting the Corruption of the New Testament: Manuscript, Patristic, and Apocryphal Evidence* (Grand Rapids: Kregel, 2011), 23–25.

13. Elijah Hixson and Peter J. Gurry, eds., *Myths and Mistakes in New Testament Textual Criticism* (Downers Grove, IL: IVP Academic, 2019).

14. Peter J. Gurry, "Myths about Variants: Why Most Variants are Insignificant and Why Some Can't Be Ignored," in Hixson and Gurry, *Myths and Mistakes in New Testament Textual Criticism*, 196.

15. Jacob W. Peterson, "Math Myths: How Many Manuscripts We Have and Why More Isn't Always Better," in Hixson and Gurry, *Myths and Mistakes in New Testament Textual Criticism*, 63.

16. For the most relevant comparative data, see J. Ed Komoszewski, M. James Sawyer, and Daniel B. Wallace, *Reinventing Jesus: What* The Da Vinci Code *and Other Novel Speculations Don't Tell You* (Grand Rapids: Kregel, 2006), 71–72.

17. After Ehrman's writings, the next leading work in this vein may be David C. Parker, *Textual Scholarship and the Making of the New Testament* (Oxford: Oxford University Press, 2012).

18. Contrast Ehrman's own work with his much more conservative revision of the standard textbook by Bruce M. Metzger, *The Text of the New Testament: Its Transmission, Corruption, and Restoration*, 4th ed. (Oxford: Oxford University Press, 2005).

19. On the gap between the church and the academy, see Daniel B. Wallace, "Challenges in New Testament Textual Criticism for the Twenty-First Century," *Journal of the Evangelical Theological Society* 52 (2009): 99.

20. This has actually happened with $\mathfrak{P}^{72}$ and $\mathfrak{P}^{104}$. I owe this insight to Elijah Hixson.

21. Komoszewski, Sawyer, and Wallace, *Reinventing Jesus*, 107.

22. Ehrman, *Misquoting Jesus*, 10, 59.

23. See, e.g., Birger Gerhardsson, *Memory and Manuscript: Oral Tradition and Written Transmission in Rabbinic Judaism and Early Christianity*, trans. Eric J. Sharpe (Lund: Gleerup, 1961); Gerhardsson, *The Reliability of the Gospel Tradition* (Peabody, MA: Hendrickson, 2001).

24. Keith E. Small, *Textual Criticism and Qur'ān Manuscripts* (Lanham, MD: Lexington Books, 2011).

25. Cf. George W. Braswell Jr., *Islam: Its Prophet, Peoples, Politics, and Power* (Nashville: Broadman & Holman, 1996), 50–53; Stuart Robinson, *Mosques and Miracles: Revealing Islam and God's Grace* (Brisbane: City Harvest, 2003), 171–86.

26. George W. Houston, "Papyrological Evidence for Book Collections and Libraries in the Roman Empire," in *Ancient Literacies: The Culture of Reading in Greece and Rome*, ed. William A. Johnson and Holt N. Parker (Oxford: Oxford University Press, 2009), 233–67.

27. Craig A. Evans, *Jesus and His World: The Archaeological Evidence* (Louisville: Westminster John Knox, 2012), 75.

28. For fullest detail, see Josep Rius-Camps and Jenny Read-Heimerdinger, *The Message of Acts in Codex Bezae: A Comparison with the Alexandrian Tradition*, 4 vols. (London: T&T Clark, 2004–9).

29. This is how I have heard him put it colloquially in public presentations. In print, his more serious and carefully stated remarks are that the original in each passage is almost certainly represented in one of the existing forms of the manuscripts that we already have, even if we aren't always sure which one it is for a given text. See Wallace, "Challenges in New Testament Textual Criticism," 95.

30. The work on the Catholic Epistles and Acts is complete, along with the paralleled passages in the Synoptic Gospels. The goal is to have the entire series finished by 2030, though that seems very ambitious given the pace of the progress so far. The whole series is entitled *Novum Testamentum Graecum: Editio Critica Maior* (Stuttgart: Deutsche Bibelgesellschaft, 1997–).

31. Dirk Jongkind et al., eds., *The Greek New Testament* (Wheaton: Crossway, 2017).

32. Peter J. Williams, "How Theological Principles in the Editing of the Greek New Testament Led to Discoveries" (paper presented at the Annual Meeting of the Evangelical Theological Society, Providence, RI, November 2017).

33. Williams, "Theological Principles."

34. Michael W. Holmes, ed., *The Greek New Testament: SBL Edition* (Atlanta: Society of Biblical Literature, 2010).

35. Dirk Jongkind, *An Introduction to the Greek New Testament: Produced at Tyndale House, Cambridge* (Wheaton: Crossway, 2019), 35–39.

36. For an introduction to the latest state-of-the-art methods in New Testament textual criticism, see Tommy Wasserman and Peter J. Gurry, *A New Approach to Textual Criticism: An Introduction to the Coherence-Based Genealogical Method* (Atlanta: SBL Press, 2017). No matter the method, confidence in the ability to reconstruct this percentage of the text beyond reasonable doubt, where variants make nothing more than the most trivial of differences, continues to grow.

37. Ellis R. Brotzman and Eric J. Tully, *Old Testament Textual Criticism: A Practical Introduction*, 2nd ed. (Grand Rapids: Baker Academic, 2016), esp. 31–64.

38. Cf. Joseph R. Rosenbloom, *The Dead Sea Isaiah Scroll: A Literary Analysis; A Comparison with the Masoretic Text and the Biblia Hebraica* (Grand Rapids: Eerdmans, 1970).

39. For what many take to be the definitive work on Old Testament textual criticism, complete with detailed treatment of the proto-Masoretic and Masoretic texts, see Emanuel Tov, *Textual Criticism of the Hebrew Bible*, 3rd ed. (Minneapolis: Fortress, 2012), esp. 24–74.

40. On this theme, see esp. D. A. Carson, "Matthew," in *The Expositor's Bible Commentary*, ed. Tremper Longman III and David L. Garland, rev. ed. (Grand Rapids: Zondervan, 2010), 9:172–77.

41. For the possibility that this may have begun with certain parts of what became the New Testament, already in Paul's statement here, see George W. Knight III, *The Pastoral Epistles*, NIGTC (Grand Rapids: Eerdmans, 1992), 448.

42. "In his reference to *the word of God*, Paul has uppermost in mind the word of the gospel, but included in his thought would be the apostolic tradition about Jesus, which was at the very time becoming part of early Christian Scripture (cf. 1 Tim 5:18) and was appealed to by Paul throughout his epistles." G. K. Beale, *1–2 Thessalonians*, IVPNTC (Downers Grove, IL: InterVarsity, 2003), 79 (italics original).

43. 1 Cor. 7:10, 12 most likely distinguish between what Paul learned from the oral tradition about the teaching of Jesus and what he did not know about Jesus's teaching. Verses 25 and 40 make it clear that he still believed he was inspired in these other instructions.

44. E.g., Robert L. Thomas, *Revelation 8–22: An Exegetical Commentary* (Chicago: Moody, 1995), 517.

45. "To 'add' to the words of John's prophecy is to promote the false teaching that idolatry is not inconsistent with faith in Christ. To 'take away from the words of the book of this prophecy' is also to advance such deceptive teaching, since this teaching would violate and vitiate the validity of Revelation's exhortations against idolatry. Alternatively, it may be best to see 'adding' and 'taking away' as a hendiadys referring to a warning not to be associated with false teaching." G. K. Beale, *The Book of Revelation*, NIGTC (Grand Rapids: Eerdmans, 1999), 1151.

46. On the other hand, as Ian Boxall (*The Revelation of Saint John*, BNTC [Peabody, MA: Hendrickson, 2009], 319) observes, if John was alluding to Deuteronomy's curses, it could be that he viewed his book itself as on a par with the Hebrew Scriptures.

47. Revelation 22:18–19 would then have been seen as the close of a larger covenantal document, as the parallel words in Deuteronomy functioned. See Michael J. Kruger, *Canon Revisited: Establishing the Origins and Authority of the New Testament Books* (Wheaton: Crossway, 2012), 166–67.

48. "These are stern words, particularly threatening for scribes forced to copy manuscripts of the Apocalypse prior to the advent of printing, or for compilers of ecclesiastical lectionaries in any age." Boxall, *The Revelation of Saint John*, 319.

49. I have illustrated this in Craig L. Blomberg, *Can We Still Believe the Bible? An Evangelical Engagement with Contemporary Questions* (Grand Rapids: Brazos, 2014), 85–87.

50. See further Bruce M. Metzger, *The Bible in Translation: Ancient and English Versions* (Grand Rapids: Baker Academic, 2001). See also Gordon D. Fee and Mark L. Strauss, *How to Choose a Translation for All Its Worth: A Guide to Understanding and Using Bible Versions* (Grand Rapids: Zondervan, 2007).

51. See further Andreas J. Köstenberger and David A. Croteau, eds., *Which Bible Translation Should I Use? A Comparison of 4 Major Versions* (Nashville: B&H, 2012); Dave Brunn, *One Bible, Many Versions: Are All Translations Created Equal?* (Downers Grove, IL: InterVarsity, 2013).

52. Bible Gateway, http://www.biblegateway.com. Once it brings up an individual verse, Bible Gateway also offers a link to see that verse in all English translations in its database, allowing you to easily compare over fifty translations.

Chapter 10 The Alleged Undesirability of the Christian Life

1. The Counterpoints series of books from Zondervan, edited by Stanley N. Gundry, and the Spectrum Multiview Books from InterVarsity provide good indications of where many of these disagreements lie.

2. A point made repeatedly by Ronald J. Sider throughout his career. See esp. his *Completely Pro-Life: Building a Consistent Stance on Abortion, the Family, Nuclear Weapons, the Poor* (1987; repr., Eugene, OR: Wipf & Stock, 2010).

3. See esp. Glen H. Stassen and David P. Gushee, *Kingdom Ethics: Following Jesus in Contemporary Context*, 2nd ed. (Grand Rapids: Eerdmans, 2016); Richard B. Hays, *The Moral Vision of the New Testament: Community, Cross, New Creation; A Contemporary Introduction to New Testament Ethics* (New York: HarperCollins, 1996).

4. John Loftus renounced Christianity after committing adultery (*Why I Became an Atheist: A Former Preacher Rejects Christianity*, rev. ed. [Amherst, NY: Prometheus, 2012], 25); Richard Carrier decided to become polyamorous after becoming an atheist ("Coming Out Poly + A Change of Life Venue," *Richard Carrier Blogs*, February 18, 2015, https://www.richardcarrier .info/archives/6737). Other factors were involved in both decisions, but the correlations should not be ignored.

5. Consider, e.g., how most of the principles in the classic self-help manual by Dale Carnegie, *How to Win Friends and Influence People* (New York: Simon & Schuster, 1934), depend on Christian ethics.

6. Andraé Crouch and the Disciples, "If Heaven Never Was Promised to Me" (1972).

7. Most poignant of all is Paul's receiving the thirty-nine lashes five times from his fellow Jews, when all he had to do to become exempt from the Jewish synagogues' jurisdiction was declare himself no longer a Jew but purely a Christian.

8. "Paul did not believe that the Christian faith was worth it even if false. If Christians believe that Christ is risen and it is not true, they are deluded and should be pitied." Thomas R. Schreiner, *1 Corinthians*, TNTC (Downers Grove, IL: InterVarsity, 2018), 311.

9. Robert W. Yarbrough (*The Letters to Timothy and Titus*, PNTC [Grand Rapids: Eerdmans, 2018], 424) captures the correct balance: "It should not be taken to be a curse when God spares his people from the 'persecutions' so near Paul and Timothy in their setting. There should not be survivors' guilt but rather gratitude. The high likelihood, however, does need to be affirmed that every life dedicated to Christ in any social setting will in the course of time attract unwelcome resistance and result in unwanted pain."

10. "This 'abundant life' should therefore not be viewed (as it has been in some Christian circles) as a 'deeper' or 'victorious' life gained by a second work of grace subsequent to conversion. It is simply a way of speaking of 'eternal life' in the classic Johannine sense of a life that is not merely endless in duration, but new life, a qualitatively different relationship to God." J. Ramsey Michaels, *The Gospel of John*, NICNT (Grand Rapids: Eerdmans, 2010), 585n71.

11. Of countless biographies of people whose lives have been utterly changed for the better by Christian love, one that is particularly dear to my heart, because it is about the former president of the school I have taught at now for thirty-four years (and whom I knew for the first twenty-four of those years), is Bruce L. Shelley, *Transformed by Love: The Vernon Grounds Story* (Grand Rapids: Discovery House, 2003).

12. For these and other examples, see esp. Jonathan Hill, *What Has Christianity Ever Done for Us? How It Shaped the Modern World* (Downers Grove, IL: InterVarsity, 2005); David Bentley Hart, *Atheist Delusions: The Christian Revolution and Its Fashionable Enemies* (New Haven: Yale University Press, 2009).

13. The congregation was Ro'eh Israel in Denver.

14. The quote is from the last line of the first verse of the American national anthem, "The Star-Spangled Banner," composed by Francis Scott Key in 1814.

15. On the Jubilee and its implications for today, see esp. Walter Brueggemann, "Reflections on Biblical Understandings of Property," *International Journal of Mission* 64 (1975): 354–61.

16. Cf. Ben Witherington III, *John's Wisdom: A Commentary on the Fourth Gospel* (Louisville: Westminster John Knox, 1995), 176–77; Marianne Meye Thompson, *John: A Commentary*, NTL (Louisville: Westminster John Knox, 2015), 190.

17. "Freedom in the Bible is not a contrast between freedom and slavery but between an inappropriate master . . . and an appropriate master—God (cf. Exod. 9:14). It was freedom *for* something more than freedom *from* something. The freedom about which the exodus is the paradigmatic instance is liberation from degrading bondage for the endless service of the God who remembers his covenant, redeems from exile and oppression, and gives commandments through which the people of God are sanctified. This is the biblical notion of freedom about which Jesus speaks. If you are not a disciple of Jesus (v. 31), then by implication you serve the tyrant of sin (vv. 21, 24, 34)." Edward W. Klink III, *John*, ZECNT (Grand Rapids: Zondervan, 2016), 429.

18. On which, see further Craig L. Blomberg and Mariam J. Kamell, *James*, ZECNT (Grand Rapids: Zondervan, 2007), 91–92.

19. In the context of civic duty, this is probably "the civil status of freedom that is the prerequisite of civil responsibility" that Peter has in mind. John H. Elliott, *1 Peter: A New Translation with Introduction and Commentary*, AB (New York: Doubleday, 2000), 496.

20. This proverb "may refer either to the false teachers who are already described as slaves of corruption, or it may serve as a warning to believers about the possibility of becoming enslaved

again by anything, outside of Jesus Christ, that might overwhelm them." Ruth Ann Reese, *2 Peter and Jude*, THNTC (Grand Rapids: Eerdmans, 2007), 159–60.

21. See further Patrick Gray, *Godly Fear: The Epistle to the Hebrews and Greco-Roman Critiques of Superstition* (Leiden: Brill, 2004).

22. For Luther's own treatment, see Martin Luther, *Galatians* (original lectures given in German in 1535; Wheaton: Crossway, 1998).

23. Not only the content, but also the syntax, of the sentence stresses freedom (because it comes at the beginning). See Craig S. Keener, *Galatians*, NCBC (Cambridge: Cambridge University Press, 2018), 227.

24. See further John Buckel, *Free to Love: Paul's Defense of Christian Liberty in Galatians* (Grand Rapids: Eerdmans, 1993).

25. See esp. Murray J. Harris, *Slave of Christ: A New Testament Metaphor for Total Devotion to Christ* (1999; repr., Downers Grove, IL: InterVarsity, 2001), 70–75.

26. C. E. B. Cranfield, *A Critical and Exegetical Commentary on the Epistle to the Romans*, ICC (Edinburgh: T&T Clark, 1975), 1:319–20; Ernst Käsemann, *Commentary on Romans*, trans. and ed. Geoffrey W. Bromiley (Grand Rapids: Eerdmans, 1980), 174–75.

27. "Notice that he is not saying that slaves are required to obey their master. He is looking at it the other way around. The master we obey shows whose slaves we are." Leon Morris, *The Epistle to the Romans*, PNTC (Grand Rapids: Eerdmans, 1988), 261.

28. The change from the 1984 to the 2011 NIV at Phil. 2:4 is crucial here. In the best manuscripts, this is not a "not only . . . but also" construction but a simple "not . . . but" construction. See Ben Witherington III, *Paul's Letter to the Philippians: A Socio-Rhetorical Commentary* (Grand Rapids: Eerdmans, 2011), 131.

29. Some scholars think Paul is forbidding the eating of all food sacrificed to idols, but this is much harder to square with his narrative flow.

30. See esp. Bruce N. Fisk, "Eating Meat Offered to Idols: Corinthian Behavior and Pauline Response in 1 Corinthians 8–10," *Trinity Journal* 10 (1989): 49–70; E. C. Still, "The Meaning and Uses of ΕΙΔΩΛΟΘΥΤΟΝ in First Century Non-Pauline Literature and 1 Cor 8:1–11:1: Toward Resolution of the Debate," *Trinity Journal* 23 (2002): 225–34.

31. See esp. Robert Jewett, *Christian Tolerance: Paul's Message to the Modern Church* (Philadelphia: Westminster, 1982).

32. See esp. Mark Noll, *The Scandal of the Evangelical Mind* (Grand Rapids: Eerdmans, 1994), 241–54.

33. C. K. Barrett (*The Epistle to the Romans*, rev. ed., BNTC [1962; repr., Grand Rapids: Baker Academic, 2011], 236) notes that Paul's emphasis was so heavily in favor of the "strong" Christian who understood this freedom that we are surprised at first that he gives the "weak" so much latitude.

34. Here Paul is motivated particularly by the themes of unity within the church and the mission to the lost world. See throughout Carl N. Toney, *Paul's Inclusive Ethic: Resolving Community Conflicts and Promoting Mission in Romans 14–15* (Tübingen: Mohr Siebeck, 2008).

35. "Paul is boldly liberal here. Even as he tries to limit the freedom of those who use it in a destructive way, his affirmation of the radical freedom of the Christian life is unmistakable." Lyle D. Vander Broek, *Breaking Barriers: The Possibilities of Christian Community* (Grand Rapids: Brazos, 2002), 101.

36. C. K. Barrett (*Epistle to the Romans*, 248) observes that Paul here returns to and "gathers up" his main theme in this overall section. Grant R. Osborne (*Romans*, IVPNTC [Downers Grove, IL: InterVarsity, 2004], 379) suggests that it may summarize the entire body of the letter, at least with respect to Jew-Gentile relationships.

37. Cf. Garry Friesen, *Decision-Making and the Will of God: A Biblical Alternative to the Traditional View*, with J. Robin Maxson (Portland, OR: Multnomah, 1980), 382–83.

38. Cf. Ronald F. Hock, *The Social Context of Paul's Ministry: Tentmaking and Apostleship* (Philadelphia: Fortress, 1980), 63–65.

39. On which, see Victor C. Pfitzner, *Paul and the Agon Motif: Traditional Athletic Imagery in the Pauline Literature* (Leiden: Brill, 1967), 82–98. See further Judith M. Gundry-Volf, *Paul and Perseverance: Staying In and Falling Away* (Louisville: Westminster John Knox, 1991), 233–47.

40. See further Craig L. Blomberg, *1 Corinthians*, NIVAC (Grand Rapids: Zondervan, 1994), 170.

41. Rollin A. Ramsaran, *Paul's Use of Liberating Rhetorical Maxims in 1 Corinthians 1–10* (Valley Forge, PA: Trinity Press International, 1996), 71.

42. F. F. Bruce, *1 and 2 Corinthians*, NCB (Grand Rapids: Eerdmans, 1980), 99–100.

43. Gordon D. Fee (*The First Epistle to the Corinthians*, rev. ed., NICNT [Grand Rapids: Eerdmans, 2014], 429) notes that "conservatives on these issues simply fail to reckon with how 'liberal' Paul's own view really is. Hence Paul is seldom heard for the sake of traditional regulations."

Conclusion

1. Or the arguments from the existence of the universe, from its design and purposefulness, from the existence of morality, and from the very existence of the concept of a Being greater than whom nothing exists.

2. The existence of something rather than nothing is empirical, as are the irreducibly complex features appealed to in the argument from design. Moral beliefs and mental constructs of God are less immediately empirical, but to the extent that they have even some connections to identifiable parts of the brain, they are also empirical.

3. See the now-classic work by P. B. Medawar, *The Limits of Science* (Oxford: Oxford University Press, 1985).

NAMES INDEX

SCRIPTURE AND ANCIENT
WRITINGS INDEX

SUBJECT INDEX